PROFILE
EDITIONS

DiRect

Tony Laithwaite

MY STORY

INTRODUCTION

When, newly arrived in France aged 19 and looking for a bed for the night, I first walked into a vineyard, I didn't think it was to be for life. But that was in 1965 and here I am, still regularly walking in that very vineyard. Not only its wine, but the wines of thousands of other vineyards around the world that I have been welcomed into, have totally dominated my life.

I never thought I would write a book, certainly not an autobiography. It's not really that, it's just memories. But I've been very fortunate; we've just had such an extraordinary half-century in our world of wine. There have never been so many changes... and I was privileged to be there, right in the thick of it for five – no, six – decades.

Writing the book has reminded me of the hundreds of wonderful characters – and the odd not-so-wonderful beings – I have met. In my mind, as I wrote, I've tasted again so many lovely wines... and also, the eye-watering stuff I used to have to endure in order to find the good 'uns, in a lifetime going around the world's vineyards. I have been reminded of the ups and downs, the joys and the sadness.

This book is certainly not a wine guide, it is not a tub-thumping collection of my views, nor is it a 'how-to-succeed-in-business', it is just me telling my stories more or less as I have all these years. Customers of mine are used to this and will know not to expect anything very profound. My mother wrote chatty letters every day of her life. Her mother, my Nana, an important figure in my life, just talked constantly... to herself, if there was no one around. I inherited the trait, so, in a way, I have been writing this book for 50 years. I know it has shortcomings and I apologise... but try reading it along with a glass of good wine. That improves it no end. As it does most things.

Tony Laithwaite

VERY IMPORTANT WINES

I have been helped over these past 50 years by several key people. But I also owe a debt to several key wines. I have picked out just ten all-time VIWs – Very Important Wines – which you will find interspersed in the text. They are not necessarily my personal favourites or indeed, still on our list, but they were all great commercial successes for us because they all became the favourites of my customers. Which is far more important. Interestingly, none of the wines are what you might call 'mainstream'. When we introduced them, all would have been considered oddballs... a bit whacky. They are all wines which altered our preconceptions and redrew the wine map for us... and in some cases for everybody. As a geographer (third class) I am particularly proud of that.

Tony

FIRST GROWTH

FLORRIE FIXES IT

It wasn't me, it was my grandmother – my Nana – who started the whole thing off, one fine day in 1965. Florrie Rudd was a formidable lady and I owe her much more than the £700 of life savings that she gave me to set up my business.

'Florrie' rather sums her up. Few people dared call her Florrie to her face but that was how she was known. No shy, retiring lady 'Our Florrie', of Horwich, near Bolton. She was as no-nonsense as that Lancashire mill town where I was born, but which I left far too early. Florrie made me a proud Boltonian. Exiled for virtually my whole life, I still always try to remain 'proper northern'. Bolton has enjoyed great renown and affluent years thanks to its entrepreneurs, Crompton in cotton, in soap; William Lever, later Lord Leverhulme (Unilever), for whom young, pretty Florrie had proudly served teas in his Rivington Barn. Now it's Warburtons bread, Fred Dibnah and Peter Kay. But it is not a natural twin for Bordeaux, the

Florence Rudd began it all.

wine capital of France, though many would say the world, sitting very proudly on the Gironde estuary, surrounded by the grandest of wine names – Saint-Émilion, Pauillac, Margaux, Graves, Sauternes, Pomerol. However...

As a teenager in the 1960s I had fallen in love with France. It wasn't the interminable French lessons of old 'Froggie' Croker. It was Chief Inspector Maigret on television, played by Rupert Davies. This great detective, always dropping into bars for a glass of *vin blanc* before climbing into his black Citroën with Lucas, lived in an exotic world I decided I wanted to join. And I also loved French humour. The French themselves admire *l'humour britannique* though they struggle with it at times, but their own humour seemed to me just as endearing. A huge hit with

Rupert Davies as Maigret in the 1960s.

young me was Jacques Tati as *le facteur*, the gangling postman in his hobnailed boots, furiously pedalling past all the racing cyclists in *Jour de Fête*. There was also the gentle cartoonist Sempé; back then I cut out all his sweet, wordless cartoons in *Punch* and stuck them all over our downstairs loo wall. People always came out smiling. There were also those French girls: Leslie Caron as Gigi, moody Françoise Hardy and of course Brigitte Bardot herself. Who wasn't in love with BB?

Then, one day in 1965, it happened. We lived in Windsor, a perfectly pleasant, but very 'southern' town where my parents Winneth and Eric had settled when they moved down south. Nana Rudd was also down that day, staying with us, when a stroke of luck – the first of many – totally changed my life. Out for a walk, Florrie came across another *grandmère*: Leina Bimont, a French tourist taking in the sights, castle and all. For reasons that never became clear, Florrie assumed this lady was lost and with her typical forthrightness took her back to our house for reviving tea. In truth Leina was not lost but merely being courteous to the force that was Florrie. Tea was served and Florrie told Leina – shouting, I expect, as she believed foreigners could always understand English if you shouted – that her grandson was very keen on France and wanted to go there to do some grape-picking. Madame Bimont kindly said she would try to find me work and was as good as her word. And... (sound of trumpets)... Leina lived in BORDEAUX!

FLORENCE RUDD: SHE BEGAN IT ALL

BORDEAUX '65: 'A DISASTROUS VINTAGE' BUT NOT FOR ME!

So, a few weeks later, on 8 June 1965, just one week out of school, that is where I arrived, to be bundled into the Bimonts' brand new white Panhard car.

On a sweltering day they drove me through a Bordeaux that seemed surprisingly shabby, the buildings all black from smoke and grime – just like old Bolton, really.

Bordeaux then, was nothing like today's cool, elegant and very lively city. All those frontages – eighteenth-century architectural masterpieces – are now nicely scrubbed up and there are so many bars, restaurants and places to visit that Bordeaux today gets called 'Europe's most exciting city'.

Sainte-Colombe's Roman stone-lined concrete wine tanks with a sump in the middle. Virtually the same as used in wineries today.

I was taken straight to the Bimonts' apartment for my first French dishes: *pot de cochon* followed by strawberries in chilled red Bordeaux, all sprinkled with sugar. A good welcome. The Bimonts could not have been friendlier, but there was a problem. The promised job at Domaine de Lisennes, just 6 miles east of the city, had fallen through after a sudden death in the family. I also learned something else – grape-picking wasn't a summer job anyway. Grapes got picked in the autumn. So there I was guiltily enjoying the hospitality of this kind couple while they ran around trying to find me another job. But wine was not a business they were involved in. André sold a scaffolding system he'd invented and Leina had just begun making and selling woven wood fence panels copied from ones she'd seen in England. They were typical of de Gaulle's thriving and entrepreneurial France. This period inspired small winegrowers as much as anyone, which was to prove good for me. The still feudal relationship between peasant producer and seigneurial wine merchant was beginning to break down as growers realised they could now bottle and market their wine directly. It's funny that France, then, was so entrepreneurial, unlike the UK which didn't at that time encourage it at all and was in a bit of an economic mess anyway. After a few days the lovely Bimonts found me work – unpaid, but *logé-nourri* (bed and board) – on an archaeological 'dig' out in a village called Sainte-Colombe near Saint-Émilion. I knew nothing about archaeology but I could dig, being quite familiar with building sites and shovels. It turned out not quite as I had imagined; the archaeologist, Monsieur Coste, gave me not a shovel but a tiny trowel and a small brush. But at least the dig was right in the middle of vineyards. Vineyards! It was love at first sight. I loved the way they looked. Neat green parallels curving gracefully over the hillsides. Vineyards then were a bit different to now. They were kept totally – but totally – free of grass and weeds. That their soil was always perfectly bare seemed, oddly, to be more important than producing healthy ripe grapes. On the other hand, they were dotted with fruit trees. Welcome shade for toiling workers, fruit for eating and distilling into digestif alcohols, especially the delicious but lethal *eau de vie de poire*. When tractors replaced horses, the trees were in the way so, sadly, had to go. Close to their houses, farmers would plant little crops of lettuce, radish, beetroot, onions and such, in the tilled earth between their rows of vines – to be harvested well before the grapes – but making the maximum use of their land. Chickens, ducks, geese and guinea fowl roamed freely. Some still do in rustic Sainte-Colombe. Verges were all neatly scythed, providing, every evening, a barrowload of food for the caged rabbits (not pet rabbits... dinner rabbits). It was the classic 'Peasant Economy', the land providing almost all the villagers' needs, with their wine bringing in cash. I've never stopped loving vineyards. Like a child wanting to be the first to see the sea, on every journey, at the first sight of green stripes, I still want to shout 'Vineyards!'. Sometimes I actually do shout.

I got my first view of the village of Sainte-Colombe when we left the main Dordogne Valley road and headed towards the ridge that runs along the valley's northern edge. Known in wine circles as 'The Right Bank', it runs from Saint-Émilion to Castillon-la-Bataille. It's not changed much, though as I remember there seemed to be more woods and fields then, with fewer vineyards than today, wine here having had a hard time of it for the previous hundred years or so. Today's great Bordeaux wine boom was still some years off. We headed into one of the little side valleys. The road wound from farmhouse to farmhouse. They were all small, with barns, built of pale stone, but every one had signs saying 'Château' something-or-other. There was only one, up on the right, that actually looked like a real château, small, with a tower and courtyard. I certainly couldn't imagine how significant that place would become for me in 50 years' time... or that I'd still be spending so much of my life in Sainte-Colombe. The dig itself was just behind the church and the cluster of houses around it: 'Le Bourg' de Sainte-Colombe. A perfectly sheltered, warm and watered spot; which is presumably why some Roman or Gallo-Roman, long ago, had built his villa there and put in a small winery. With my brush I helped excavate its stone tanks – smaller but remarkably similar to the concrete ones used today.

But in another stroke of incredible good fortune – I have had way more than my share of luck in my life – I was billeted up the hill, with a late-middle-aged couple: Jean and Geneviève 'Ginette' Cassin, who had agreed to take me in.

STE. LOCOMBE.

Lussac Coop?

My first workplace,
La Cave Coopérative
de Puisseguin-Lussac-
Saint-Émilion.

Well, not quite 'in'. A cautious couple, they put me in the barn. There was a bed, though. A big bed with ancient linen sheets, very thick and coarse – wonderfully cool on hot nights – which bore Madame's very elaborate cipher, embroidered by her own hand, apparently. There was a bowl on a washstand with a big jug to fetch water from the pump in the yard. The rest of my bathroom was 50 yards down the vegetable garden. It was not what the French call a *watair* (WC). It was an earth closet. The vegetable garden around it was, of course, exceptionally bountiful.

I spent just a week or two monotonously brushing and scratching Roman stones in baking sunshine and sleeping in the barn. But there was a bonus: Madame Cassin was a brilliant cook, so I ate very well. I was actually allowed in the house to eat and over those meals I discovered that Monsieur Cassin ran a local co-operative winery. So one evening I confessed that I was no archaeologist and it was so hot out there, so perhaps there might, possibly, be a job, please sir, in the cool, in the co-operative? Why should he listen to me, a 19-year-old English schoolboy with no experience of anything really? But he did.

Monsieur Cassin rang his *maître de chai*, Monsieur Lafaye, and a day later the first Laithwaite started in the wine business as a *stagiaire* with the not very romantic – but, I felt, quite key – job of rinsing out the bottles. From the moment I stepped inside the cavernous, concrete co-operative

I was hooked. Wine co-ops mostly began during the Depression, years after the First World War, and were built of reinforced concrete, in a brutalist style. Inside they resemble old-fashioned prisons like the one in *Porridge*. The prison cells though, were cuves and contained wine, not felons. So the doors were much smaller. A person could still get through those doors if they were small and prepared to enter head-first and horizontally. They went in – someone has to – when the vat got emptied, to shovel out the sediment which drops out of a wine after it ferments and begins to settle. My 'minder' at the co-op was Serge, a small, wiry, and very kind man, who did this job. It was the work I immediately yearned to do. You will know how pleasant it is to inhale the aromas in the bowl of a glass of wine. Imagine then, climbing into a damp, dripping tank only just emptied of lovely wine. Pungent? The aromas are, quite literally, mind-blowing. You reel. Very happy work if you can get it. Alas, I was stuck on the bottling line instead, and became a robot.

I stood beside the small line, on which I placed the cleaned, empty bottles. That is all I did hour after hour, day after day with little Monsieur Ferrere, Marcel hair *en brosse*, and ancient Monsieur Poli. There were also two small, dark, pretty young sisters who, alas, found me utterly hilarious and unbelievably stupid as I was incapable of stringing more than two French words together. The banter around me was continuous and witty, I think. I just couldn't understand it. But by God, I wanted to. The little sisters succeeded where 'Froggie' Croker had failed; they made me desperate to learn French.

But at least there was the wine. There were a hundred taps in the immediate vicinity and only a few – those painted red – dispensed water.

The bottling machine broke down fairly frequently; it was a primitive machine. However, if it didn't break of its own accord, Marcel knew how to make it break, because Marcel regularly needed to light up one of the horrible brown cigarettes that were perpetually glued to his protruding lower lip. And he needed a drink. Marcel was *un mec qui aime le pinard*, he had *un penchant pour la bouteille*, he was a lover of *la picole – un arsouille*, in fact.

Actually we would all have a drink. Except the girls. France doesn't do tea breaks. But every *mec* needs something to make the monotony bearable. So I began my career as a wine taster.

Opposite: The old bottling machine.

As time went on I began to be more discriminating, stopped drinking straight from the tap and used a glass. This was the grimy wine glass Marcel kept hidden in the tool cupboard. It had lost its foot and the broken stem was embedded in a wooden barrel bung. We all used it. I learned to discriminate, noticing that the others didn't just go to the nearest tap. They would run the risk of being apprehended by Monsieur Lafaye just to get to one particular tap. But Lafaye had only one eye; so you just had to stay on his left.

This, I suppose, helped me understand something that has been invaluable to me: tanks of wine may all look the same, barrels may all look the same... but they're not. Not at all.

Wine isn't made by a machine. It comes, via grapes, out of the earth and every little patch of earth is a unique mix of soil and rock, and that makes grapes – and wine – vary accordingly. Even cloned vines vary, and so far no one has managed to clone a grape-grower. Growers all work in different ways, on different days. Result is, every vine produces a slightly different wine to its neighbour. To most of us, the difference is not readily discernible initially but by the time the wine is in barrels or tanks, the differences do become discernible. To make the commercial quantities of wine required by Big Retail today, many different wines must be blended together. The bigger the volume needed, the more wines must be blended: the delicious with – inevitably – the less delicious. So don't ever buy big blends, was what I was given to understand very early on. Cherry-pick that extra-special tank or barrel, like we, back then, picked the best tap.

When I did launch my wine-importing business four years later, I started with a wine from Monsieur's co-operative. But I didn't launch with its standard blend – I checked with Marcel which tank was currently the favourite. 'Never just buy what you're offered; taste the whole cellar first... then choose,' has been my exhaustingly pleasant modus operandi ever since.

I absolutely adore wine cellars. To this day whenever I walk into the cool, echoey darkness of any traditional winery, smell that smell of wine and wood, and hear those sounds, the tock-tock-tock of the pump, the clink of bottles, all the clatterings and swooshings, my heart still surges a little.

The co-operative was in Puisseguin, about 4 miles away, and Monsieur Cassin drove me to work in the morning. We bounced along in his old canvas-topped Citroën 2CV, and then back again for lunch, *le déjeuner* – what everyone called *la soupe*. Then back again to work and home again in the evening. I had no idea then of just what Jean Cassin – simply 'Monsieur' to me forever after – would mean in my life. It was the beginning of a lifelong collaboration. He became my adopted French father. Even in those very early days he would talk animatedly about wine production, the history, the geography, the marketing, with lots of arm-waving, as we bowled along the old RD 17. I drank in every word that I could understand.

MONSIEUR CASSIN
MY GREAT MENTOR

Opposite: Monsieur decanting a bottle of something very old with a candle behind the bottle neck so he could spot when the copious sediment threatened.

I was really and truly lucky to get Monsieur as my mentor, supporter and guru. Of all the thousands of people running wineries in France – and I've met a lot of them – I don't think anyone could have helped me more into the business. He drummed both wine lore and business wisdom into me. That took a lot of drumming. He had this habit of repeating everything three times, to make very sure it went in. He spoke excellent English but only used it when all else failed. He insisted I speak French or at least try to. I tried; I had to if no one would speak English. My brain hurt but, after a month or so, weirdly, I found myself beginning to think in French and by the end of the summer I could speak it quite passably. Half-man, half-parrot, me. Not that I necessarily *knew* exactly what I was saying. The cellar lads taught me some very bad words. I once greeted a roomful of Madame's refined ladies from the Secours Catholique with a new phrase

21

Grandad Rudd.

that made all their teacups jump in their saucers. I'm quite fluent now, especially in *argot* – slang – though I still have trouble reading French.

Only now do I fully appreciate that with my family background the chances of me ending up in France, let alone becoming an entrepreneur, were ridiculous. I know if it hadn't been for a whole series of fateful, fortunate meetings my world would never have moved beyond England.

I was born in Bolton in 1945, the only child of Eric and Winneth Laithwaite. My mother had to give birth on a trolley in the hospital corridor (the baby boom had just started) and didn't enjoy it one bit. Hence no more babies for her, thank you, just the one – very spoiled – boy. We moved south in 1950 when my father, the youngest of three rugby-playing brothers (Bill captained St Helens, Albert got capped for England), was told that there was no room for him in the family firm of A. Laithwaite and Son, Builders' Merchants, St Helens. He had a degree in Building Science and got a job in London, working for British Aluminium at its headquarters in St James's Square. I was very close to my Nana Rudd, so for most of the journey south I screamed at the thought of losing her. As my mother was a teacher and my father had gone back to college after demob from the RAF, it had fallen to Nana to raise me. She had set up a corner shop selling her home-made cakes and bread, after Grandad Rudd, a joiner, erecting pit-props, was totally deafened by a mine explosion and invalided out. He had then set up his own carpentry business in Westhoughton in an old black allotment shed that smelled of wood-shavings, glue, linseed and tar, and which I loved. He let me light the stove to boil kettles. He made furniture and replacement windows, but Nana said he was too soft always to insist on payment from the hard-up old folk of Westhoughton. I remember him fondly as a very kind grandad. Nana was different; strictly cash, was Our Florrie! Did I pick up any business sense from her? I doubt it. After all, I couldn't see over her counter. She was always baking and didn't have

Old Labrut tipping grapes into a duy.

time to read me stories, but on the other hand, was always encouraging me to come up with stories to entertain her, like describing our future life in the ideal house we'd all live in one day, and the journeys we'd go on. Maybe this is why I got a reputation, very early on, as a dreamer or, to teachers, a dozy sod. 'Laithwaite, what was I just saying?' Whack! Ow! I was known as 'Nod' Laithwaite, not Tony, right up to when I left university.

My mother taught domestic science, and was forever trying out foreign recipes. We would holiday abroad. I remember trips to Holland, Denmark and Sweden – though not France – and the food. Oh! The smorgasbord and the Danish open sandwiches! She got me keen on interesting and varied foods. My first vague interest in wine came about when my father, whose office in St James's seemed encircled by wine shops, began to bring home bottles. One day he returned with a little book on how wine was made. I had a look and saw a picture of pretty harvesters laughing in sun-drenched vineyards. I clearly remember how that book – well, mostly that one picture – set a train of dreamy thoughts in motion.

SAINTE-COLOMBE

When I actually got to rural France it was more different to my life back home than expected. In Sainte-Colombe, for a start, their day's priorities were sort of the other way round to ours.

At home, meals were fitted into busy lives. Here, very obviously, life had to fit around meals. They seemed to live just for eating and drinking. All work seemed to be done with the basic aim of ensuring at least one very good, long, slow meal every day. The whole day revolved around that midday meal, wine, and the nice *sieste* after. The big siren, away down the valley in Castillon, would wind up and moan every day at noon, and everybody would immediately drop everything, and head off to *la soupe.* The countryside would fall silent – apart from the cicadas – for two whole hours.

The week had set days for market, the various vineyard tasks and church. The month had its lunar cycles that dictated how the sap rose or fell, hence when to plant and when to harvest. Almost everyone had at least a row or two of vines, right down to the postman and the fishmonger. But most were full-time growers. In the vineyards there were far more oxen, horses and mules than tractors. People worked together a lot. Families would get together to help each other with major tasks like uprooting old vineyards or dragging great rocks out of the earth to get deeper soil for planting. There was lots of bawdy laughter, which, sadly, seems gone now that tractors rule.

The whole year revolved around wine and food. Everything had its season. Winter was out pruning vines: a long, solitary, slow, cold job – just a little warmth from the burning cuttings. Evenings were in the winery, racking and topping up. Spring was for protecting the new vine shoots; summer was keeping rampant vines in check and hopefully healthy. Autumn of course was *la vendange*: the vintage, fermenting and all. Hunting game – well, anything that moved and was edible, really – and picking mushrooms (*cèpes*) in the woods had to be fitted in too and making hams and pâté de foie gras. Basically, I was a townie but I had developed an early passion for country life, going to collect hundreds of eggs and fetch the cows in at Uncle Noah's Top o' th' Hill Farm on the moors up at Rivington near Bolton. As a child, I was always dream-escaping to that place, but this was even better. Not a bad way to live. Not bad at all.

But my life had to carry on and university beckoned. I had been extremely lucky again. My father's job had taken us from Windsor to Birmingham and I had moved to Bishop Vesey's Grammar School in Sutton Coldfield, one of the best grammars in the country. Scholastically I'd been a disastrous embarrassment to my parents but I did better at Vesey's. It was such a confident, successful school in a confident region; thriving industrially just then, turning out E-types and suchlike. Even though I wasn't the greatest student: 'Not really an academic, are we, Laithwaite, mmm?' 'No Sir.' But I loved it there, because it really was a great school, and because I suddenly found I could run faster than anyone else in Birmingham – the sort of thing that gets you real prestige in a boy's school. Being Speedy Laithwaite also got me into the 1st XV – a very successful rugby team. In my final year, an unbeaten season culminated with a tremendous win over Rugby School itself... as I can never stop reminding the surprising number of Old Rugbeians in the wine world – Hugh Johnson, Steven Spurrier and all. So while I was and remained academically 'nul points', it was sport that helped me build the cocky confidence which is so useful in business.

So when my parents moved back down to Windsor I stayed on at Vesey's, which had a small boarding house. Although I liked the school, I had no real idea what I wanted to do. Possibly architecture? Maybe? I applied to schools of architecture. When I left school in 1964, I was keen to get away from the regulated life and be my own man now... except it didn't happen. My A levels! Two Es and a D. So forget architecture, then. I had to go through the ultimate humiliation of returning to school, two months after leaving. 'Nod' Laithwaite crawled back to Vesey's for an extra year.

I still cringe when I think about that. But had it not been for lousy A levels and going back to school I would have missed out on Nana Rudd's Bordeaux job-hunting. Odd to think, if I had been brighter and worked harder, life might have turned out duller.

Those three months in Sainte-Colombe among the vineyards were to define my life. I loved everything about rural France. Yes, some romantic notions were shattered a bit. Not every girl looked like Brigitte Bardot, there were black Citroëns but no Maigret. The Moulin Rouge might still be the epitome of excitement and naughtiness but then I never got as far as Paris. Sainte-Colombe didn't have a bar with a basket of croissants on the *zinc* and the aroma of coffee and Gauloises hanging heavy in the air as glasses of *rouge qui tache* were raised and clinked by men in berets... *'Santé!'*. It didn't even have a shop. It was definitely not sophisticated. But then neither was I. As an introduction to French life, for me, it was near perfect. And also a step back in time. In Sainte-Colombe only the Cassins had a car. No one else had anything much that might be called modern, like a fridge or TV. Apart from the Cassins, nearly everyone still wore wooden clogs. Men wore berets and *bleus*. The women floral aprons or black, if widowed. All kept pigs, chickens, ducks and geese, and horses or oxen to plough. There was bottled gas but some still cooked on open fires, sometimes in rooms with earth floors. They grew virtually everything they ate and drank. Each tiny patch of land, even a single apple tree, or walnut, or acacia copse, every bit of woodland that might produce fruit, game, *cèpes* or posts for the vineyard, was owned, meticulously mapped on great charts in the village hall, watched over, guarded and cared for. Every bit of valuable earth was tended so as to produce its best, the best of whatever it was suited for. All this done so as to go on producing it for sons and daughters and grandchildren. They hadn't yet invented the term 'eco-friendly', but the folk of Sainte-Colombe really understood what their precious, life-giving land needed. Men did the heavy stuff, what were called the *grands façons*. Steering a plough in and out between each vine, behind their horse, with the reins looped round their neck, created a breed of men with huge shoulders and massive necks. Pruning thick vines with secateurs developed huge hands. Women did the *petits façons*, which would be mostly tying vines to post and wire. After work the men would go to their wine cellars to taste their tanks. The women would tend their animals and kill something for supper.

Madame kept a cow for milk and a horse for work. They lived side by side. But then Madame employed a Spaniard from the far south in Andalusia who spoke no French and his jolly wife Mercedes who did... non-stop. They came with their huge family: three beautiful daughters Maria, Paquita and Isobel, only son Carlos, and two or three infants. They all moved into the two barn bedrooms next to me. The horse didn't like being constantly cursed in a language he did not understand. So he died. Madame found a replacement: a big mule called Charlot (the French nickname for Charlie Chaplin).

She bought him, plus a big old cart with two massive wooden wheels. They had to be fetched many miles from a farm beside Michel de Montaigne's château just over the line in the Département de la Dordogne. That was a long, long day. A mule that understood only French, a farmer speaking only Spanish, and his assistant speaking only English. We got so lost in the woods.

It was a time warp of a landscape and I realise some people might have found it dull. But by pure chance I had landed somewhere that would remain an enormous part of my life, all my life. It wasn't cool Paris, it wasn't the sexy Côte d'Azur or Provence. It was the Bordeaux bit of the Dordogne Valley, and I loved it. I fell for that life of vineyards and cellars governed by the seasons and the cycles of the moon. And also the long brown and, come to think of it, actually quite Bardotesque legs of the girl who rattled her milk-pail past my window every evening.

Winching a duy onto the roadside platform from which it would be collected and taken to the co-operative by lorry (all far too slow – not good for the wine).

Antonio, Charlot and my van by the La Clarière vineyard in Sainte-Colombe.

Living? It was like being in a novel, a historical novel, and I never wanted to leave. Weekends, I made hay with local families, and I mean real hay; with pitchforks and rakes, whole families working together, with the cackling old ladies telling me undreamt-of facts of life. The boys and girls took me to the summer *bals*. Every village and hamlet had at least one weekend-long summer *bal* a year. *Orchestre*, dancing, feasting, flirting, fumbling, boules and bike races. And for big-town excitement there was always Castillon-la-Bataille just down the valley. Well, at least it was a town even if not that big... or exciting.

It seemed longer than just three months I had spent there, so much had happened. I got the train home, taking with me an illegal number of bottles of claret for my father and his friends. I had loved it all but my resits had finally earned me a place at Durham University and the lure of what I'd been told would be a wonderful undergraduate life drew me home.

DURHAM

I was off to read Geography and for that I have to thank Brian Roberts, the Geography master at Vesey's. Not being naturally gifted academically – and according to Brian, the laziest boy he ever taught – I needed a nudge in the right direction.

Brian gave me more of a shove towards Geography at Durham. *The* place to go, apparently, was Hatfield College. None finer. It was of course where he had been. That was good enough for me, so off I went to the North East. And he was right; I had a great time with all the Geordie staff and the bright northern students. (Durham University then wasn't at all as posh as it can seem now.) There I gained a confidence, met so many clever people, and of course made lifelong friendships. I always saw myself as a bit thick – and I still do – but I did go to my lectures even if I – Nod, remember – couldn't usually stay awake. I got a third-class degree not because I was a 'sportsman' but because it was the best I could do.

The social side was brilliant with dances and balls, and these, actually, gave me my first 'business'. This was something I'd started at school: building and painting stage sets. I pitched in on designing the settings and backdrops for the bands who tramped round the university circuit in the 1960s. Before stadium rock got invented, all the top acts we heard on the radio played only in small clubs and university halls, so we could actually dance to them. It was a golden age. Chuck Berry for £4 anyone?

Even The Who performed in front of a Laithwaite set. I was given £20 to spend on a set. I used unwanted end-of-rolls of newsprint, old paint, discarded wire and glue. I made monsters, Greek gods, giant hands and birds of paradise – all sorts. Didn't make money but I got to show off, had a backstage pass, and it gave me my fondness for doing my own, unhindered thing.

As my university time ended I started to look for a job. I drew a total blank on the wine trade. British Airways and the BBC looked exciting. Nothing doing there though. I had a few brief interviews but nothing came of anything. I suppose my lack of enthusiasm for any job that meant a lifetime in a dull office (they were truly dull, back then) didn't impress.

So everyone in college but me landed a good job. I had loved Durham and I had learned a bit about geography. Unfortunately I couldn't regurgitate it to order. However, I have always believed that geography, even my very basic geography, has helped me to find good wines – and wine, they say, is bottled geography. I assess landscapes and microclimates pretty much automatically, and working out the human geography of a place – proximity of markets, transport links, politics – is just as useful in helping to search out overlooked or undervalued wine districts. But Durham gave me much more than advanced map reading. It gave me something more important than all the rest put together. There was this one, very attractive girl... mind you, there were a lot of attractive girls. But this was a particularly feisty girl. Perfect legs for the fashionable miniskirt. Rag Queen of 1967. Sadly, she didn't seem to like me much and fended me off. Fought, as they used to say, for her honour. We did not get on. We did, however, become friends a few years later. Then, she came to help me run my business. Then, we married. She was Scottish. And there's me, always so determined to marry a French girl! Barbara Hynds and I both left Durham with questionable academic records. She, although very clever, was also really dangerous in a chemistry laboratory. Mind you, despite her demolition work she still landed a great job. But I didn't. Luckily.

I hadn't got even a nibble of a job. What to do?

I had gone back to Sainte-Colombe every summer while at university and I spent 1967, the Summer of Love, researching my geography dissertation on 'The Wines of Saint-Émilion and Surrounding Areas'. Monsieur's introductions enabled me to go round and interview winemakers from the smallest *coopérateurs* to the owners of large estates like Château Troplong Mondot. I got to meet future 'great men' like the young Christian Moueix and his winemaker Jean-Claude Berrouet, the men behind Château Pétrus. I had begun to learn how the wine trade worked. And it fascinated me. But I hadn't yet decided that wine was going to be my life. In the end, it wasn't my decision; it was life, and my situation, that decided I was going to do wine.

Jobless, in the summer of 1968, what could I do? After a building-site job at Eton College (I built its theatre) I went back to France, to Bordeaux, to Sainte-Colombe, to the co-operative, to the bottling line and once again flung myself on the hospitality of dear Monsieur and Madame.

THE CASSINS

Jean Cassin was born in Castillon, called Castillon-sur-Dorgogne until it was flamboyantly renamed Castillon-la-Bataille to commemorate the decisive battle of the Hundred Years War in 1453 when, after 300 years, the king of England ceased to rule this part of France.

Aquitaine had come under the English crown as part of Eleanor's dowry when she married our King Henry II. Today, every year, tourists flock to the town as over 700 Castillonais re-enact the Middle Ages and their great battle in a vast and amazing *son et lumière* spectacle on a hillside above Castillon and remind everyone that the locals actually fought not for the French but for the English king. Alas, the French king won, mostly because, for the first time, his army had effective cannons. Not fair, really. Not cricket at all. Castillon's great château was razed to the ground as a punishment.

After the First World War, in which his handsome elder brother was killed, the small, slight, bespectacled Jean was sent off by his mother to Africa at just 14 to seek his fortune. He did well and ended up at Kano in British Northern Nigeria, running a large French trading company. He became French consul and a thorn in the side of the British colonials. They saw him as that 'damned uppity little Froggie'. He saw them as Arrogant British Colonials. Nonetheless he became a great Anglophile. He loved *le cake*, *le Chester* cheese (as the French call Cheddar), proper tea, Black & White whisky, and *le pudding*.

Back in France he had joined the army at the start of the Second World War, but was captured immediately and spent five years as a POW, eating, he said, nothing but turnips. He used this time to learn most of Shakespeare off by heart. It became a passion that lasted through his life. I remember at Domaine de Lardit, his house in Sainte-Colombe, he kept a *Complete Works* by his bed, the left page in French and the right in English. He read and memorised one page each night. Proud Frenchman that he was, he thought there was no one to rival Shakespeare. Years later I took him to see *Hamlet* at Stratford-upon-Avon. He really loved that; and there was this bizarre sight of a Frenchman, mouthing every line along with the actors. He never again ate another turnip.

Above: My room chez
Cassin.

Right: Monsieur,
Madame et moi at work.

It was not a great war for Monsieur but his imprisonment brought Madame into his life. French girls were encouraged to write to any POWs they might know. Madame knew shy little Jean from the local tennis club, and so a correspondence began that turned into a romance – Shakespeare must have been useful there – and a wedding in 1945.

Little Madame then trotted off with her new husband to Kano. She was proud to be unashamedly what they called *Vieille France*. Parisians use the term disparagingly but she saw it as a compliment. She ran his large household and was, as I knew, the perfect hostess. Their lives changed when Monsieur suffered a heart attack in 1958, and they returned to France. They had intended to retire and enjoy a quiet life, but hadn't counted on the powerful president of the local wine co-operative. It was struggling... more than struggling: its 200 farmer members were bankrupt. An experienced returning businessman, even one who'd had a heart attack, was a godsend, so the president, a forceful man, asked Monsieur Cassin to rescue them.

The co-op had got into its desperate financial difficulties by making the mistake of selling most of its wine to just one American merchant who had gone bust – not an uncommon story.

To organise a recovery was a big challenge but Monsieur took it on. The future of 200 grape-growers depended on him. Like Madame, Monsieur was small; a stooped man with the tummy of one who clearly loved his food. 'Mole', I used to think, of *Wind in the Willows*. Like Moley he wore thick glasses behind which you could just see weak but piercing eyes. He was always, always reading, often with a magnifying glass and frequently giving me his advice, with that wagging finger. '*À mon avis, à mon avis, à mon avis.*'

BACK TO THE CAVE COOPÉRATIVE

I went fairly happily back to working at the co-operative. Before, I had been a *stagiaire* – cheap labour – bottling, cleaning tanks, sweeping floors, filling bottles, stacking bottles, labelling, packing and dispatching wine.

After university I was still a *stagiaire*. No promotion for being Laithwaite BA. But I now also worked out in the vineyards, mostly spraying copper sulphate from a backpack. I would end the day stained blue, which amused Monsieur; 'I 'ave nevair seen zat: *un Anglais bleu! Ho! Ho!*'

The co-op did its own brand of wine that was now well known and sold throughout France. Independent wine merchants would come and taste their way through the cellar, trying tank after tank till they found what they wanted. One memorable day I was sweeping the cellar floor when it began to rain wine. Two storeys above me on the upper catwalks, Bernard, the deputy director, and several merchants were sipping, gurgling, tasting and spitting over the catwalk railings... on me! I found this exceptionally motivating. It would, I thought, be much better to be up there spitting than down below, being spat upon. So Monsieur kindly gave me Mondays off to do a day-release wine course at Bordeaux University under the legendary Professor Émile Peynaud, a great man who did more than anyone to drag Bordeaux out of decades of doldrums into a splendid new golden age where the top châteaux – though not necessarily all the others – have resided ever since. Indeed Monsieur himself had studied under Peynaud to learn more about wine when he started his co-operative rescue. I used to taste wine under the Prof's guidance all morning, then go off to join the student riots in the afternoon; 1969 was not as riotous as 1968 but rioting – *la manif* – was still all the fashion. I had no political views but was still trying to get off with French girls. The most important thing that the Prof taught us was simply not to trust our own untrained human palates. He had a clever way of teaching us humility. Many of my classmates were heirs to *grands* châteaux and not overloaded with modesty. He gave us all just two wines to taste and compare, and asked us, one after another, to tell the class how they compared, and which we preferred. He let us all hang ourselves; we all agreed the second was far superior and all waxed lyrical. Then, smiling, he informed us that both

Port of Bordeaux.

The Port of Bordeaux – home of the largest trade the world had ever seen; claret... mostly to Britain.

glasses came from the same bottle. I've not totally trusted my palate ever since. I've also never really believed in people claiming to be born with 'wonder palates'. Tasting skills have to be learned, and that takes many years. The 'two wine trick' has been useful to me, more than once, with overconfident, cocky new staff. Works every time. Try it.

In the 1960s in the Libournais (which is the general term for all the right-bank vineyards that cover the ground around Libourne, Saint-Émilion and Castillon), the winegrowers were basically just farmers who grew grapes and fermented them, very simply, in concrete tanks. They then waited for a *courtier* (the rather splendid title the French give to their wine brokers) to call, taste, take samples away and hopefully get a merchant to make an offer. When a deal was closed, the merchant sent a lorry or a tanker and collected the wine. The farmer's job was then over; the merchant looked after things from then on and usually made nearly all the profit that was to be made. The growers remained poor. Actually this was the system throughout all Europe back then.

Monsieur was a pioneer and went in a different and innovative direction. His Coopérative de Puisseguin Lussac was the first in Bordeaux to start bypassing the merchants and do the whole process: making wine, ageing it, bottling it and marketing it around the world. As a result he was not the most popular figure with the great wine houses of Bordeaux, the likes of the Calvets, Cordiers and Cruses. These intermediary merchants, sitting pretty between simple wine farmers and small wine retailers, had dominated the wine trade for centuries. But then, it was really they who created the great Bordeaux trade, not the *grands* châteaux who rule today. But those merchants were ruthless, not least towards Jean Cassin and his new ideas that were beginning to sideline them. They did not take kindly to him. He told me one day that the merchants had 'sent me to Birmingham' – meaning Coventry, of course – because his co-operative dared to cut them out and go direct to the first large shop chains appearing in France. In today's Bordeaux the great merchant houses along the waterfront, Les Chartrons, have all disappeared or become shadows of their former selves. The wine producers, the grand châteaux and co-operative groups, have dominated recently. Who knows what the future holds? Monsieur the ex-African trader (the merchants disparagingly called him the *marchand de cacahouètes* or peanut vendor) had created a new way of working. And not just in his approach to marketing. In the early 1960s Monsieur had the co-operative accounts computerised by the only computer then in Bordeaux. This seemed a bit of a contrast with his general frugality. His habit of watching every centime meant his PA, Madame Coste, and her assistant, young Jeanette, were instructed to reuse every envelope arriving at the office. They were all to be split open into sheets, hole-punched and tied together with string to make the scribble pads on which he drafted all his letters and did his sums. Monsieur considered notepads an extravagance too far for a bankrupt co-operative. His methods – which I had to learn – worked, and the co-operative got back into the black and eventually became a huge success. All this helped influence me, I suppose.

While he worked his wonders, Madame was delighted to be back where her family had lived for centuries. They were a contented couple, respected in the village where Monsieur, despite strong political views (he claimed to be a Bonapartist, whereas Madame had always wished for the king to return), never involved himself in the political life of the area. But he was seen as a surrogate *maire* by the locals. They came to see him for advice on money, taxes and all sorts. Though they had no children, Madame taught all the Sainte-Colombe children their catechism at Sunday school, so knew them all and consequently pretty much everything that was going on in the village.

Madame, a small, birdlike figure, was never still, always fizzing with energy. She drove the lanes furiously, but would slam on the brakes for any small bird sitting in the road. She would pick up injured ones and take them home to nurse. She had been educated at Le Cours Saint-Seurin (a bit like Cheltenham Ladies' College apparently) where all the posh girls went. So she knew Madame la Baronne de Marcillac and the other little aristos of the area, and took tea with them. This part of France is so English; they have, since Queen Eleanor, been known as the 'Anglo-Gascons'. Madame was not an aristocrat but perhaps thought herself the equal of those who had grandiose titles but were really only very minor members of the French nobility. But certainly her family was further up the social ladder than her husband's, as she was in the habit of reminding him.

She was never really happier than wearing her apron, in her kitchen. It was a kitchen that had not changed down the years... and still hasn't. Her niece Catherine now keeps it – and indeed the whole house – as a sort of shrine to Tante Ginette and Tonton Jean. She was so fond of them. I remember, also fondly, being allowed indoors to eat with them: Madame on my left, closest to the kitchen and the large fireplace, in charge of all food; Monsieur to my right, in charge of the wine. I can still see the picture so clearly. The polished, old, round oak table with everything gleaming, the old cutlery with the blades of the knives resting on tiny glass trestles, the water glasses ordinary and modern but the wine glasses ancient, made of thick glass, with straight sides. On special occasions the really fine glassware came out, which meant about six glasses per setting as important guests would get a different wine for every course, from dusty, encrusted bottles from their vineyard going back to the 1920s. Madame's vivacity and Monsieur's erudition attracted fascinating guests from the cinema, fashion, literature and operatic worlds. Their great favourite was Alain, Baron de Condé – Madame insisted he was really a prince – an Oscar Wilde sort of figure – a searingly witty restorer of paintings.

But I was amazed at the frugality of the daily servings. Brits like me have a tendency to gulp our wine like it was beer. Properly brought-up Bordeaux wine people do not gulp. They sip, look thoughtful a while, then eventually swallow and quietly sigh. The first time Monsieur poured wine for me, he poured about an eighth of a glass. I thought he was flattering me; asking me to check it to see if it was corked. (I was taught that the ritual of sommeliers giving a taste to the 'one who knows about wine' was solely to enable them to detect any cork taint – not then uncommon. Cork taint has all but vanished these days. But the ritual persists. Even with screwcap bottles!) I'd seen people do that tasting thing in restaurants so it was gone in one swig, with me nodding that it was perfectly fine and looking expectant. Nothing doing; that small serving was 'it'. The bottle remained untouched for ages before Monsieur poured another miserly eighth.

Furthermore, Monsieur would only ever pour wine *after* we'd started eating, *never* before. As he explained, good Bordeaux wine, red wine, is only ever drunk with food because it is dry and quite tannic. On its own, its tannins can make the inside of your mouth feel rough, sort of pebble-dashed, which is not *agréable*. But when you've already chewed on some meat or cheese the wine actually seems to sweeten, and the drying tannins just vanish (it's to do with a reaction between tannins and the amino acids in meat and cheese). The wine will then enhance the food and slip down *parfaitement*, Monsieur assured me. It truly does, and that, especially today, is worth remembering. We now have sweeter, richer and less tannic wines in abundance, from Australia, California and the like, which have got people used to drinking red wine that doesn't need food at all. A red Bordeaux opened and poured straightaway without any food, can come as a shock and, sadly, as a result never be ordered again. This is why it is important for us wine merchants to make clear which of our wines only taste their best with food.

While wine seemed to be rationed, we drank plenty of water. Spring water from the pump. At this table it was water for your thirst, wine for your pleasure and of course your health. Bordeaux: *le vin médecin*! But *toujours* in moderation. I had to learn this habit. That was hard, but maybe it has helped me and my liver survive the wine business for over 50 years.

Mind you, everyone else in the village drank more, much more. Well, certainly the men did. The working countrymen of Sainte-Colombe – and

I still raise a few geese every year. Vicious but delicious.

indeed the rest of France – were all alcoholics according to some, and 2 litres per meal was not uncommon. This showed clearly in their bright red faces and warty purple noses. But the women were not big drinkers; indeed most wives did not drink wine at all. I never really understood why. But they lived long, while their husbands didn't.

While Monsieur kept the wine bottle out of my reach and pushed the water jug towards me, little Madame, a ball of energy, would be bobbing up and down attending to the food. Breakfast was simple. Just *le toast*. Croissants were a town thing, as were baguettes. In the villages it was the *gros pain de campagne*. Truly *gros*: a loaf the size of a small child that lasted all week and which you cut into thick slices by clutching the great thing to your chest – as if it was indeed a child – then sawing the knife scarily towards your heart. The Cassins served marmalade but most other people just rubbed a raw garlic clove on their morning toast. I was reminded of this every time I boarded the crowded – and eye-watering – early-morning train to Bordeaux to do my wine course.

Apart from special occasions lunch, *le déjeuner* – or in patois *la soupe* – was the big meal. *Le dîner* in the evening was relatively simple. Like eggs or cold meat. *La soupe*, though, was at least five courses followed by coffee. On her stove Madame kept a big stockpot. It was always there... 5 litres' worth at least, filled with vegetables and bones of all sorts. Constantly replenished. Her *domestique* Fernande (an enthusiastic

Opposite: Harvest scene. exception to the non-drinking wives' club) would have it on low heat all morning and Madame would then take ladlefuls to combine with tomatoes, potatoes, vermicelli, or whatever she planned to make her soup of that day. The recipes were many and varied but always finished off with a big lump of butter. I've never had soups that good anywhere else.

There was a special thick black soup we got in winter when they killed the pig: *guimbora*. So incredibly rich; it was, apparently, mostly pig's blood with red beans, vegetables and lots of pepper. *Guimbora* time was when you met the village and you saw how important it was then for villagers to be a real community. Every year, every household raised its pig. It lived in a sty by the house and ate all the leftovers. Quite sensible really, as there were no green bins back then. Not sure there were any bins at all. Certainly no bin men. When you kill a pig there is an awful lot of meat and offal, all at once, but back then, there were no freezers. So you would salt-cure the hams and hang them from the rafters in linen bags. You'd make jars of pâté and rillettes from the small stuff. That left the guts and blood that could not be conserved, but were much too nourishing to waste. So what the villagers did was cooperate and swap. When, say, Madame Trepout next door killed her pig, the village would be notified (probably everyone had heard the shrieks of the poor thing being despatched anyway). That evening after she had slaved away all day over the *carcasse*, someone, often a child, from every family turned up at her door with a jug. This was filled with the hot, peppery soup, all beans and vegetables, and was – once you got your head adjusted to the blood thing – utterly delicious. The child also took home a pack of black puddings or *boudins noirs*. More blood. The whole village would feast that night on the innards of Madame Trepout's pig. People who work manually out all day in the vineyards in winter, maybe steering a horse plough constantly in and out between vines – far harder than straight-line ploughing – need very solid nourishment. The following week it's Madame Parinet down the road who kills her pig. So all share her pig's innards. And so it goes on around the village: every household, every pig. Sadly, it doesn't seem to happen any more; it may even have been banned. But then the villagers don't cooperate so much now and go to the hypermarket instead.

After the soup, there were *hors d'œuvres*, which could be a salad, endive or *niçoise* or tomato, or perhaps beetroot and shallot, grated carrots or artichoke, or the other type of artichoke that you ate by peeling it leaf by leaf, dipping each in vinaigrette and scraping the soft part off with

41

your teeth. The main course could be chicken from the yard, head and feet still on, or duck or guinea fowl. On Fridays we always had fish. Lampreys on special occasions. Best of all, though, was steak. The dining room fireplace was important, less for its warmth, more for the *grillades*. Mostly entrecôte bordelaise to which the people of that region are devoted. There was a ritual – Madame's ritual. She just loved putting on the show that Monsieur and I would always enjoy. And not just us, people came from far and wide for this performance and the steak. Let me take you there.

It involves not a fire as such but just a *sarment*. Everyone puts away a big collection of *sarments* to see them through the year's *grillades*. Willow was, and for some still is, what vines are tied to the wires with. You still see rows of willow stumps dotted around the vineyards sprouting bright yellow shoots. These shoots are harvested every summer and put into streams to soak so they become pliable enough to knot. Wonderfully ecological.

The *sarment* just fits in the fireplace and is lit by Madame with a crumpled sheet of newspaper. She spreads the rest of the paper in front of the fire to catch the dripping fat. The *sarment* blazes fiercely for a minute or two, then dies to a thin covering of glowing red embers, giving off a sweet 'dried herbs' aroma. A large iron grill with a long handle and four short legs is plonked on this, to be cleaned and sterilised. Madame now wipes the red-hot grill with more of the newspaper to remove the last of the old grease and lies the grill before the fire.

Then one very large, very thick entrecôte steak with many veins of fat is slapped on the hot grill. It about covers it. The petite but amazingly strong Madame then arranges the embers and lifts the grill on to them. Oh, the aroma! I can smell it now. It doesn't grill for long, as they like their meat fairly rare. When she turns the meat, she spoons a generous layer of raw, chopped shallots on to the cooked side. They ooze into the hot steak. Then she seasons it with sea salt and plenty of fresh-ground pepper. The timing is immaculate, though Madame doesn't really need to worry about overcooking because the embers quickly lose their heat and the steak then sits relaxing and soaking up more aromas and shallot juice while Monsieur and I do similar with a little wine. The steak is cut up and served. *Frites* are the only accompaniment. You get a salad separately, afterwards. Oh my! Oh my! I would drive 500 miles for that steak. And I did for 40 years, almost every month, at one time. Madame also conserved everything that could be conserved. Not just lots of jams but lots of pâtés too; rough pâtés done in *bocals* – Kilner jars – and matured for years like fine wine. Rillettes also. And lampreys. Oh, the lampreys! A French delicacy – ugly fish that exist by sucking blood from other fish. Bought at the market in season, cooked in their own blood with leeks, spices, red wine and a little chocolate. Served as the first course, with croutons, on all special occasions. A dish unlike any other. Fit for a king. As we were taught in school. A bit too delicious for old Henry I, dying, as he did, from a surfeit of them.

The Cassins took me with them to a few very special feasts with local farmers, when a crazy traditional meal of ten courses or more was served. You could see what you were in for on arrival. When you sat down there was a high pile of empty plates before you, one for each course.

The first course went on the top plate, and when you finished, it was removed. The second course went in the next one down, and so on. You worked your way down, plate removed after each course. These days some restaurants serve their 'taster' menus of many courses. But what you got back then was not a thimbleful of flower-decorated lamb. The old country folk would have been ashamed to offer such miserly portions. No, these were *grandes bouffes*... Surfeit of lampreys? This was a surfeit of everything. Mind, these were not refined bourgeois folk. These were the ordinary farming folk: big strong people of amazing capacity. And they had invited the little English chap who was silently groaning and praying for the end. These bashes didn't happen often. Just as well, really.

That year from the summer of 1968 to the summer of 1969 was idyllic. Rioters may have been ripping up the cobbles in the streets of Paris but Sainte-Colombe and Castillon remained calm, untroubled backwaters. This wasn't known as *La France profonde* for nothing. It was the deep heart of the country. People had their set ways and were proud of them; the land was their life and they did not want or seek change.

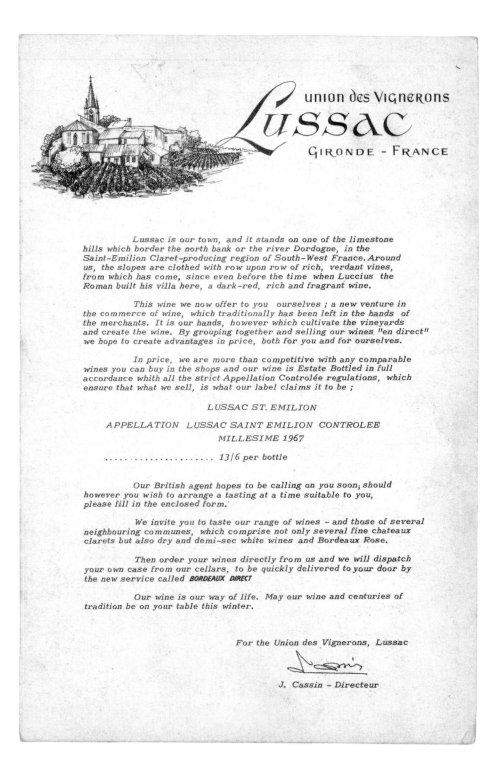

UNION DES VIGNERONS

Lussac

GIRONDE - FRANCE

Lussac is our town, and it stands on one of the limestone hills which border the north bank or the river Dordogne, in the Saint-Emilion Claret-producing region of South-West France. Around us, the slopes are clothed with row upon row of rich, verdant vines, from which has come, since even before the time when Luccius the Roman built his villa here, a dark-red, rich and fragrant wine.

This wine we now offer to you ourselves ; a new venture in the commerce of wine, which traditionally has been left in the hands of the merchants. It is our hands, however which cultivate the vineyards and create the wine. By grouping together and selling our wines "en direct" we hope to create advantages in price, both for you and for ourselves.

In price, we are more than competitive with any comparable wines you can buy in the shops and our wine is Estate Bottled in full accordance whith all the strict Appellation Contrôlée regulations, which ensure that what we sell, is what our label claims it to be ;

LUSSAC ST. EMILION

APPELLATION LUSSAC SAINT EMILION CONTROLEE
MILLESIME 1967

.... 13/6 per bottle

Our British agent hopes to be calling on you soon; should however you wish to arrange a tasting at a time suitable to you, please fill in the enclosed form.

We invite you to taste our range of wines - and those of several neighbouring communes, which comprise not only several fine chateaux clarets but also dry and demi-sec white wines and Bordeaux Rose.

Then order your wines directly from us and we will dispatch your own case from our cellars, to be quickly delivered to your door by the new service called **BORDEAUX DIRECT**

Our wine is our way of life. May our wine and centuries of tradition be on your table this winter.

For the Union des Vignerons, Lussac

J. Cassin - Directeur

Opposite: The very first of many sales letters.

THE BLINDING FLASH

This was the time before the UK was in the EEC and I was only allowed to stay with a temporary work permit as a temporary *stagiaire*. There was a time limit.

I tried to find a permanent job but French wine merchants turned me down as fast as had their British brothers. They were at least nice about it. Calvert, Cruse, Cordier and Eschenauer all said nicely, '*Non!*'. I did get a job with the CIVB (the wine producers' organisation) as a wine guide on bus tours for English-speaking journalists. But that was far from permanent.

Better than when I had tried to get into the UK wine trade. Going off to the biggest outfit of all, Grants of St James's – who, strangely, were based in Burton upon Trent – proudly clutching my 'Wines of Saint-Émilion and Surrounding Areas' dissertation. That might impress them, I thought. The large man in the three-piece pinstripe sitting behind his huge, highly polished desk interviewing me, burst out laughing when I showed it him, and straightaway tossed it back across the desk. That was a motivating moment! Stayed in my mind a long time, that did. I was so keen to work in the wine business and it was about the only thing I knew anything about, and here was this man showing such contempt. He symbolised the established wine trade and his attitude cut very deep. From then on I gave up trying to join any other UK merchants and avoided them for years. But far from putting me off wine, that laughter simmered in my guts for years. It gave me a real motivation to prove him wrong, to show the old bugger. A while ago, I met up with a whole roomful of entrepreneurs invited by the Government – I forget which one – to a drinks party in Westminster. Left hanging around for hours by a Minister who was clearly far busier than we were, a group of us discussed our business lives. It turned out that all of us had, early on, been laughed at and that an indelible memory of being humiliated was a large part of what had driven us on. But bottle washing in the co-op wasn't really on the fast-track, career-wise. If I was going to sock it to the bastard in Burton, I really needed to find something else – anything else – fast.

Life in France was so good but I knew it couldn't last. Monsieur Cassin had taught me about wine; working as a *stagiaire* had shown me the business from the bottom up. It had been invaluable. But the really important lessons came in the talks in Monsieur's car on his way to the co-operative and around the dinner table. Here, I was being drip-fed the intricacies of the business of wine. Monsieur repeated and repeated and repeated how a business worked, the way he had made his co-operative change. And I was slowly taking it all in.

Then, one day came the Blinding Light! My particular road to Damascus was that winding RD 17 between Puisseguin and Sainte-Colombe as Monsieur drove us home one warm evening. He suddenly suggested that if no one else would give me work in wine, I should try selling his wine. What he meant was become a 'rep', what in France they call a *multicarte*. I should go around calling on restaurateurs, shopkeepers and wine merchants – basically set up as another of his freelance agents. But I immediately saw something very different and crazily exciting. This was – and still is – a trait of mine. In almost everything I undertake, for some reason it seems I must always take the unexpected direction rather than the logical, sensible one. The academic result of this had been that even when I could remember some facts, I never gave examiners the answers they expected. That habit scores very low. But, it seems, for an entrepreneur this lateral-brain stuff is a great advantage and can score big. That's as long as you also have a sensible person or two around and they are prepared to back you... sometimes but not always. By no means always. Monsieur provided me with a good counterbalance of sense, and thankfully, many others have since done the same.

I have maybe embroidered the story over the years in the frequent retelling, but his suggestion in the car that evening seemed to explode something in my head. It ignited a fireball of ideas: a string of plans to do with writing letters to people – not businesses but actual consumers – with an offer of a free wine tasting in their homes, telling them all about Monsieur's co-operative and its wine, collecting lots of orders and sending them back to Bordeaux, shipping the wine to the UK, delivering it, maybe actually earning some money and never ever having to go for another humiliating job interview.

Monsieur did not disagree but weighed in with stern practicalities. We talked on in the car and talked and talked into the night, sitting in that old 2CV now parked up inside Monsieur's darkened garage. A worried Madame eventually had to come out and drag us into dinner, so hard

My first wine and my first – and last – hand-drawn label.

did the idea bite, so long did we sit, plan and argue. The next day a sales letter was drafted – I still have a copy of a version.

We wrote it together, me persuading Monsieur to leave his quaint English grammar in the letter. He let me choose which bottling I wanted. He let me draw my own label (a very odd, hand-drawn thing, when I look at it now) and letterhead and got it all printed for me. The prices were all worked out. He did that; beyond my abilities, that sort of thing – and still is, actually. Monsieur always believed it was very important to make a profit – no half-price deals for him – but that it should never be an excessive profit. He believed it was important that the margins were fair all round. Too little margin, and service and quality would inevitably drop for lack of funds. Too much, and the customers would get upset and leave. He said that you develop a nose for where your price should be. I still believe he was right. However when you see the astronomical prices now reached by some Saint-Émilions, I do have some doubts. But at that time, in 1969, even a superstar wine like Château Cheval Blanc was only £3 a bottle in the shops. It was a different time. But though I didn't know it then, it was a very good time to start a wine business in the UK.

2

BORDEAUX MIXTURE

TIME TO GO HOME

I began to plan my return to England. I produced my label, saw my wine bottled, prepared a dozen sample half-bottles with my shiny red label on, printed a box of sales letters and saw a glorious vision of what I was going to do.

Previous page: André Velletier, a wonderful winegrower in Julienas, Beaujolais. He kept to the old traditions such as fruit trees still growing in his vineyards, for the workers – and he still had the old manual wine press because he loved the noise and laughter his student harvesters brought to his little cellar.

I had found a name: 'Bordeaux Direct' – simple, straightforward and no nonsense. It said what I intended to do: bring the wine of a Bordeaux wine cellar directly to consumers. I had taken it from a signpost near a fork in the road south of Castillon; it was either 'Bordeaux par Langon' or 'Bordeaux Direct'. I'm sure I made the right choice. I think we might have been the first of so many companies to use the word 'Direct' in their name. Certainly caught on, didn't it?

I wrote to my parents and explained what I planned to do. My father must have looked at me, his only child, no money, no car, no work and planning to live at home, and no doubt wanted to tell me to pull myself together and get a proper job, but he didn't.

He was actually quite enthusiastic about the wine part. Perhaps they thought that in time I would become sensible, but for now they encouraged me and offered what help they could: free board and lodgings, and occasional use of the car. Nana Rudd helped even more. She 'lent' me her life savings of £700! That was my vital starter capital. A couple of years later, there was more. She had long been widowed, but after a passionate courtship between pensioners (my girlfriend and I frequently found the front-room sofa already occupied), she'd

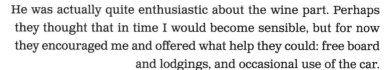

Opposite: Jojo, master bottler in the Appelghem Chai.

gone and married my other grandfather, also a widower. Keeping things in the family! Five years later, these two retired entrepreneurs gave me a formal loan of £7,000, a huge sum, and at a fair rate of interest, when I was suddenly in need and no bank would even look at me. This demonstrated the usefulness of 'family' in business. New start-ups are such tender things. Like little seedlings need watering and protection, they do need love and a bit of money. Today, it's wonderful that such help and advice is now available to young start-ups who don't have family backing. I have seen what help from the Prince's Trust can do for the most unlikely of start-ups, and I've seen through doing stuff with Oxfam the amazing effect the tiniest of loans can have in the poorest parts of the world.

I was ready to go. But I really didn't want to go back to Britain because life in France just got better and better. That summer in France, they still refer to as *l'été érotique*. Well, they would know. It was a wild old summer for me. Through playing a season for the Castillon-la-Bataille rugby team I had made many more friends in the town, one result of which was being offered a tempting job down there. Monsieur was fine with me leaving the co-op and going to work for Établissements Appelghem who supplied wines and beers to local bars and restaurants in Castillon and some way up the Dordogne. My bottle-washing skills were not up to those of their little Jojo so I was entrusted with bottling the special barrels. Real wine work at last!

I worked alone in a dark corner of the cellar, crouched down beside that day's barrel with my lamp, my bottles and my *tireuse à quatre becs*. This ingenious little device fills four bottles at the same time by gravity without spilling... in theory, at least. It took me most of a day to fill, cork, capsule, label and pack a barrel: 300 bottles in theory. But we were always a bit short. Evaporation of some sort. Happy days. Some barrels were Saint-Émilion, some were Côtes de Castillon, but mostly – because that was what the locals really loved – it was a thick, black, 15-degree wine from an Algerian wine region called – would you believe – Mascara. What a wine. Sadly, it doesn't exist any more. (But I have found success over the years with quite a few wines that we now classify as 'Black-Reds'.) Hazy days were followed by hazy nights as a late-night barman at *Le Dancing de la Gare*. Terrible bands but wild old parties. I camped out in a vast, empty, deserted old château just along the railway line. Château Gaillardet fronts on to the main Bergerac road and Monsieur Appelghem wanted to turn it into a showcase for his wines. That never happened, but he let me legally squat there in return for cleaning up

and restoring old wine equipment and making him a tasting room-cum-museum in my spare time. This somehow became my main job. What a summer! The sun shone, the Beatles on the juke box sang about the 'Sun King', and that was me. Then one day, my boss's son, Jean-Pierre Appelghem, just loaded me and my samples and stuff on his lorry up to Calais near where he bought his beer and, as he has told everyone ever since: '*Je l'ai foutu dehors*' ('I threw him out').

A SLOW START

The return home was sobering. I remember clearly the moment in October 1969, sitting at home in my bedroom in front of the electric fire, laying out my sample half-bottles of the claret from Monsieur's co-operative in a neat row on the bed.

This was what my wild dreams had come down to. I had the 12 samples, my reps' sample case, my sales letters, my slender wits and a pit in my stomach. It looked bleak, and scary. But there was no way I could avoid giving it a go. I had done a lot of hitch-hiking and it felt a bit like I was setting out on a long hitch. I got the same nerves, the same tense guts. You have to pluck up courage to hitch, you must forget fears and just take your chances on the open road. You are sure no one will ever give you a lift or turn out to be a murderer, but you just hope, and eventually a car does stop, and they are always very kind. It was similar now, exciting as well as scary. But I didn't have a business plan that would impress television's Dragons in their Den today. I wasn't even sure how to get my letters out to people. Finally I decided on nothing more sophisticated than taking 100 names from the local telephone directory. I opened a page at random – it was the Ds – wrote the names and addresses on envelopes, posted them, and prayed hard. Not hard enough; I got just two replies. Oh disaster! Things looked SO bleak. (It was only later that I discovered 2 per cent was a perfectly respectable return on a 'cold list' mailing.) To me at that time, it seemed dreadful. But I borrowed my father's Austin and set off in my suit for my first free tasting with a couple just up the road in Burnham. It seems mad now that I could go off for a wine tasting with just one wine. But that kind couple bought my first case. I think they felt they had to, perhaps feeling sorry for this hopeless guy. They said:

Dancing de la Gare poster.

'Mmm, very nice... we'll take a case.' Probably just to get rid of me. But it was my first order – a case of 1966 Lussac-Saint-Émilion at the grand sum of 13 shillings and sixpence a bottle (£8.10 in today's money). It was a start. That seems very cheap today, but back then Averys of Bristol was selling premier grand cru classé wines for £3! A wine similar to my Lussac, today, would cost maybe ten times as much as it did then. But any first growth will now be at least a hundred times more.

CHÂTEAU LA CLARIÈRE LAITHWAITE

THIS IS MY FAVOURITE WINE. ABSOLUTELY. IT HAS TO BE. IT'S MINE!

It's from the very vineyard that started the whole wine thing off for me in 1965. It's been hugely important for the Company and is the favourite of thousands of customers virtually every vintage. Especially the thousands of Confrères with whom I share both the place and the wine. And it has also made my Company what it is. Because when I bought La Clarière and became a wine producer it soon made me a much better wine buyer. I lost a good bit of arrogance and learned to listen to my suppliers more. And learned to understand and trust them. Because I now knew what they went through to produce good wine. One taste of a wine and many wine buyers think they 'know' it. They assess it immediately. But they can't, really. Because wine is alive. Like us. It has its good days and its bad. At the same time, according to Professor Peynaud, WE too, even us 'experts', have our good and bad days. So all in all it takes more than a quick sip to get to know a wine. Certainly if you're going to place a large bet, like ordering thousands of cases. And, just as importantly, when you really get to know it, a familiar wine becomes like a friend. A real friend you're always happy to see, whom you never tire of. I don't know if it's a particularly addictive wine, but I do know once they've enjoyed a case of La Clarière, the Confrères' annual delivery day becomes a regular, and much looked forward to, date in the calendar for them.

My second tasting was in an office on a trading estate in Windsor with the local baker, Roger Denny, who had gone into property development. I think my genuine enthusiasm for Monsieur Cassin's wine plus my total naivety as a salesman actually worked. Mr Denny was won over. He dragged some of his team into the office and between them they ordered an amazing five cases. These guys were experienced salesmen, but they do say that no one is easier to sell to than a salesman. When I eventually delivered the wine, they were very happy and even rang other friends while I was there, to tell them they should meet this odd wine guy and his one wine. From that day my base of customers slowly grew. Everyone noted down on an index card to be phoned back or written to when I guessed they might want another case. It's called 'looking after your customers'; nothing is more important, said Monsieur.

I came to realise over the next year or two that I could not have been luckier (again) in my timing. These early customers were people who had recently been over to France on the new car ferries, had drunk the local wine, liked it, and realised that it didn't taste the same as the wine they were getting at home. There was a reason for that. Back then almost all wine in Britain was imported in bulk and bottled here by British wine shippers in a very British sort of way. We sort of overcooked it in the same way that the French thought we overcooked our beef. As a result UK bottled wines came out rather oxidised and dull-tasting, with a brown tinge. Many British shippers thought we didn't like wine with any sort of bite to it so they let the air get at it. Suddenly there was this bloke sitting awkwardly in front of them in his tight suit offering wine that was bottled by the people who made it and who liked their wine more natural. It had a fresher, more vibrant taste; you could actually taste a fruitiness. It even looked different: bright red with a blue rather than brown tinge. It stayed fresh in the bottle, often tasting better the next day, many said. Also it came from a village I knew, made by people I could tell them about. So they got the whole story, and liked that. I didn't realise it then but it's clear now that acquiring this habit of telling the stories of wines was another key to eventual success. Other merchants, at that time, didn't do that. I was different. Word spread. People came. Not many, but 'business' had at least begun. I was an entrepreneur. Friends were amazed. Nod? An entrepreneur? I was a lazy boy, a daydreamer. I didn't do paper rounds or set up businesses as a child. I stayed in bed for as long as I could. I did found a club at school, called the 'William Club', a fan club for boys who liked *Just William*. But I didn't do that for money, just for fun, though I did mix and bottle a ghastly luminous lemonade to sell to club members which stained their mouths yellow. Not a success.

But I doubt there is actually an entrepreneur 'type'. They come in all shapes and sizes. You meet many who have been employees for much of their lives, then start something up on their own later. For them it was a courageous move. For me it wasn't brave at all because I had nothing to lose. There certainly has to be a passionate desire to achieve something. You have to keep in your head a very pleasant picture of what your dream result looks like. And usually, I have discovered, this isn't simply a pile of money. The pursuit of just money can actually get in the way; it can lead you away from pushing for the dream. The money path is not the same as the dream path. It will cause you to make very obvious decisions, which help the opposition to see you coming. Following dreams leads you to take unexpected decisions which they won't see, so you can make a breakthrough. Disruption, it's called now. By disrupters. Going in odd, unexpected directions. Which is fine as long as your ultimate dream goal remains fixed in your head. When I eventually bought the van and began driving wine back from Bordeaux myself, that was not a money decision. But you do need to be prepared for the change entrepreneurship will make in you. It's a drug and like any drug you get addicted. Terribly addicted. You won't get to lie in bed much. Or if you do – and I do these days – it's only because lying there quiet and alone and musing on business while half asleep is when I get my best ideas and ideas are what an entrepreneur must produce. They don't produce widgets, they get other people to produce the widgets. They don't even necessarily produce the idea for better widgets but they'll have had the idea about how to set things up. So creatives will have the ideas and the organised types will make the things for talented salespeople to sell so the number-crunchers can get in the money to pay everyone and keep them happy. But the entrepreneur doesn't aim for all that at all; his or her dream is just the perfect widget and he or she is driven by an inability to bear the thought of anyone else beating them to it. Entrepreneurs are obsessed. They can't stop. You think that Branson is lolling around on his island during long, idle days in the sun? No way. He's always working. I had a meeting with him once, in London. He doesn't relax much. Funnily enough, I was told afterwards that he was surprised by how relaxed I was! But that's because when I'm nervous I can't stop yawning. It's a strange tic. One that got me into trouble at school but has since helped me negotiate some good contracts.

THE FIRST YEAR

My dad put word round his golf club that his son was now in wine. So thanks to him I soon had orders for just short of 20 cases.

But a small legal problem had appeared. Rather late in the day I realised that selling any alcoholic beverage in the United Kingdom required a licence, which I didn't have. I also didn't have any suitable shop premises that the law required and that the local magistrates would demand. I would have had to appear before the court for the licence and wasn't optimistic. They would be looking for mature, steady and experienced applicants. They would just see me as a young renegade about to incite mass inebriation in the local population. Because there would also be 'the Opposition' that always turned up in court. The existing licence holders in town would always object to anyone else moving in on their patch. They would convince the 'Beaks' that my new shop would spell certain debauchery in Windsor.

My adventure thus seemed doomed at a very early stage. But the Luck of Laithwaite prevailed. One customer (via my dad) was a barrister, Norman Henderson, who knew of something that could resolve my problem. This was the little-known wholesale licence. It restricted sales to a minimum of 12 bottles, or a case, and didn't require any shop premises and it seemed I could easily get one. Wonderful thing, our British law – all those powerful legal brains at work. They deduced that while selling one bottle of wine in a proper shop would risk the fabric of society coming apart, selling 12 bottles from home obviously posed no such risk. Five pounds to the local police station for a slip of paper made everything legal. As it had never occurred to me to sell anything less than a case, the wholesale licence seemed just made for me.

Others, I found, used the same astuce. Indeed, I believe Majestic Wine started that way some years later.

This was the first of many, many lessons about the shipping and selling of wine in Britain. Another example: I thought all I had to do was get the orders and send them off to Monsieur Cassin who would then send the cases back. Not that simple. For my first load, I got the wine sent from Bordeaux to London by boat to the East India Docks – or West India

*Opposite: Not a wine
I sold, but a poster
from the '60s, when
advertising was just
getting creative and
youthful.*

Docks – not sure now… or then, for that matter. The whole area is now part of Canary Wharf, but the cranes were still working back then. I rented a small van and drove to the London offices of Thomas Trapp and Son, the agents for my shipment. I had to complete reams of paperwork before I set off through what remained of the docks after the wartime bombing. Blackened walls, a lot of car parks and scrap yards. My first challenge was to find the right warehouse. The second challenge, when I got there, was finding that my 20 cases had now become 17, thanks to pilfering. That was quite a percentage to lose. I complained and just got a shrug of the shoulders; this was what inevitably happened in the docks before today's strong steel pilfer-proof shipping containers were invented. Clearly this was not a great way to import wine in the small quantities wanted by Bordeaux Direct. Nor was it going to be a profitable way.

'*Quoi faire, Monsieur?*' Well, there was a solution and Monsieur found it; my second shipment avoided London altogether. It came into Shoreham-by-Sea, Sussex – a small harbour with an honest reputation. Shoreham received regular cargoes of wine from Bordeaux on a boat called the *Zephyr*. I went and collected *all* my 20 cases. From then on I made regular journeys down to Sussex. I even bought my own car, to the relief of my father. Nana Rudd had 'lent' me her savings. That £700 kept me going, and some of it now helped get me a battered but serviceable Cortina estate from my garage mechanic mate Merv. I did the Shoreham run about once a month – for 20 cases a time. It took me a month to do enough tastings to sell that many. This level of sales meant that, of course, I wasn't earning anywhere near enough to live on, but Mother managed to keep Father from throwing me out. Just.

In order to bring in some extra money – I didn't want to use up all Nana Rudd's money – I took a Christmas job at Simpsons of Piccadilly. Me, one of the most sartorially challenged men ever, in one of London's most upmarket clothing stores? But off I went to the shop that was the inspiration for the sitcom *Are You Being Served?*. I especially loved that television series when I read that its writer, Jeremy Lloyd, had worked there too. It was truly like Grace Brothers. People really did call 'Are you free, Mr Laithwaite?'

My stint there helped prevent the deep midwinter becoming even bleaker. Apparently I was good enough in the job for them to keep me on

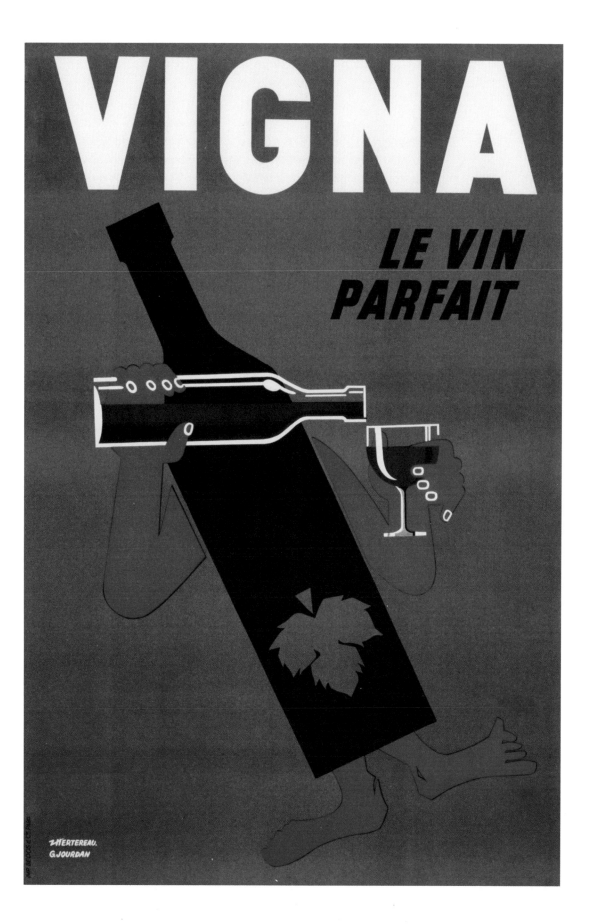

after Christmas for the January sales period. I enjoyed the bustle and the laughs of that little interlude. But then it was back to my own extremely nascent business. Where I felt very lonely. There wasn't much to do. I went out and rented an office for a fiver a week, behind a junk shop in Victoria Street, Windsor, just along from the barracks. I made furniture out of pallets and other abandoned junk. Spent days doing it. Killing time really. Because no one came to see me. I spent hours arranging and rearranging that office. Hiding from reality I suppose... Business was SO slow. This was when I came closest to giving up. But this was the period of the Apollo space programme. I followed it avidly. Watched every blast-off, moonwalk and splashdown. I had the time. Business being what it was. Or wasn't. But sending men to the moon must surely have encouraged me to think that selling cases of Bordeaux was not at all impossible. It was an optimistic world back then. All was possible. The future was bright.

But I was knocked back by a dinner at Eton College. My down-to-earth Yorkshire mate Dave Lowther was, somehow, now a Geography teacher at Eton. He kindly invited me for dinner at Baldwin's Shore, the house he shared with other young teachers. Free meal? Sure. But, he said, one of them 'knew about wine'. This was not a pleasant evening for me. This man obviously felt I might threaten his position as 'the wine expert round here' and went for me. It was a fight. A serious verbal fight. He was going to trounce me with his superior wine knowledge. He wanted to show me up. To expose me as ignorant. His full-on attack threw me, this was just so completely new to me. Monsieur and his friends never did this. Certainly the lads at the co-op never did. They all knew lots about wine. But they didn't hit you over the head with it. I had no idea that in Britain some people used wine as a social weapon to keep out the lower orders. He came out with stuff like 'Of course everyone knows the '64s from Pauillac are not up to the Margaux level, except of course for the south slopes... you do, of course, know that Anthony Barton will only ever use well-toasted oak... so what side of the hill do you think this comes from?' I held my end up... just. I had, after all, worked in Bordeaux for some time, and I had actually met Anthony Barton, the most delightful man in the Bordeaux trade and owner of Château Langoa Barton, while this dreadful man just got his stuff from books and articles in the papers. But if this duelling and snobbery was what selling wine in Britain was all about, I thought I'd maybe just give up now.

What got me going again was a letter from my other even more down-to-earth Yorkshire college friend Tony Parkin. I'd written him a moaning letter. His reply began

> *Dear Nod, Thanks for telling me your problems. Can I just say that in Yorkshire we have a saying: 'Tough Titty!' Look, old son, you chose the wine game, and there are many worse problems than yours. Stop moaning and just get on with it, will you!*

I suppose I could've reacted badly. But as I remember it I near fell off the loo with laughing. Only Parkin could say that. Only a bloody Yorkshireman. So no question of a Boltonian giving up after that!

The Eton dinner, I eventually decided, had been a good thing. I now knew how I was going to do wine, or at least how I was not going to do it. There would be no wine snobbery from me. I'd speak plainer than plain. No flowery stuff. From me a spade would be a bloody shovel. I'd also learn more and more. First hand. Not from books. I'd judge a wine by tasting it 'blind', not looking at its label. I'd focus on just my customers and act accordingly. I'd ignore pseudo-experts. And my job would be to draw into wine all the people – most of the population – that this man and those like him would try to frighten away. I stopped faffing about in the office and went out looking for customers.

In order to give my business an image of actually being an up-to-date sort of venture, I decided to invest in something amazingly new: a 'pocket' calculator – the first one ever sold, apparently. I couldn't – and still can't – manage even the simplest mathematical calculations so this new invention was for me. It seems ludicrous now but it cost me £200 to buy the Sharp Y200. More than the car. It did make some sort of sense, I suppose. Though to call it a 'pocket' calculator was rather wide of the mark. It was the size and weight of a house brick, but it was very new and it did my sums so I could actually give my customers a proper bill. Then I went mad and bought two Philips mini-cassette recorders – hard to believe now but they were cutting-edge stuff too; hey, this was the very beginning of the high-tech world! I sent one to Monsieur Cassin in Sainte-Colombe, the other stayed with me in Windsor. The idea was to send the cassettes to France where Monsieur and Jeanette, his secretary, could play my spoken order instructions. It kept us in touch. I missed France so, and the thing was, I couldn't actually write French.

It lifted me to hear his recorded replies... and lectures. What you have to realise is that back then the phone was all but useless for overseas calls. In those days if I – or anyone – wanted to phone abroad, you had to call the International Operator the day before and book a time for a call. Then, when next day the operators eventually called back and put you through, you had to pray they didn't cut you off mid-conversation. The operators of Castillon were notorious for this. I had my office which was fine and my tastings kept going along but when I met up with friends from school or university I felt embarrassed. I would actually try to avoid them. They all had jobs and incomes; they were doing well while I, even with my calculator, was struggling.

But slowly the number of tastings increased. Roger Denny had put me in touch with friends of his who lived in Weybridge. Suddenly my horizons were expanding, into the affluent Surrey stockbroker belt: St George's Hill where John Lennon lived. They had laid on a big party for the tasting. It went well, so now I was heading up to more than 20 cases a month. That took three or four good tastings. I don't think I ever repeated the phone-book mailing idea that got me my first two customers, it was just too expensive. Now, I relied on word of mouth and being passed on by friends, plus a lot of doorstep leafleting. But I realised there was a limit as to how long I could carry on selling just the Lussac-Saint-Émilion. It was a wine I believed in, but had its drawbacks. I knew it was well made and honest and had not been mucked about with en route like so much that was bottled and sold in the UK. My wine would last – improve, in fact – over the next two or three days if you put the cork back in: the sign of a well-made wine. Customers were impressed by this. Mine was a popular wine in France but it was tannic, hard-edged and fairly uncompromising – the way the French liked it. It was best with a rare steak. Customers told me I needed different, softer wines.

I also now realised that I didn't really need the office; it was an extravagance, so I gave it up. Instead I rented the much cheaper cellar below. This gave me somewhere to store cases and I opened it up to intrepid customers on a Saturday. A sign-board 'Wholesale Cellar' outside drew in the odd, curious passer-by but it was mainly people who had met me or heard about me through the tastings who dropped in. My routine grew to two or three tastings a week, plus a lot of leafleting and knocking on doors, Saturday visitors to the cellar, then a monthly trip to Shoreham and delivering the wine orders. It was hard-going although getting more enjoyable... but not that exciting. I pined for sunny Bordeaux, for the easy paradise I had known. Then it came to me – another of those flashes – that the solution lay there. Why didn't I simplify everything, bypass Shoreham, drive onto one of the new (lucky timing again) roll-on/roll-off ferries and go down to Bordeaux to fetch the orders myself in the old Cortina? This would mean that the wine was truly Bordeaux Direct. There would be no more shipping in through Shoreham but instead a nice day's drive down through my beloved France. And back. I didn't stop to consider if it was financially practicable. Because it clearly wasn't. But, there would be such nice peripheral benefits.

Customers seemed to like the idea of delivery coming from Bordeaux directly. They would not only get the wine delivered straight from its vineyard but a happy delivery man babbling about the latest happenings in the vineyards. Cheaper prices? Well, I was certainly going to cut out a lot of middlemen. Wine had traditionally gone from grower to *courtier* to French merchant to shipper to importer to English merchant to retailer (not forgetting the unofficial 'levies' taken en route by dockers). I would now cut out all those costs. So I just did it. I was very nervous. I think I drove all the way to Bordeaux without a stop. When I got there I had trouble prising my hands off the steering wheel and couldn't stop shaking.

But the Cortina and I made it there and back alive, and I really, really loved doing it despite a lorry shedding its load of logs in front of me. Luck again; my bonnet had come loose as I followed that lorry and I'd had to stop. The logs came off before I'd caught up again. Thank you God. The happier more chatty me, gabbling on about the trip, seemed to help sales move up towards 100 cases a month.

But the old Cortina was hardly the transport of a burgeoning business. It was seriously limited on capacity. So I took the next big step and hired a Ford Transit box-bodied van from Godfrey Davies in Reading for four days. Again, I drove to Southampton, then on the Thoresen ferry to Le Havre. But it worked well. I was more relaxed now. So I splurged the last of Nana's money on my very own van... with some unexpected help.

THE VAN

On my first trip Monsieur told me he had arranged for me to meet a few fellow wine producers from as far afield as Bergerac and Saint-Émilion.

These friends Monsieur introduced me to were part of a loose association of like-minded independent winemakers in different areas of France. They had all met at France's wine *concours* (competitions) as judges, had got together and started bottling their own wines. They wanted to export. Great timing. Great luck for me. Soon I was offering tastings of more than one wine and bringing back van loads of several different wines. There was a dry white from the neighbouring Côtes de Francs. There was a red from Bergerac which was as good as any Bordeaux but cheaper, and a couple of dry whites like no customer had ever tasted before: a zingy, fresh Sauvignon Blanc from the new co-op at Duras and an even better dry white from the beautiful little Château de Panisseau at Sigoulès, near Bergerac, which became a huge seller. The owner, Madame Becker or 'the widow Becker', had come from Alsace and brought that region's high standards of white winemaking south with her. She made a lovely wine. Very unusually, it was always a blend of the new and older vintages, such a sensible idea, but one I don't think I've ever since come across elsewhere in quality wines. It was made all the lovelier by the picture of her tiny turreted Dordogne château on the label. She became my top seller, this severe, little old wizened lady. Very formal and correct. I would have to take tea with her, for what seemed like hours... sitting very upright in uncomfortable chairs. One time, Barbara, who didn't then understand either French or winemaking, fell asleep on her chair and slid quietly to the ground. One way to speed up our departure.

There was also Château Magence, a bone-dry Graves – an unusual wine for my customers, used as they were to British-bottled Graves being sweet more often than not. Owner Dominique Guillot de Suduiraut was a pioneer of cold fermented whites in Bordeaux. President of the Institut Technique de Vin, he installed what I believe were the first ever stainless steel tanks in Bordeaux. They were cooled very simply by cold water running down the outside. Being able to ferment white wine at cool temperature to retain the fruit flavours was revolutionary in Bordeaux at that time. He inspired many, notably Denis Dubordieu

My first big success was this white from the Dordogne.

who took his work to new levels after Dominique's sad early death. One morning during the harvest when his tanks were in full ferment, he had entered his cellar and was immediately asphyxiated by the carbon dioxide which had accumulated overnight, because the vents had not been left open. Tragic. The same thing nearly happened to me when I got my own winery. Carbon dioxide hits so quick like a hard punch in the head and... you are gone. I, though, was being cautious because of Domique's fate and managed to drag myself out just in time. But every vintage there are deaths due to CO_2.

My new favourite wine was Le Vieux Château Guibeau at a whopping 18 shillings and sixpence a bottle. Guibeau is a wine we still sell today, buying it from lovely Brigitte, granddaughter of the old original owner, Henri Bourlon. And she is a brilliant winemaker. She likes to call me her *père anglais.* I have come to know the whole Bourlon family very well. Surprising really because I didn't get off to a good start with old man Bourlon.

That summer I'd hired a Velosolex. A model they don't make any more. Unsurprisingly maybe. Basically it's a solid bicycle with a two-stroke motor hanging from the handlebars. Pull the cord to start, get on, pedal

Above: One truck at Château de Selle, Provence.

Opposite: Later we had a fleet!

off, then lower the motor's flywheel on to the front wheel. *Voilà!* Just not too easy to steer. And don't even think of braking hard on that front wheel. Turning into Château Guibeau the machine and I messed up our cornering and somersaulted into the vines. Extricated – half-garroted and dazed – by the family, cleaned up and revived with good cognac, I was ushered in to meet old Henri, very stern, behind his huge desk. When going to talk to an important winegrower it is best not to start by demolishing part of his vineyard. How odd is life, though. He became a great mentor to me and the Bourlons have been my longest-serving suppliers. I could never imagine not having Le Vieux Château Guibeau on our list. One day soon I expect we will be dealing with Brigitte's daughter, the great-granddaughter of the man I first bought the wine from. I must be SO old!

Looking back, it seems crazy that these winemakers would trust this one-man business, especially when the man was an Englishman and very young. But back then the big merchants totally dominated the sales of wine and were actively opposed to any wine producers who sold direct. None of Monsieur's group had any presence in the British market and I, my van and tiny cellar in Windsor offered them a chance they were prepared to take. They hoped it would mean bigger sales in the long run. They too liked the very simple, direct selling route. They were great people to deal with and I was lucky to meet them. Monsieur Bourlon, Monsieur Gouzon, Monsieur Guillot de Suduiraut and Monsieur Bernard. They all taught me so much, but they also did something so generous I still wonder at it today. They got together and bought me most of my new Ford Transit. They all chipped in £200 each, so did Monsieur. I put in the same – the very last of Nana's money – and for £1,200 I got a shiny new, aluminium box-bodied, 35cwt Ford Transit. With double wheels at the back! It could carry 100 cases of wine and I was now getting close to selling 100 cases a month. This was huge. My customers reckoned that for me life was just one long holiday and in one way it was. With the range now up from one to six wines, the sales increased as I had hoped. Also, my 'backers' gave me other financial assistance. Monsieur Cassin gave me 90 days' credit and convinced the others to do the same. I needed that. It was how I financed the business. I more or less only bought and imported what I had already sold. And my customers had paid me when they'd ordered. So I avoided cash flow problems. Usually. Such was Monsieur's help, that to this day I struggle to comprehend it. I think he was proud of what I was doing – after all I was his pupil. And,

LE VIEUX CHÂTEAU GUIBEAU

GRAND VIN DE BORDEAUX

Le Vieux Château Guibeau

PUISSEGUIN SAINT-ÉMILION

APPELLATION PUISSEGUIN-SAINT-ÉMILION CONTRÔLÉE

2016

S.C.E.A. BOURLON DESTOUET
33570 PUISSEGUIN - GIRONDE - FRANCE

MIS EN BOUTEILLE AU CHÂTEAU

THE SECOND WINE I SOLD, THIS TAUGHT ME MUCH BY COMPARISON WITH MY FIRST.

Henri Bourlon showed me that wine isn't necessarily all about the difference between one patch of soil and another. It is mostly about different levels of skill and dedication. Many people realise this now, but few did back then. Me, for one. My first two wines were made within a mile of each on the same soils in the relatively minor appellation of Puisseguin-Saint-Émilion but Henri Bourlon, a winemaker well ahead of his time, showed me amongst other things how taking the risk of letting grapes hang longer on the vine produced a riper, rounder, darker and more complex wine. Customers agreed: Guibeau has remained a popular wine of ours for 50 vintages now. No other wine of ours has a sales record that comes near. Henri also, very generously, liked to offer his guests the pick of his extensive cellar of very grand Saint-Émilions to drink alongside his own wine... which always came out very well by comparison. That's something I learned to do too.

sort of, his adopted English son. He was doing what he did to help me. It was certainly more than just a business opportunity for him and the co-operative. I also wonder why the others all helped me, but they did. Would I do that today for some young start-up entrepreneur? I hope so.

My routine was that I would leave Windsor at 6pm for Southampton and the tiny, by today's standards, Thoresen overnight ferry, that you could actually drive on (up to then, when you went abroad with a car it was winched on by crane). It was a Norwegian boat, so you got a nice smorgasbord, then a bit of kip, and off at 7am into the industrial port of Le Havre. Once over the Tancarville Bridge though, it was all pretty and rural. Cows, apple trees, black-and-white cottages and whiskery old guys on bikes fetching their baguettes. The Pays d'Auge. How I loved that trip. 'Brown Sugar' belting out of my cassette player (I screwed appallingly big speakers into that van!) tonking along: those old Transits really could shift. Narrow windy roads; Pont-Audemer, to Bernay, to Gacé, to Alençon, to Le Mans (down the race course's Mulsanne straight, knocking 90) to Tours, Poitiers, Ruffec, Mansle, Angoulême, Chalais, Saint-Médard – names gouged deep in my memory – and finally into the vineyards, past the old Puisseguin co-op, Saint-Genès and finally Sainte-Colombe around 6pm. Just in time for a cool *vin de noyer* – Madame's home-

Posing with Madame Coste and Le Président de la Cave Coopérative.

made aperitif made from a liqueur of young walnut leaves macerated in brandy, then blended with young red Bordeaux and sugar to taste – and a long chat with Monsieur, while Madame, clattering in the kitchen, got supper.

By now, four years after first arriving chez Cassin I was allowed to sleep in the house. And use a real bathroom, not the pump and the terrible earth closet in the vegetable garden. Though... being inside was not all good. French internal walls are very thin and the Cassins snored. How they snored!

Next day was my 'rounds': first stop Libourne for some Saint-Émilion and Pomerol. Then south over the two rivers – the 'Deux Mers' – to get the Graves and Sauternes, then east to Sainte-Foy-la-Grande and along the Monbazillac road up the Dordogne to get the Bergerac wines. Then back west on the northern valley road (to avoid the lethal main RD 936) to Le Fleix, Villefranche and then the co-op of Francs. They were such lazy buggers there. I would drive right inside the cellar and load up myself while they finished their little *grillade* outside. They enjoyed a lot of *grillades* there. I didn't stick with their wine too long, though I really liked old Conchou, their long-suffering president. Unsurprisingly, that little co-op is now defunct.

Then on to Puisseguin, Le Vieux Château Guibeau and my own dear old co-op. A full van-load in one great day, plenty of gossip, and many tastes of this and that. But I couldn't then just drive home. There were *les papiers* and *les formalités*. The UK was not yet in the EEC. So with every wine I had to collect papers: green *acquis verts*. (Getting caught by the gendarmes with wine and no green papers meant prison.) The next day I had to drive the 30 miles into the big customs hall in Bordeaux with my *déclarations* for export. It was just along from where the great new Cité de Vin has just opened. Exports to the UK were under Transports Internationaux Routiers (TIR) rules. With dread, I would climb the stairs to where the 'Dragon Lady' sat and glowered behind the huge array of rubber stamps on her desk. She hated me. She hated everyone. All papers had to be in perfect order or got thrown back... with a twisted smile. When all was finally OK she would perform with her stamps a routine that would have impressed any rock band. She was the Keith Moon of rubber-stamping. Bang, bang, bang-etty, bang, crash, thud, repeat and repeat. I learned it was very necessary not to grin during this percussive display. A final scowl after eventually finishing, and I was free to go, but only once the van had been quarantined with a lead seal. All that took a whole day. A less good day. But still good as it was back to Madame's for dinner and sleep, snoring permitting. Then an early start to get to Le Havre docks before 6pm when the freight office closed. The return overnight sailing was taken up with even more form-filling for the UK Customs and Excise. That administrative workload was vastly increased later when, due to a run on the pound in the early 1970s, the Government slapped on a load of emergency currency and import controls. To raise cash and help the balance of payments by curbing imports, they brought in this scheme – where all importers were obliged to lodge a deposit of 50 per cent of the value of their desired importation with HM Customs to be returned at a later unspecified date or whenever the authorities got round to it. Alas, I just didn't have the money to carry this surcharge.

But, luckily (yet again), I discovered that imports under the value of £50 were exempt. Customs and Excise said it was permissible for me to divide my cargo up and 'import' every customer's order as a separate 'consignment'. My wines sold for between 13 shillings and sixpence and 18 shillings and sixpence, and the average order was two dozen bottles. So it worked. All orders came in under £50, so no import deposit was needed. But it was no sleep for me on the ferry as I stayed up filling in import documents for Mr Smith, Mr Brown, Mr Jones and all, to ensure their orders never came over 50 quid. On arrival in Southampton I would put this huge mass of papers in the in-tray of the quietly furious customs men in the Long Room. They hated so much paperwork for so little tax, and always made me wait till last. So I'd plenty of time to park up the van, and walk into town, to Barclays, to withdraw the necessary duty money. Sometimes this was not immediately forthcoming and I'd have to find a phone box and plead with my bank in Windsor. No money, no clearance. But Barclays – such decent chaps they were – always relented… after delivering the ritual lecture on the need for fiscal probity. Then back to the Customs Long Room, deposit the money and pray they wouldn't shout for a 'full turnout'. But inevitably they did. So then I would have to drive into their shed, and wait for a team of dockers to roll up from the cosy Dockers' Club over the road because, of course, I wasn't allowed to touch the seal or anything. However, at least these were good dockers. Maybe they could see I was earning a lot less than they were. They took pity on me and behaved impeccably. The customs man would do his count, sign me off, the dockers would carefully reload absolutely every bottle, and then, finally, I could get off home, ready for the next month, delivering and hopefully taking further orders.

Customers liked their very direct delivery a lot. Some would invite me in for a cup of tea and a chat. They wanted to hear about Monsieur and the others. This taught me something that has been immeasurably valuable to me: for a surprising number of people, it is not really 'tasting notes' they want, but some knowledge of how their wine is made, where, by whom, why and how they do it like that. I was a long way from running a proper business, but I'd found my passion and people to share it with, which was a big deal. Not everyone is blessed with the gift of work that evokes their real passion, where work doesn't actually seem like work at all. Selling was fairly hard – I don't think I'm a natural salesman, but it wasn't too hard and people were really nice to me. Maybe it wasn't so much that the wines were nicer than they were used to, but maybe they just liked to help a young guy with a new idea. Anyway, they bought. Thank God.

People these days often ask if I ever saw it becoming a big business and I say, 'No, of course not.' I didn't look any further forward than the end of the month and the next trip. The trip was my reward. Sure, I wanted enough money to be able to hold my head up and buy my round with mates, all of whom had better paying jobs than me. Certainly I needed to pay rent on my cellar, and contribute a bit to my parents. At that time I never expected to do more than just get by. Anyway, in those days it seemed to me you were actively discouraged from trying to make money. The top rate of income tax was 98 per cent, for heaven's sake! So what on earth was the point of trying to make money? Better you didn't aim at making money but just aimed to enjoy yourself. See if they could tax that! I had also heard, many a time, the old wine trade saying: 'The only way to make a small fortune in wine is to start with a big one.' Added together, these things caused me to mould my business into something that I enjoyed but which was never really aimed at making big profits. Just getting by. And I succeeded brilliantly in that respect. For 20 years!

Graft for three weeks selling 100 or so cases of wine. Then as reward, jump in my van and bomb down to Bordeaux – sunshine, good food, my friends and my lovely France for a few days. Initially, I actually wanted to form a co-operative like the one I had worked in. But Monsieur counselled strongly against that; he knew the problems all too well.

But it is easy to forget that starting a business in the 1960s was not really the thing. Not cool. Encouragement to set up in business? None. Advice available? None. Small, starter premises? None. Finance? You are joking! Computers? None smaller than a barn. Phones? Wait two years. So everyone went off to be a lawyer, accountant, teacher, union leader or banker. Fine people, all. But that didn't get the country very far economically. It was not until years later that somehow the idea spread that running your own business could actually be the best fun there was. Ever since, I have tried to keep the level of fun high in my business. Wry smiles and winks all round at my constant refrain 'but it must be FUN!' Bonkers Chairman Tony on his hobby horse again. Maybe I worked for peanuts – well, Mother's cooking, actually and also Madame's. But I bloody loved it all.

Money did get tight as sales grew and I sometimes got my buying and selling out of kilter and the bank was not so sympathetic. But then I had a bright idea: I decided to sell what I called 'loan stock'. I was told afterwards that it was probably illegal. I honestly never knew, one way or the other. Ignorance was financial bliss. I said to customers that if they would lend me £100, in return I would give them a 'loan stock certificate', and they would get £20 off £100 worth of wine every year. Quite a few people did take it up and that certainly helped for a while. We eventually closed the scheme down, and were surprised how much that upset the customers. They had loved it. It wasn't a bad business model... early crowdfunding of a sort. Perhaps I should have stuck with it.

As I now had my very own van, I decorated it with the words 'Bordeaux Direct' and my company logo – a cockerel coming out of a wine glass. I cut it all out of black paper and used a lot of glue. (I had kept up my artistic efforts since Durham.) During a very cold week in my early days working at the co-op, Monsieur had talked about getting some wine labels designed and I had begged for the chance. He had taken pity on me and let me into the warm office where I scrawled out a selection for him. Some were chosen and used, some were not.

Haggling in the vineyards of Saint-Émilion.

The cockerel coming out of the glass was a reject. So when we started Bordeaux Direct I asked if I could have it as my logo. It was simple and straightforward. But not simple enough for a French lorry driver waiting one day with me for the ferry at Le Havre docks. He peered at the cockerel symbol and the words *'Du producteur au consommateur'* and asked: *'C'est quoi que vous vendez... du vin ou du poulet?'*

I was still very much a one-man show, with friends helping occasionally. And I eventually wore my father's patience too thin and was ordered out of the family home. At 24, it was long overdue. But I got a room in the house next door so I could still nip home for the odd meal when the Old Man was out. He was a good man, my dad. I admired and respected him a lot. He tried to instil his strong morality in me. Like when I found half-a-crown in the street, and he made me take it to the police station. He was like that. I lived next door with old Mrs Slingsby until she asked me to leave too. I was too noisy. But the sweet old-fashioned thing was kind enough to offer me another home: a four-bedroomed flat in Trinity Place, Windsor – almost next door to my one celebrity customer, Michael Parkinson. The flat had spare bedrooms which I then let out to some

French friends in return for a bit of help in the business. Bernard, a great, gangling *mec* from Provence, did the cooking. Very cheaply. It was always, always *nouilles* – pasta which he imported by the sackload – and cheese.

It was my van journeys to Bordeaux and back that gave my business its own individual slant on wine, its image, its USP or Unique Selling Proposition. The old van image is still used today and tells the story better than words.

In it, I began travelling more and more, further and deeper into the vineyards, meeting new producers, hearing their stories and finding new wines. I realised my focus on winemakers as much as wines was, certainly back then, something unusual. Most professional wine buyers bought from tastings set up in London by producers, agents and importers. They still do. I have tried going to those but working like that doesn't suit me. I am reluctant to buy simply on taste, my taste. I had, after all, been taught by Peynaud in Bordeaux to be wary of my taste. My palate was perfectly fine, but I knew it varied from day to day so I was unwilling to place large commercial bets on what my palate was doing on any particular day. For safety I needed to taste a wine several times and I had to know the producer, the vineyard and the winery. I thought it better to take the trouble (no trouble at all, a pleasure, really) to go and meet the producer, check out his vineyard and cellar, and learn his history and track record. There are many clues in cellars and vineyards which tell you if this winemaker/grape-grower is really reliably on top of their job. If I got all enthusiastic, I would try an order or two on the customers and then, if they seemed happy, settle down to buy the wine year in, year out. I guess this is all because I had started on the production side of the wine trade, not the retailing end, so knew personally what life was like for wine producers. I didn't want to behave like the buyers who would buy a wine one year but not the next simply because they went off it. I believed my good, and very professional, producers would likely make a good wine every year. True, there are always annual vintage differences but that is part of the fun of real wines. Comparing, seeing variations, evolutions and patterns. Most drinks, after all, are standardised. Coke and Pepsi never vary. Heineken doesn't vary. Single vineyard wines do vary. That's why they fascinate us more than lager. Lager refreshes wonderfully, but nobody talks all night about a lager. Do they? Hugh Johnson's clever definition of a fine wine is that it is 'a wine worth talking about'!

It's not necessarily a fault if a vintage got less sun than last year, so the wine has turned out lighter. It might be more delicate. It might show subtleties last year didn't have. So if it's sound and well crafted, I'll buy it, knowing that there are customers waiting because this is 'their' wine, one they love. If one of our producers had a vintage really messed up by frost or hail or pourriture or all three, I was sure he'd warn me before I even saw a sample. However, I don't recollect that happening often. Good winemakers don't mess up much. I have always believed in forming great and lasting wine friendships and, through me, my customers do too. 'Wine is personal' is what we say a lot these days.

Through my van journeyings, my circle of wine contacts, friends and acquaintances really was growing rapidly. I suppose they liked the fact I believed so strongly in French wine from small producers and saw that I could help them into the growing English market. The 'at home' tastings increased in number. Yes, offering more than one wine was certainly an astute move! And one common characteristic was beginning to show, one that we still see today. It was our 'wine next door' thing: our marked tendency to prefer the less well-known – and less expensive – wine that lived in the shadow of its more privileged, well-known neighbour, which was not necessarily a better wine. This was not just my preference; these were the wines I saw that my customers preferred, if given a choice... and a taste. Maybe it's just the traditional British preference for the underdog. But for me it is 'the Sainte-Colombe Factor'. For me, and consequently Laithwaite's Wine, this has always been a HUGE influence.

CASTILLON V. SAINT-ÉMILION

'My' village of Sainte-Colombe – indeed the whole Castillon wine region – and I were so well matched.

There was young me struggling to be taken seriously as a wine merchant and there was Castillon struggling to be taken seriously as a wine region. I was a newcomer trying to get into a business dominated by companies that had been there a very long time, just as Castillon was trying to persuade people it could produce wines as good as those at the other western end of their *côte* (ridge). Castillon's vineyards occupied the eastern end of this limestone escarpment, and everyone had once considered their wines to be Saint-Émilion or Saint-Émilionais, but they had been cut off in 1936

4. CASTILLON — Le Port

Loading wine on gabares in front of Le Chai au Quai. Castillon was one of the major wine ports on the Dordogne until well into the twentieth century.

when a canton boundary drawn during the reign of our bad King John (he ruled just as badly here too) for administrative reasons only, was chosen as the eastern boundary of the AOC (Appellation d'Origine Contrôlée). No one has ever explained why. By chance I had landed just over that border, not in wealthy Saint-Émilion but in the 'underdog' village of Sainte-Colombe, lying within what was now a little-known wine region, Côtes de Castillon, that felt cheated out of its birthright. This seems to have conditioned me for life. From my first days in the region I heard loud and clear the grievance felt by all around me: their sense of having been done out of what was their due. They were all angry at being banned from calling their wine Saint-Émilion. And I took on their anger.

As the song said around that time, 'Time was right for revolution'. The post-war generation was making its mark through music, literature and theatre. Old, established ideas were being overthrown. The 1960s were 'Angry Young Men' times. So many, at this time, started to get angry about social injustice, race discrimination, whaling and other seriously important things. I just became the Angry Young Wine Merchant! Not quite such an important global issue, I understand that, but it was my very own issue. I was incensed about a dubious choice of boundary drawn hundreds of years before! I wanted to tell everyone that Sainte-Colombe and its neighbours had been unfairly excluded from the Saint-Émilion appellation. I wanted to explain how their place had been taken by a vast flat area on the Dordogne's alluvial plain which up till then was used for cattle rearing. It's just not good vineyard land, down there. Never will be. Too wet. Wine trade people know this. But they rarely tell the customers. It is something I believe in as fervently now as I did half a century ago. And don't get me started on Saint-Émilion grands crus. How come the title grand cru in Burgundy is bestowed upon only a tiny handful of the finest vineyards – less than 5 per cent – yet in Saint-Émilion every single estate is or can be a grand cru? The term simply means it's a Saint-Émilion that's a touch stronger. And most grands crus are to be found down on that flat alluvial plain. It's not a classification, it's an appellation. The classified châteaux are the crus *classés*. There I go again. I'm still the angry wine merchant. Just not a young one any more. There is, I believe, a mental condition known as 'monomania' and I certainly have it. Oh yes. But I'll calm down now.

However, my condition has meant that wherever I go for wines, I'm always looking out for the just-as-good but usually overlooked wines next door to the famous. And that's worked well for us.

THE FIRST BIG TRUCK

Within a year business had increased to the rate where the once-a-month 100 cases that the Transit could hold was not enough.

I had also stumbled on a rather different market – Christmas gifts given by companies to their valued customers. It was perfect for my wines: I did two, three or six bottles in nice 'presentation packs' and their success turned my Decembers into very frantic months. I did well in the industrial estates in Slough, Feltham and High Wycombe because no one else was doing this. The packs were so popular it meant I had to book a very big articulated lorry that could carry 1,200 cases of 12. It came safely from Bordeaux but hit a logistical problem in Windsor. Where to store it? My cellar in Victoria Street was already becoming stretched by just the Transit van loads. I sometimes ran out of room. The cellar was so full of wine there was no passageway through it. Mostly, if I wanted to get a case (it would, of course, always be on the far side), I would have to burrow my way to where I thought it was, haul it down the tunnel I had made and then shove all the cases back. I could have been entombed down there. So I had a full cellar, and a big truck on its way with 1,200 cases. There was only one answer: Merv the Swerve.

When you enter the world of small business you enter a hidden world, the inhabitants of which quietly look after each other and can fix almost anything. Not necessarily in orthodox ways. My great new friend Merv could fix anything. He was a real-life – and much more successful – Del Boy who worked out of the garage opposite and knew many others who worked discreetly in garages and sheds all around town, that outsiders knew nothing about. Merv lent me a lock-up which may or may not have been his: a sizeable shed on the outskirts of Windsor that would hold all the wine until I delivered it. But there was a slight security worry, I thought. So Merv borrowed this caravan from someone and I planned to sleep in it beside my wine for most of December that year. But a delivery of 14,400 bottles of wine still posed problems: the truck tried to reverse in and began to demolish the gateway. So we had to arrange for it to go to the lay-by next to Windsor racecourse and Merv and I shuttled the cases to the shed in our vans. The police screamed up within minutes. ''Ullo, 'Ullo, 'Ullo, what's going on here then?' Luckily Merv knew the boys in blue well and I had, at his suggestion, contributed the odd bottle to their Christmas tombola.

But it became clear that the shed, caravan security and the cellar in Victoria Street was a hotchpotch that didn't offer a long-term solution. It was not what you might call a viable business plan. I wanted to stay in Windsor but needed a safe space and somewhere where my wine business would look like it was 'for real'. I also felt happier surrounded by the wine I was selling. But these were the days before anyone thought of building 'start-up' business parks with offices, workshops and storage on the edge of town. I just wanted somewhere without caravan security or the risk of being buried alive.

The answer, at the rent of £20 a month to British Rail, was Arch 36. Central – actually under Windsor & Eton Central station – practical and cheap. All the 50 or so arches were full of little businesses. I thought No. 36 looked particularly right for wine, I didn't need to tart it up, it looked terrific as a shop. Customers loved it: they sat on cases at 'tables' that were just more cases – it looked like a wine cave. Smelled like one too. Majestic started the same way, some years later. There was no running water but electricity came from somewhere or other. Might have been via Merv. He certainly found me his mate, the phone engineer, who got me hooked up – perhaps unofficially but at least a year sooner than the good old GPO (Telecom) was then able to manage officially. There was no loo which meant a swift run across Victoria Gardens to the public toilets. The Arch became 'a venue', it was our 'wine theatre', it had a presence. People came. Famous people came – Michael Parkinson for one. Canny buyer. At last Bordeaux Direct had a proper home and it proved to be a launchpad for the business. We had a proper base where the wine could be stored in ideal conditions and people could come to me for tastings. Saturdays were the big day. Coachloads came in the evenings for big tastings. Women's Institute, Rotary, works outings, amateur winemaking clubs, all sorts.

BARBARA AND RAILWAY ARCH 36

And around then came the biggest ever change in my life. By chance, Barbara, that feisty girl with the legs from Durham, crashed back into my life and started to take me over.

She was still lovely, but she was awfully free with advice. She would come and watch me work and just couldn't help keep saying, 'No, wrong. You should do it this way.' She was always telling me I needed to keep accounts. So of course I said, 'Well if you're so bloody clever then why don't you come and do it?' Unexpectedly, she did. And, dammit, she was right. And she did do it better. I have been doing pretty much what she told me to do ever since. Except in wine. That was my bit. I did wine and words. She did numbers and people. My reunion with the girl who evaded me at university came about, of course, by another stroke of my luck. Barbara's sister Helen, also a friend from Durham, had gone to South Africa to marry. On a trip back to England she decided to hold a party at her sister's flat and invited old friends from Durham, including me. So there was Barbara, now a successful young executive in London and there was me struggling to make ends meet in Windsor. Barbara was a city girl, and claimed she lived in Bayswater (Paddington really... well, it was on the border). It didn't seem promising but something clicked and we started going out. It became a working partnership in January 1972 when she gave up her job and joined Bordeaux Direct. Things would never be the same again. She had always been a bit crazy but she had a very good job and was earning proper money. She worked for a company that compiled the JICTAR (Joint Industry Committee for Television Audience Research)

Arch 36.

TV ratings. But she gave it all up. They told her she was mad. Her boss was furious. Now she was going to move into a... railway arch! She came to work with me at the same time as I moved to the Arch. While Arch 36 had lots going for it – if you didn't mind the lack of water and loos – it also didn't have an office. But there was an answer: the caravan which had provided security accommodation now had a new lease of life. It came with us to the Arch to be the office. I went off next day to France and Barbara turned up on her first day and the caravan was gone! Our papers were strewn all over the floor. Presumably the guy Merv 'borrowed' the caravan from hadn't agreed to it going so he came and collected it. Funny how often similar disasters would occur just as I had gone off on a trip to France.

*After a tasting at
the Arch.*

So we needed a new office. By chance I had seen a very large empty
packing case further down the arches. I took it off the hands of the
owner to turn it into a store. Now I set about making it into an office. I
cut a door in one side and installed a desk and a light. Barbara was not
enthusiastic. But she cleared all the papers out of my 'filing cabinet' –
(the glove department of the van) – and an old schoolmate of mine, Pete
Bendall, who had become an accountant, was drafted in to turn them –
creatively – into accounts. The Arch rapidly filled up. I was now keen on
shipping in whole trucks and we could store at least 2,400 cases in the
Arch. It got pretty full, so eventually I had a mezzanine floor built by a
friend of Merv's so I could take customers 'upstairs' for tastings with a
view... of wine boxes. Health and Safety would have had a fit, but luckily
they hadn't been invented yet.

I was beginning to get pretty proud of my business. I could hold my head
up with my friends. I was earning a living. And I wasn't alone. I lived in
a rented a flat with my French mates – Barbara refused to move in –
and the success of the business meant my parents could feel a bit more
relaxed about me and just enjoy the odd bottle of my wine.

To get our little business known, we did more and more leafleting... by hand. That seemed to us the cheapest, most effective way of finding new customers. No way could we afford to advertise in newspapers. So it looked like we had a business, but would likely remain a small, local one, and were happy with that thought. We still hoped to earn more money, as it was a hand-to-mouth existence. A good sale and we'd blow it immediately on a meal over at Signor Pattochi's La Taverna. No sales and it was a bacon-and-egg butty at the Goswell Greasy Spoon. But we were young and in charge of our own destiny. Our bosses were our customers. And they were good to us. At this stage we – love's young dream – were just thinking 'This is not bad', and it kept growing and that kept us excited. The real motivation for me was finding new wines, going to new places. I hadn't really searched beyond France yet, but France has an extraordinary number of wine regions, many of which had never sent wine to the UK. I intended to visit them all. And eventually I did.

I don't think we thought about what would happen if the business collapsed. Why worry? We didn't really have anything to lose.

The tastings in the Arch proved popular. There was an atmosphere. To give it more of a sense of theatre, good old Merv 'acquired' some flaming wall braziers. Really flaming. He got them – legit, honest – from the nearby Bray Studios, where the Hammer Horror films were made. These would give some 'atmosphere' to the tastings, he thought. Too right! Within minutes of being lit, the flaming arch filled with smoke and the customers left choking. One lady had come to the tasting wearing her mink! It was a moment that the Crazy World of Arthur Brown – of the big hit 'Fire' – one of the most popular rock acts of the time and just then appearing at the Windsor Race Course Rock Festival (the world's first ever rock festival), would have enjoyed. The Arch was becoming my theatre.

I tried to spread the Arch idea. We didn't have the resources to go round opening more arches but I had my keen customers. So I wrote and asked if any would want to open their own arch and have me supply them. We thought we'd be franchising. We'd read about franchises. Though maybe not read quite enough. A dozen couples volunteered to open what we decided to call Saturday Cellars. We knew we did over half our weekly turnover between Fridays evening and Saturday night, so we reckoned people with proper day jobs could do pretty well on just one day a week.

Opposite: We also sold barrels to those who liked to bottle their own – sometimes I needed help from my Arch neighbours.

Sunday trading was illegal then. Anyway we ended up with cellars in arches, garages, sheds and all sorts in Tunbridge Wells, Winchester, Tetbury, Ringwood, Stockton-on-Tees, Kinross, Reigate, Manchester, and Leeds. Interesting mix.

For a while they were fun and sort of worked. But we'd not understood that for franchises to work they have to be very tightly controlled or the all-important 'brand image' gets lost. And ours did. All but one eventually started buying in cheaper wines to make, they hoped, better margins. The customers drifted away and they all eventually folded. Except George Lane in Winchester. George was different. A lovely man, slightly eccentric, and a hilarious teller of jokes who had served in all three armed forces. Major Lane we called him, Major Lane Ahead. Prior to us meeting he'd tried doing wine on his own and had a van like mine. But it hadn't quite worked so he was someone who understood that doing wine wasn't as simple as just buying some bottles and hoping they'd sell. So he stuck with us, and for many years ran his little cellar in Winchester. It worked for him and us till he retired. But George was a very much a 'one-off'.

So forget franchising then.

But we were beginning to be noticed. The first newspaper piece about us was when the great John Arlott wrote nice things in *The Guardian*. He was as keen on wine as he was on cricket, renowned for taking bottles into the commentary box. Several years later, Ade Bentham, a cricket nut who now runs our US office, told me a good story: he remembered a worried trainee in our Thatcham shop, saying that a tramp had come in. Ade went down to eject him but ended up selling him a couple of cases of Cru Beaujolais. It was John Arlott.

GOING BEYOND BORDEAUX: MEETING A LEGEND

Having got me buying from his winemaking friends in Bordeaux, Monsieur Cassin encouraged me to go round the whole country and meet his friends in other regions.

He and others had set up a sort of club of like-minded, ambitious wine producers who knew each other from meeting up at wine competitions in Paris, Mâcon, Bordeaux etc. where they all hoped to improve their reputations by winning loads of medals. Their leader was a bit of a legend called Jean Dubernet. Together they'd started marketing their wines under the banner '*Race et Fidelité*', which means, I suppose, making wines the right and proper way. Fraud was not uncommon back then, and lower standards were becoming common. These guys all believed in maintaining standards and were firmly opposed to cutting corners. So they were always a bit more expensive than the market. But then they won all those medals. Monsieur Cassin said I could do worse than go and see these people, learn from them, buy from them, and maybe copy them a bit. He said I could trust them absolutely. So off I went in the trusty Transit, the old rock 'n' roll cassettes blasting away. I met them all and bought from most. Great people. Trustworthy. Then I had to add new finds of my own, which was harder but great fun.

So my work fell – well, still falls – into two parts: in the UK trying to ensure we sold our wines, and travelling abroad looking to find wines that would sell. So I set off on the vineyard wandering, or 'Wine Treks' as they came to be called, that have occupied me ever since. It's what I do, it's what I love. Aren't I the lucky one? Nana always said I was born under a lucky star. (My much-lamented assistant Clare was always more forthright: 'Lucky Bastard!' was, I always thought, a term of endearment.) After half a century I'm still doing the Wine Treks round the vineyard. Why ever would I stop? What is it I do exactly?

At a co-op winery after the *bonjours*, I'll typically be given a glass and taken climbing up the metal stairs and gantries to the top, right up under the great roof. Walking across the tops of the concrete tanks, the *directeur* will flip open dozens of trapdoors, plunging his bottle on a pole into the gleaming black pools for samples. Each time I'll hold out my

glass, then sip and suck the freezing wine. It's cold because everywhere is cold. Buying is almost always done in winter. Tasting, then, is not easy. You have to hold the wine in your mouth for it to warm up, otherwise you can't taste much. It helps if you can learn to carry on talking while holding a little wine in your mouth. I'm now quite good at that. It was Burgundy wine-broker and Yorkshireman Tim Marshall who taught me the trick. Not surprising. Takes more than a mouthful of wine to silence a Yorkshireman.

The other necessary skill is spitting. Most people are embarrassed about spitting. Wine professionals are not in the least embarrassed. Indeed it is the way to earn respect in the wine trade. A bit like small boys having peeing competitions against a wall, full-grown wine chaps and wine women like to demonstrate their prowess, powerfully projecting a neat, cohesive little globule of tasted wine accurately into any convenient drain. Practise as I might, I have never become a great spitter. My lips just don't work right. I've ruined many a good suede shoe in my time. I've noticed, these days, that winemakers usually cart around a great big slops bucket. For cellar hygiene probably, but maybe also because they've heard about my spitting.

A private cellar will usually be smaller and below ground, so a touch warmer in winter. Take one in the Rhône Valley, for example, the Plan de Dieu... February. Mistral howling outside. Feeling freeze-dried. Below ground it's quiet. This is not a showpiece cellar. This isn't California. It's a working cellar, harsh fluorescent lighting, and 30 old *foudres* to taste, all with wood taps, plasticined around to stop leaks. No frills, and clean. Written in chalk on the fronts of the *foudres* are things like '*Rasteau 2017 Grenache Syrah Mourvèdre en coteaux*'. The winemaker is going up his ladder to reach each bung, then stick in his siphon to give us all a squirt of cold wine. Nice big bucket to spit in. He is laughing at my appreciative gurgling noises when we hit a real good 'un. He's pleased.

THE MIDI

From early on I had gone south from Bordeaux and discovered and loved the strong, dark red wines of Gascony, the wines from south-western regions, from what they called the Haut Pays, which had helped create the reputation of Bordeaux but which, over the centuries, the unscrupulous Bordelais had managed to lock out of their port long enough to favour their own wines.

I had read that, in the Middle Ages, the English market much preferred the inland wines from the Haut Pays which were richer, stronger and darker than the pale (*clair*) wines of Bordeaux itself. These, back then, went by the name of 'Clairet', only in later centuries becoming the darker 'Claret'.

There's the little region of Madiran, that when I first went in 1974 had shrunk to but a handful of growers of which the wine of the Laplace family was the only one you ever saw mentioned. I turned up at their place one bright autumn morning to find three generations of the family out in the yard having a bottling day. They are big people in this region (where rugby first took hold in France) and Grandfather in his *beret basque* and clogs, with his big moustache, was clearly still the patriarch. But his son now ran the show with his wife and their teenage children. Everyone had their role and all the men wore the big Basque berets. I got shown their huge old 100-year-old vines, then invited in to eat round their enormous kitchen table. I loved everything about this family.

Cahors up the River Lot from Bordeaux was then less exciting. Older customers were always keen I should get some wine from there. So I did. The only source back then appeared to be the co-op at Parnac. Nice wine. Customers would swirl the palish red wine around their glass saying, 'Ah! The black wine of Cahors.' Amazing, the power of suggestion! In people's minds, Cahors seemed always black, when clearly it wasn't. I heard that the phylloxera bug had wiped out all the ancient vineyards on the near-vertical, bare scree slopes north of the river, which had produced tiny quantities of small black grapes which made the true black wine. In recent times the area had fought its way back into existence, but had replanted its traditional Côt or Malbec vines on the flat, fertile 'easy' land south of the river. Made a nice wine, but no way was it black.

From Cahors, what became my most regular route east would then take me on up to Gaillac, a 'lost' region where a couple of giant co-operatives made what were the cheapest, honest wines in France. By 'honest' I mean the wine was what it claimed it was: from the vineyards of the co-op members. It was always possible to buy cheaper wine from specialist 'cheapo' mass-market merchants. But I'd been warned off these places... more like factories than wineries. Gaillac White became my House Wine for some years. These days Gaillac now produces a very impressive range of exciting wines often made from grape varieties only found in this region like the Len de l'El – in the old *langue d'oc* of the south. In modern French that means *loin de l'œil* or 'far from the eye'... which I have always thought a delightful way of conveying that this variety produces very small grapes!

I learned that in Gaillac a great injustice had been visited upon the gentle, kind and remarkably intelligent man who became a hero of mine and many others: Jean Dubernet, the oenologist who revolutionised winemaking in Languedoc and Roussillon.

DUBERNET
ANOTHER GREAT MENTOR

Apparently, when he left his easy life as a consultant in Bordeaux, seeking more of a challenge, he first of all took the job of running the biggest wine co-op in France at Labastide-de-Lévis in Gaillac. The place – indeed the whole region – was really struggling. Unlike the hot Midi, the high Gaillac district is a cool climate region, which meant that some cold years the grapes did not ripen quite enough to make decent wine. Cold years also happen in Bordeaux and Burgundy. But they had – and still have – a remedy: sugar. Appellation Contrôlée regions have the right to 'chaptalise' their wines... they can add sugar to their grape juice. Sugar ferments into alcohol very well, so if you add it to watery grapes you get a stronger wine – admittedly with the problem that fermented sugar has no flavour. Nonetheless chaptalisation (named after clever Monsieur Chaptal) was widely practised in the period we are discussing. It is much less done these days. Thankfully.

Gaillac had the problem that it was not an Appelation Controllée region but fell into the second division of VDQS. (It has since become AOC.) So then it was not allowed to add sugar to its grape juice to obtain a satisfactory level of alcohol in the wine, meaning, some years, its wines were unsaleable – a ruinous problem for an already poverty-stricken region.

Dubernet found a solution. By putting a proportion of the winery's juice through a sort of pressure cooker that he invented he was able to concentrate it. This rich concentrate he could then add to the normal juice, instead of sugar. Which you would think a better solution: more authentic, more flavourful. But the Appellation Contrôlée regions did not see it that way. They saw it as a threat to their exclusive right to be able to boost the strength of their wines by adding sugar and persuaded the authorities that Dubernet was about to unleash a torrent of rather good wine from regions which were, officially – therefore unquestionably – inferior. The great and good of Bordeaux, Burgundy etc. had, of course, excellent connections in Paris. Gaillac did not.

A young Jean Dubernet.

XV DU PRÉSIDENT

❋

THIS IS JUST ONE OF MANY WINES FROM THE FRENCH MIDI THAT HAVE BEEN SO IMPORTANT FOR US.

The Midi, or Languedoc-Roussillon, has long been our No. 1 source of wines. This high-strength Grenache, our first 15 per cent wine and our first really big seller, was discovered in sun-baked Opoul – the warmest place in France, and a rugby-mad village. Hence the label. That extra degree or two means Grenache from schist-based vineyards becomes round and *gouleyant* (rich and purplish) after just six months, without any need for barrel-ageing. (We tried barrels but they just thinned out the wine and were quickly abandoned.) It still sells well but has been overtaken by Cabalié, a wine a bit like XV and from the same region but with a touch of the *vin doux naturel* (VDN) about it. VDN is Roussillon's port-like wine made, we believe, since long before port itself was invented. Cabalié is not a VDN but is a wine that has not quite fermented out to total dryness and this succulent style has proved, unexpectedly, very, very popular with customers. But for me the great joy of Midi wines cannot lie in just two wines, however popular, but in the fact that the region has the world's largest and most diverse range of affordable wine.

Dubernet was arrested, tried and imprisoned... for trying to make a better wine and help impoverished winegrowers. Monsieur Cassin and directors of wine co-operatives throughout France were incensed at this and mounted a 'Free Dubernet' campaign. Which worked. But Dubernet had to leave Gaillac. He left behind his legacy of the lightly sparkling Gaillac Perlé – his invention – which to this day is the best-known wine of Gaillac, and moved down to Narbonne where he started his next campaign: to get the winegrowers of the much vaster Midi out of the parlous situation they too were in.

My regular journey would then continue on from Gaillac through the next town of Castres and over the Montagne Noire down into the real hot, dry Midi.

I remember on one occasion early on Armistice Day I had left a grey, damp Castres full of grinning old war veterans watching drum majorettes going through their paces. Driving east, the green countryside was positively English. To the south a looming dark mass topped with raincloud came closer: the Montagne Noire. Maybe it's the dense covering of chestnut, oak and pine that earned it the appropriate name. But just after Ferrals – with its field walls of upright stone slabs – a big change occurs. The clouds are left behind and behold a vast sunny vista! Ahead were the Minervois, the Valley of the Aude, Corbières and Roussillon; on the left, the Mediterranean and in the far distance Mont Canigou and the Pyrenees. I was already in the Haut Minervois – all stones, scrubs and abandoned vineyards. Up here any kind of cultivation is really too difficult. But when I pulled off the road the scent of wild garlic was strong where the tyres had crushed the little plants. Suddenly in a matter of yards the climate and landscape changed and the countryside went from green fields and cows to dry stones, scrubby bushes and lots of pointy cypress trees. I then went on through the seemingly endless Mediterranean vineyards to old Narbonne and Dubernet.

The Midi was my first big new region outside Bordeaux. It is very big. If not now, certainly then, the biggest wine region in the world. The Midi is a vague concept but wine people generally consider it to be made up of the two biggest and most productive French regions: Languedoc and Roussillon. I was pushed towards it by my Bordeaux suppliers. I remember old man Bourlon, at Château Guibeau, exasperated, crying,

'*Tony... Arrêtez! Toujours* asking for cheaper wine. Any Bordeaux wine cheaper than ours will only be cheaper because it has something wrong with it. If you must have cheaper wine, go to the Midi... go see Dubernet.'

The reality was that many of the suppliers of 'cheap' Bordeaux were not at all like the winegrowers that I had met through Monsieur. Massive merchant factories, huge bottling plants (with no vineyards) blending stuff day and night from far and wide in vast volumes, immediately sent out in truck after truck, wine that didn't taste like I thought it ought to... nothing like what I knew as real Bordeaux. I wanted to stick with my kind of dedicated, obsessed, passionate winegrowers. So I insisted on 'Grower-bottled wines only'. That's what I put on my letterhead. Not only were the wines nicer, they were honest. I knew these were wines made with loving care. They were more exciting and interesting. Self-interest, maybe, but I always found that as long as I took the trouble to tell my customers about my winegrowers, tried to get my customers involved, and offered them as much of the fun that I enjoyed as I could, then it worked.

Anyway, Dubernet was the perfect choice, by now a great man in the Midi. Jean Dubernet had risen above that unpleasantness in Gaillac. Here was a top Bordeaux oenologist (a wine vet, if you like), personally trained by Émile Peynaud himself. A rising star, he suddenly abandoned the comfy life of consulting to the great Bordeaux châteaux and headed towards the wild south, 'to make a real difference'. He spoke quietly amongst the noisy, shouty, angry, violent, cellar-wrecking men of the Midi but nonetheless revolutionised winemaking in the region. All these years on, the Midi still provides more of Laithwaite's wines than most other wine countries.

This was where the very first vineyards in France were planted – with vines, one imagines, brought by galley from the Middle East, where wine began. The now mostly abandoned terraces on which they grew can still be clearly seen on the hillsides near the coast. Vineyards were planted on the steep slopes where only vines can grow, while the flatter, more fertile land was reserved for essential food crops... that was the general rule.

Those wines, one imagines, were really rather good. Then, in the middle of the nineteenth century, disaster struck: some idiot imported a bunch of American vines which contained the little louse called phylloxera which promptly destroyed almost every vineyard in Europe. This at a

*Railway Arch 36.
The UK's first wine
warehouse?*

time when every working man in southern Europe was putting away litres of the stuff every meal. So suddenly... no wine! Winegrowers soon worked out that they could graft their vines on to louse-resistant American rootstock, but of course that took time and the population was going mental. Whoever could get back into production first would make a fortune. So there then occurred something like a wine gold rush. Ruined winegrowers from all over France figured out that they would be better off moving to the vast spaces of the Midi, where land was cheap and sunshine plentiful, and there planting something, anything – American hybrids, whatever – that could produce lots of wine FAST! Never mind the quality. Get the quantity. The desperate market would drink ANYTHING vaguely wine-like. Vast fortunes were quickly made.

If you drive today through the lower parts of the Midi countryside you will see it is still dotted with vast mansions and châteaux, built in the nineteenth century by the more successful nouveau wine barons, the oligarchs of their day. They led the wine rush, planted every hectare they could and just churned it out.

It was *vin ordinaire*: carafe wine bought by the demijohn or later in those five-star, plastic-capped litre bottles which we Brits took to calling 'plonk'. It stained your teeth, *le rouge qui tache*... it stained your clothes! Dubernet called it Industrial Wine and hated it. I'd assumed it would be something like plonk that I'd be getting from the Midi. At that time in Britain it had become quite cool to drink *ordinaire*. The big guys were importing wines in litres with plastic caps called Vieux Ceps, Carafino or Hirondelle.

But Dubernet, the missionary who believed he could change the Midi, had other ideas. He took me on his 'rounds' in his gas-suspension Citroën DS bouncing sedately down the lanes and tracks, up into the hills to small villages that looked ruined but still supported plenty of life. One village we stopped at was Berlou, high in the Saint-Chinian hills.

It has strange purple 'soil' – just flakes of prettily coloured mica, really. But vines do miracles in it. Not much else does. Anyway this schist stuff produced with little human help a low-acid, non-bitter, not tannic and therefore 'round' red wine. With no need for expensive barrel-ageing, it produced what they call *gouleyant*: rich, purplish wine. My customers adored it immediately. It was fantastic value.

In the vast crumbling Château de Luc, Dubernet introduced me to a gentle, brownish wine; the result of being made in a gigantic old wooden cask the size of a small house. Then in Fabrezan there was a shop where the village pharmacist made a really juicy-fruit red using the traditional *macération carbonique* technique where the grape bunches are left to macerate then ferment in a carbon dioxide (oxygen-free) environment. It's the same method – more or less – as used to make wines in the Beaujolais region.

None of these wines were made with anything special in the way of grapes. Not 'noble' grapes. Cinsault, Carignan, maybe a bit of Grenache. Replanting to produce better wines was way beyond people's means, back then. They had to do the best they could with whatever they had. And Dubernet was there to help.

The next wine I collected on this exploratory tour of the Midi was called Château de Durban – the château may still have existed but it wasn't obvious among the ruins. Another wine made by the *macération carbonique* method, it came from the village co-op winery.

I took the plunge (in those days I had no one around to tell me it was too risky) and bought a tank of each wine. These wines were appealing and cheap but they came with a drawback. The châteaux or co-ops of the Midi didn't sell them in bottles. Dubernet said no one in the Midi sold wine by the bottle.

I find that hard to believe these days when everywhere you go there are estates with signs saying '*Vente directe, dégustation gratuite*', and when some wineries have shops that would look fine in Mayfair. But back then the Midi was purely bulk wine. Wine left the region mostly in a rail tanker on trains which could be up to a mile long... a whole mile of wine! Imagine. They went to the heroic drinkers of Paris and the north and got bottled or carafed up there. But of course it gave us a problem.

Our solution came in the shape of the one local bottling centre, a big old steam-driven thing in Perpignan, and Dubernet arranged for the wine to be taken there and bottled under his supervision. That was 300 cases of each wine. They filled an entire articulated lorry. They filled my railway arch. There's a photo of me in there with cases towering around (see p.99). That was these Midi wines. And they went down so well with the customers. They were at a good price and people just loved that easy style. You didn't have to cellar them. Splash them into a jug... same as they do in the Midi cafés.

But Jean Dubernet warned me... it could be hit and miss. Next year maybe these particular wines wouldn't be so good... but others would. There would always be something good in such a vast place. Trick was to find it. Eventually, we drew this weird-shaped wine label and created a brand called *L'Épervier* or 'The sparrowhawk'. You see these little birds hovering all over the region, looking for a juicy morsel. And that for me was what Monsieur Dubernet did, and also his partner in the practice, Old Monsieur Demolombe and his wild son, Jean – who became a very great friend. And Jean's assistant, and then successor, Andrée Ferrandiz, who continued to find wines for me till she retired. Even then she continued to phone occasionally to tip me off about a new wine she had heard about. She still does. The customers took to the weirdly shaped label and every year saw new villages from the Midi reach the British market. A new name and village and style, but all were produced by passionate people.

Being taught how to taste grapes by Georges Bertrand.

I was lost in this vast region – that I came to love even more than Bordeaux – and I always would be… anybody would be. Even Hugh Johnson's *Wine Atlas* Midi map had little detail. The region's wines just were not mapped. And this is the most geologically complex part of France. So I had to have these helpers, my hawks. From this point on, the 'Bordeaux Direct' name became somewhat misleading. However it was many years before we plucked up the courage to change it. I could, I suppose, have bought Midi wines bottled in Bordeaux. Saved myself many long drives. But it would not have been the same. Bordeaux merchants would tanker in a lot of Midi wines. Whether they sold them as Midi wines, however, was another matter. As the weaker Midi *ordinaires* were always 'improved' in the old days by rich red imports from Algeria, so the Bordeaux merchants knew that pale, poor vintage Bordeaux could be made more saleable by a bit of good rich Corbières. That is what my disapproving Bordeaux winegrowing friends would tell me, anyway. The authorities knew this and did their best to control provenance, to make it impossible to move wine without permission. Every shipment, every truck had to be accompanied by papers that detailed what went from where to where and on what day. There were roadblocks and checks. And prison.

*Jean Cabrol made a
very easy-drinking
Minervois. Access to
his cellars was via a
trapdoor under his bed.
Madame was never
happy with this.*

Legend has it that ingenious wine merchants always found ways round the roadblocks and checks. This was a business where the rewards meant it was worth beating the system. I have, of course, no idea if it was true but they told me about 'the motorbike scam': early morning, a full tanker would leave Béziers with correct, stamped and dated papers and be in Bordeaux around noon. Its papers would immediately be handed to a biker who would rush them back to Béziers, where a second tanker would set off with the same, apparently correct papers to arrive before midnight. *Le voilà!* Within the specified 24 hours, a whole extra tanker of good, untraceable Midi wine with which to improve or 'stretch' a less-than-wonderful Bordeaux! It's all changed now of course.

Recently I was stranded for hours in Bordeaux airport by a yet-again delayed flight. The only consolation was a bottle of Midi Chardonnay from the lounge fridge made by a guy called Gérard Bertrand who used to play in the back row for France. Which was weird. Because I was just about to write another story about my wine hunting in the Midi... and the next name on my 1976 list of suppliers: Georges Bertrand, father of the above Gérard. So I quietly enjoyed that bottle, typed the story and hoped a plane would turn up sometime.

Georges Bertrand was a *courtier*. These are the very active guys who spend their days visiting winegrowers, tasting and collecting samples of their wine. They take these to the merchants and attempt to sell a tank or two. They will, if they can, take a small commission from the producer, and from the merchant. If they are sharp they can do well. Georges was sharp and had an office in Gasparets near Lézignan. Super-fit, he had been a good rugby player and was now an international referee. Sharp he certainly was. He quickly cottoned on that I liked the soft fruity style of red and, instead of supplying me from one of his producers, realised he could do better himself. His *macération carbonique* Grenache-Cinsault-Carignan from his vineyard was lovely. But had no name. Few wines did back then. They just had tank numbers. Anyway my 'off-the-top-of-my-head' idea 'Cuvée Georges Bertrand' seemed OK to him. So, with a quickly sketched-out label, away it went... to wide acclaim. When we launched *The Sunday Times* Wine Club, Georges's was the most popular wine. We sold a ton, and established a style which continues to be popular to this day.

1987

Château
de Pech Redon
Côteaux du Languedoc
La Clape

Appellation Côteaux du Languedoc Contrôlee

Mis en bouteilles par Jean DEMOLOMBE
Propriétaire à 11100 Narbonne France
Produit de France

12 % alc vol 75 cl e

L'ÉPERVIER®

12 500 bouteilles
bouteille
N° 06025

ROSÉ DE SAIGNÉE

We shipped many different Midi wines under our signature label, L'Épervier.

Some time later with Dubernet, we three then came up with a follow-up idea: a lightly sparkling rosé, to be called 'Rosé Perlant'. When a wine has a lot of bubbles, the French call it *mousseux*... as it foams, or mousses. With fewer bubbles, it gets called a Crémant – creamy. Even fewer bubbles make it *pétillant* – it prickles. With only a few bubbles or 'pearls', it's *perlant* or a *perlé*.

Georges was, as I said, sharp, but I haggled a great price out of him and felt good about that. However... when 1,000 dozen turned up in Slough, for our next *Sunday Times* offer, they had labels... but no capsules (things that cover the cork)! 'You didn't specify capsules' said Georges. 'But, but, but bottles always have capsules'... splutter splutter... but it was futile. We were stuffed. We had just one day to pack and despatch 6,000 mixed dozens containing two bottles of a wine looking really cheap because it had no capsule. Our desperate solution was to send someone round every Boots in the Home Counties, to clean them out of the capsules they sold, back then, to amateur winemakers. It was an all-night job with those bloody capsules and the end of quite such a cosy relationship with Georges.

But his wine continued to sell well. Some years later I got the dreadful news that Georges had aquaplaned off the autoroute at Narbonne, fatally... one of an alarming number of wine suppliers I have lost in road accidents in France. Great, great shame. Great guy, if a touch sharp. But also great to see his boy doing so well. That was not a bad Chardonnay... the bottle had a capsule, too, and my plane came.

3

WINE PRESS

THE SUNDAY TIMES

I'd found the way of life I liked and thought I would live happily ever after just driving round vineyards. I had Barbara in my life, and she was doing all the hard bits. We had the Arch that acted as office, store and tasting venue and I was soon even able to get a mortgage and buy my own flat in Windsor.

Opposite: Poster for the first ever wine show in the huge new Bordeaux Exhibition Hall. It's now called VINEXPO.

So as far we were concerned, life could just continue on in this rather nice way. Little did we realise what the future held in store for us.

Back in the 1970s newspapers fulfilled roles very different from today's social media world which provides access to news as it happens. Those were gentler, slower times, and newspaper readerships were in their millions. Papers lived in an unchallenged vibrant, innovative world and investigative journalism was going through something of a golden age.

No editor was held in higher regard than Sir Harold, then just 'Harry', Evans of *The Sunday Times*. In 1972 he had launched his historic campaign for proper compensation for the thousands of victims of the thalidomide drug meant to help pregnant women overcome morning sickness but which led to thousands of babies being born with malformed limbs.

The Sunday Times had written exposés about a whole range of other topics, including malpractice in the wine business. I had read those avidly. It was started by Nicholas Tomalin who did a piece about people importing plonk from North Africa and labelling it as whatever they wanted to. Then some time later – well, years later in 1972 – he did another piece and on the spur of the moment – just one of those things – I wrote a slightly witty 'Dear Editor' letter to Harry Evans, saying

thanks for doing this. And he only went and printed it. I still have the cutting:

> *Thank you, Insight Consumer Unit, for another wine exposé on dishonest labelling (Look! last week) – only six years after the last.*
>
> *Could you not do a few more? There are some of us in the trade earning a hard and precarious living importing and selling only château and estate-bottled wines which compete in price with the London-bottled brews.*
>
> *To do this commercially and compete against those of our big brothers who apparently learned their trade bootlegging in Prohibition America, we've had to cut out absolutely everybody and everything generally associated with the fine-wine trade.*
>
> *We live in a railway arch and do nothing finer or more esoteric than driving one great truck between vineyard and consumer – it's hard and not at all the life wine-trade executives are supposed to lead.*
>
> *We can and do sell really good château-bottled clarets from châteaux that do actually exist – no fantasy at all – at well under a pound, and many other wines too. Château-bottling, as opposed to merchant-bottling either in France or this country, is the only reasonable guarantee of authenticity and quality.*
>
> *The French think the average Englishman knows nothing about wine – they are right, and no matter how many full-page 'guides to a wine label' the British trade prints it has not the slightest intention of doing anything to improve the situation until it's dragged screaming into Europe.*
>
> *Tony Laithwaite, Bordeaux Direct, Railway Arch 36, Goswell Road, Windsor*

That letter was very spur of the moment and it is quite possible

July 16th 1972

THE SUNDAY TIMES,

Chateau wine on the cheap

THANK YOU, Insight Consumer Unit, for another wine exposé on dishonest labelling (Look! last week)—only six years after the last.

Could you not do a few more? There are some of us in the trade earning a hard and precarious living importing and selling only château- and estate-bottled wines which compete in price with the London-bottled brews.

To do this commercially and compete against those of our big brothers who apparently learnt their trade bootlegging in Prohibition America, we've had to cut out absolutely everybody and everything generally associated with the fine-wine trade.

We live in a railway arch and do nothing finer or more esoteric than driving one great truck between vineyard and consumer —it's hard and not at all the life wine-trade executives are supposed to lead.

We *can* and do sell really good château-bottled clarets (from châteaux that do actually exist— no fantasy at all) at well under a pound, and many other wines too. Château-bottling, as opposed to merchant-bottling either in France or this country, is the only reasonable guarantee of authenticity and quality.

The French think the average Englishman knows nothing about wine—they are right, and no matter how many full-page "guides to a wine-label" the British trade prints it has not the slightest intention of doing anything to improve the situation until it's dragged screaming into Europe. **Tony Laithwaite**, Bordeaux Direct, Railway Arch 36, Goswell Road, Windsor

blazer! Warm in winter and cool in summer. Don't tell me that they are in fashion now, for it isn't the same.—**Joanna Nash**, Wallington, Surrey.

● Elaine Grand asks, Why shorts? My query is, Why longs?
My elder son has outgrown a ankles and discarded thre otherwise perfectly g four terms. In

that I wrote it after a couple or more glasses had fired up my courage. It was quite the Angry Young Wine Merchant again taking on the established wine trade. Mr Wound-up of Windsor. I was sure they would never print it. But I bought my copy that Sunday morning and started reading it in a cubicle at a service station on the M6. My whoop of joy must have worried the other gents. It was given the little headline 'Château wine on the cheap' and this blatant bit of self-advertising appeared on Sunday, 16 July 1972. A date I really should remember. But odd to read it as today all the screaming is about *leaving* Europe.

As a result we got hundreds of letters expressing interest and support. We sent them all our very short wine list. It was really our first national newspaper 'ad', and in those days *The Sunday Times* had a readership of 4 million.

Sadly, the man who wrote the article, Nicholas Tomalin – who really was one of the foremost journalists of his generation – was killed a year later in Israel by a Syrian missile while covering the Yom Kippur War. It's hard to remember that back then in that pre-EEC time, the French Appellation Contrôlée (most other countries didn't yet have such things) was not legally recognised in Britain. Many in the wine trade still maintained that names like Pommard and Châteauneuf-du-Pape were indicative of 'styles' rather than specific geographic locations. It had worked well for them that way for centuries. However, various bad lads were now going too far: shipping a tanker of good old plonk and baptising it variously as Beaujolais or Pommard or Châteauneuf or Pomerol or whatever. But everything we sold was bottled by the people who made it, fully conforming to Appellation Contrôlée rules. So it was honest, but also more expensive.

The publicity was all very well, Bordeaux Direct received a welcome boost with extra sales and our customer base expanded as did our sales area. But we couldn't expect Harry Evans to print regular advertising letters from Arch 36. It seemed as though the letter and the boost to the business was just a happy interlude, but what happened next was exhilarating and then terrifying for us.

A figure I can only describe as a Svengali appeared in our lives. He was a customer and his name was Chris Dolley, a name I will never forget. It turned out that behind his smooth, charming exterior he was a bit of a cunning genius. But how were we, two naive innocents in the world of business, to know? He liked to come round and have a drink and chat. He was extremely friendly, though he had a terrible laugh. That laugh should have warned us. He impressed us because he was sophisticated and also chairman and managing director of Penguin Books. He even said he had a chauffeur.

MR DOLLEY

We were in our early 20s, with no business training. It did seem likely this man could help us to grow faster. He could name-drop for hours and he really did have a chauffeur.

So far no catch, but then Dolley came up with a business plan where he said I should set up a Limited Company. So we did, and I gave shares to Barbara, Monsieur, and my mum and dad. Barbara became Managing Director. It seemed best. I became Chairman, an easier job, I reckoned. All very grand. Then Dolley said he would like to buy some shares too. Seemed like a good idea at the time, so we sold him 20 per cent of our business for the – to us – huge sum of £10,000. In those days we had never actually had any surplus money, we still lived hand to mouth. So that really was a huge sum to us. It started well. After *The Sunday Times* letter, he said, 'I know Harry Evans well, I will give him a call and ask if we could do a Reader Offer.' Bold as brass, he went off to *The Sunday Times* and got them to let us do one of the reader offers that they often did with wine merchants for a mixed box of a dozen bottles. They called them 'Instant Cellars' and had been doing such offers for years. Anyway, I got together a case of 12 bottles, two of each of my latest range of six best-selling wines. Dolley wisely hadn't mentioned to them the packing case office in the old coal-arch. But quite sensibly *The Sunday Times* sent someone down to check out this Bordeaux Direct outfit.

He was a lovely chap called Bruce Howell. He came down and looked round Arch 36. I am not sure it was what he was expecting but luckily he was as mad as us. Slightly anarchic too. Actually... maybe more than slightly. We got on well. He blithely told his bosses that we were well up to the job. He was either a lot more confident than we were, or just wanted to see a how big an explosion he could create. In truth, none of us had any real idea just what the results of the newspaper offer might be.

The Sunday Times got the guy who wrote their 'Atticus' column to write the copy. This was another stroke of luck as they normally had their resident wine writer do it, but she had just left – fired, I think. We never found out why. But that meant our copy went out without any opinions or judgements from a wine writer. 'Atticus' was in those days a guy called Allan Hall who did a really good job for us because he was witty, and wit sells wine much better than banging on and on about the tastes of blackcurrants and cinnamon and all that. The offer worked a treat. The wines were ones that readers had maybe heard about but not been able to buy easily. There was Château de Panisseau, my favourite Bergerac white, the Sauvignon Blanc Nouveau from the co-op of Duras in the Lot-et-Garonne, a Muscadet from old Monsieur Dugast, an Alsace Dry Riesling from the co-op of Kientzheim-Kaysersberg, a Château du Trignon, a Côtes du Rhône from André Roux, a Côtes du Rhône Primeur from the co-op at Chusclan, a Château de Durban Corbières, a Roc de Lussac, a Monbazillac from the co-op, and the sparkling Vouvray from Château Moncontour. We sold – and I still struggle to believe it – 3,000 cases in one hit. It was a stupendous number for us but also a logistical nightmare. The Arch was just not capable of taking that amount of wine. And there was no way we could handle it with one small van or even a lorry load. We just guessed a number, and ordered three big 40-foot articulated lorries that could each carry 1,200 cases. To store it, we took over the handily empty old NCL warehouse between Slough station and the Horlicks factory. As the order forms poured in, we worked day and night, packing and stacking till we dropped. We didn't have a forklift truck, just our muscles and those of any friend unwise enough to let themselves be roped in. It stretched not just us but also our meagre finances to breaking. We rented the warehouse for just a few weeks and put all the wine in there, repacked it, prayed hard, and – phew – sent it all out a few days later. We used NCL to deliver the wine... and we still do (although now it has gone from National Carriers Limited to being Yodel). The enormity of what we had achieved through this offer affected every aspect of our lives. No longer was it a one-man show, or a one-man-and-one-woman show, because we needed a lot of help. The orders all came in by post, with cheques for the wine. They had to be taken to the bank, labels had to be typed and stuck on each case, and then despatched on the right truck.

This was a huge leap that could really break a small firm and often does. It was physically exhausting. I had three sturdy, hard-working typists, sitting on my bed in the flat with typewriters on their laps, doing address

My first Vouvray supplier – Château Moncontour.

label after address label with another load of people in the living room opening envelopes. *The Sunday Times* had never had a wine offer go so well. We sold twice as much as any previous offer. They took a royalty on each case sold, and were very happy indeed. So Bruce, still totally unfazed by it all, said: 'Well, go on then, do another one.' We repeated the exercise some months later... different wines but still from the little French regions I had made my own... and it worked again! These were heady times. In a little over six months we had sold quantities of wine that six months earlier we couldn't have imagined possible. I had been walking around leafleting and relying on my mezzanine tastings in Arch 36 for orders. Now they were coming in their thousands. For a while we were outselling everybody in the wine trade bar perhaps the Wine Society. We hoped that there would be repeat business from the orders.

But then we had a better idea, and made an even more fantastic breakthrough. On the strength of the readers' response, our Svengali Dolley was sent back in to pitch the paper to create a whole new concept: a 'Wine Club'.

They liked the idea, and proposed a joint venture. It was Barbara who did the contract negotiating, backed up by David Wright, and they achieved something remarkable which underpins everything we have been able to achieve since. You'd expect a deal between one of the world's leading newspaper groups and little us in our shed under a railway arch would be a bit one-sided. But Barbara saw that a one-sided deal would never last. Because they never do. *The Times* newspapers put in many clauses to protect themselves and their reputation. They insisted that if we stopped trading for any reason then they could continue the Club alone. Barbara agreed but asked that this be a reciprocal arrangement, and this caused some mirth. (I wasn't there, was kept well away.) How could anyone dare imagine the mighty *Sunday Times* ceasing publication? But she got her way. And a few years later, what happened? The newspaper shut down for months during its fight with the print unions. But during that time we were able to keep the Club going and indeed widen its audience to the benefit of the newspaper, us and, above all, Club members. I am not aware of any joint ventures that have succeeded as well and as long as *The Sunday Times* Wine Club, launched in 1973 and now in its 45th year.

Instead of just doing intermittent reader offers, there would now be a permanent presence. With lots of things going on to entertain and educate a public which was getting increasingly interested in wine. The newspaper went for it, even though by then they all knew about our railway arch headquarters. At that time there was no such thing as a wine club. True, there was the grand old Wine Society which had been going since the 1800s, but an all-singing, all-dancing wine club, like we envisaged, had not yet happened. With such a club we could send out a regular wine list every quarter and a magazine where we would talk about wines, and try to help and advise people new to wine... which seemed to be just about everybody. *The Sunday Times* could get top journalists to write it with wit and flair. We would call it *Wine Times*, and with the magazine members would get more special offers as well as a wine list. We would organise tastings around the country and wine tours abroad.

And that is just what we did. It all happened so fast, we were carried along with those ideas and had no time to think about failing. We just believed it would work. I had to hire my first 'executives' (apart from Barbara that is). Martin Wright became Wine Club Manager, and Tim Bleach helped with buying and shipping. Both were fresh out of school, but then we were a young company. We moved from the Arch to an old First World War munitions factory (that had more recently been a bra warehouse) of 6,000 square feet in downtown Slough. We traded there from 1973 to 1979 and the business grew fast. It was now officially called

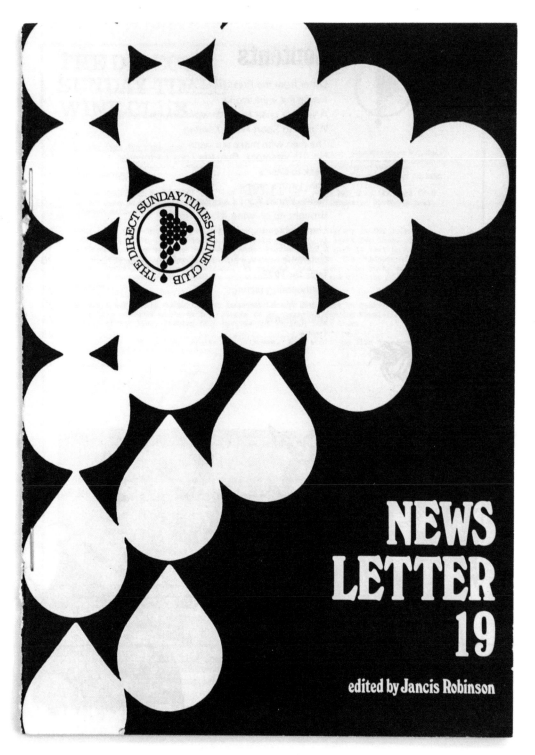

THE DIRECT SUNDAY TIMES WINE CLUB

NEWS LETTER 19

edited by Jancis Robinson

Young tasters Tim Bleach, buyer, me and Hugh Johnson.

Direct Wines (Windsor) Ltd. Not the name we wanted. But we were forced into the change by one of our less charming customers. He had gone off and registered a company with our name 'Bordeaux Direct Ltd'. He then invited me over and, all smiles, said I could have the company he had registered – if I gave him half the shares. I left, furious, but also in a panic. But then I remembered that a friend from school had become a lawyer. Dave had been our rugby captain and was always considered a bit of a 'hard man'. On the field he often had to be restrained. I thought he might sort this man out. But, instead of getting violent, Dave calmed me down and told me that as I had been trading as Bordeaux Direct nobody else could use the name without being done for 'passing off'. So relax, he said, just use another name for the limited company. So we became Direct Wines (Windsor) Ltd. The wine world know us now as Direct Wines. Though the customers don't.

Once the Wine Club was launched, 5,000 signed up straight away, and it was not long before we were at 20,000 members. We were now definitely the second largest mail-order wine company in the country, still chasing after the Wine Society. We overtook them eventually. We set up tastings and wine trips within a month or two of launching. Soon we were even selling tickets for a wine cruise round the Mediterranean. It was, in retrospect, a phenomenal period. But at the time we didn't know it. We had an idea; we did it. There was a great sense of urgency. We were like runners who thought we could hear footsteps behind us getting closer. No longer did we have nothing to lose. Now we had a lot to lose.

The Club had also acquired a President in Hugh Johnson, the wine author. *The Sunday Times* thought he would be a good addition and he was. Not just because of his remarkable *World Atlas of Wine* which had recently been published but because of his long-standing links to the paper. He had been wine correspondent back in 1962 and also travel editor. Perfect. As a relatively young newcomer I really looked forward to meeting this venerable old legend of the wine business. But I was completely thrown when Hugh first arrived at a Wine Club meeting in Printing House Square. I was expecting the elderly, presidential-like figure whose whiskery old face adorned the cover of his first book, *Wine*, rather than the bouncing mid-30s chappie who burst into the room, with a 'What ho, Chaps!'. Apparently the face on his book cover belonged to the revered *maître de chai* of Château d'Yquem, not the author. The picture of Hugh's arrival in that sunny boardroom is still very clear in my mind. He was full of affable Woosterish bonhomie. Hugh's enthusiasm for 'his' Club was very evident from that moment, and it still is. His marvellous maps and the way he can take the boringness out of wine writing changed everything in the wine world. For the first time we could all see our world. And for the first time it wasn't scary. It was the start of an enduring friendship based, I like to think, on a sort of mutual respect. I look admiringly up to him as the Greatest Wine Writer Ever. He looks fondly down on me as his 'Lad' from Bolton.

The sheer volume of wine suddenly needed to satisfy the Club's demands meant that we needed a larger range. I could no longer just rely on Monsieur Cassin and his friends. Hugh obviously knew a lot of people in the UK wine trade. So we started buying from them, which rather changed the model, as previously we had bought everything directly from producers. We needed a sherry or two, so we bought it from Averys. We bought quite a lot of different stuff from different people as we had to keep the quality up and keep the supply going. If you are doing mail order you can't afford to upset your customers by not delivering either in quality or in time. It was a frantic period of fast growth. We made mistakes; we got things wrong. It was flat out all the time; I remember the pain… whole days busting for a pee, just couldn't find time to go. But we got through. I still managed to do my 'pootles' (Hugh's term) round France in spite of the pressure. Although now there was no point in bringing back 100 cases at a time. The days of the Cortina and the Transit van were long gone. But I was still going abroad at least one trip a month, often two or three times, to find new stuff. I started by going to just over the border into Spain for Rioja, then over the northern German border and down the Mosel with Hugh, then over the Alps into Italy – like a web, my journeys and contacts gradually sort of spread outwards. So much had to be sorted out, and had to be made to work. It was luck with Dolley and Harry Evans that we got *The Sunday Times* deal but it was not luck that kept us hanging on in there during that wild ride. Dolley was the only 'outsider' involved. But that we survived was no thanks to him. It was in spite of him. After a while, he started trying to take us over completely, and did some devious things. Not content with *The Sunday Times* Wine Club he went to see the *Sunday Mirror* and set up the *Sunday Mirror* Wine Club without telling us or involving us. He did it with a bunch of lads in Peckham! Yes, true Del Boy stuff. We went to see them as we were worried about what was going on. They were friendly enough, we got on. Nice lads. But there were no offices and when we asked how they coped with customer problems, queries, complaints and all, they took us to a small brick shed, and opened the door to reveal a huge pile of letters. 'The Complaints Department', they said, and roared with laughter. Dolley also went to United Dairies and set up a wine club delivering on the milk floats. Neither worked.

At the same time, he kept encouraging us to overtrade. Go on, buy another truckload! The bank will be fine about that. I am sure now he intended we'd lose the plot and get into a tight fix. And of course we did.

We were right at the end of the Christmas rush in 1974 when thousands of cases went out as presents through both the Wine Club and the still-growing company gift market. Barbara and I, Chairman and Managing Director, had our grand titles but were both working in the warehouse packing non-stop, and were shattered by Christmas Day. But the holiday offered us the chance of a day or two of respite. In fact everyone in our small team worked incredibly hard, particularly during the rush, and would always be dropping with exhaustion on Christmas Eve. That was when we habitually all got ill. We could never afford to be ill at any other time – it was just not possible. We had started to run out of cash. Nana

Vertiginous harvesting on the Mosel.

Rudd had tried to help. She and Grandfather Laithwaite lent us £7,000... I still have the document. But it wasn't enough. So there we were, slumped and exhausted in the flat on 24 December when we had a visitor – Dolley. It was about to become a Christmas we would never forget.

Dolley came armed with figures; he knew all the details of the Company as he was on our Board. He said: 'I am afraid you have overtraded, technically you are insolvent, and the bank is now going to foreclose on you.' Dramatically he went to the front door, opened it and there was our bank manager hovering in the hallway outside my flat. He looked sheepish. Dolley marched him in with papers all ready to sign over the Company to him in return for him bailing us out. That was quite a moment. We had already seen the other side of Dolley as he had become very critical of our ways and made it clear he thought he could do it all better. Now he was trying to force us to sell out completely to him. He'd ensure we still had nice jobs, he said, but now it was to be his company! This Christmas Eve was his *coup d'état*.

I don't think we even hesitated, our Company was our baby, and you just don't sell your baby, do you? You don't just give in. So we said no. But he was determined to have it. We refused again and again, we wouldn't sign. He went away. Cross. Very. For us there was no Christmas that year, just a crisis. There was just one person we could turn to – the man who had helped me so much and inspired me to start the business. I got on the phone to Monsieur and he said '*Le Salaud!*'… a French term meaning something like 'The Bastard'. When I told him what had happened, he said 'Toneee, leave it with me' and over Christmas he phoned up all the producers he had introduced us to who were still the majority of our suppliers. He explained the problem and they all immediately agreed to give us an extra three months' credit. Just like that! It was an extraordinary feat that bought us valuable time. That year we made sure we had a MASSIVE January sale and sold everything and paid off the overdraft. Then we focused on selling hard every month to raise the money to pay the growers back and so survive. Then we changed our bank. Back to Barclays. We were OK, just, but were convinced Dolley had to go. I could've killed him, but Monsieur said that wasn't businesslike.

It was an experience that had a lasting effect on us. In the long term we benefited. For never again would we let ourselves get into the position where outsiders could threaten to take our Company from us. Never again would we allow outsiders to take a share of our baby. Never. So in a way all this unpleasantness turned out to have been a sound lesson. At the time I wondered where my famous luck had gone. But I see now, it hadn't, it came back, for soon we did get completely rid of Dolley and got all of our Company back. (There really is no doubt of the need for a lot of luck in business.) The good fortune came when our Svengali got into financial troubles of his own and urgently needed to raise cash. He had got it into his head that he was a genius businessman who could start up a whole empire of companies. There was a furniture company, a clock company, all sorts of other stuff, but he got something badly wrong and overreached himself. The bank was then after him not us. Barbara and our legal 'heavy', David Wright, negotiated – I know not how – to buy back our shares for the exactly same money he had paid: £10,000. With one bound we were free again! On the one occasion we met him afterwards he was unrepentant and said that if he hadn't been desperate we would *never* have got it back from him. But we did and that is why today we have no outside shareholders – the Dolley episode had scared us so much. We had offers from people wanting to buy our Company almost every week in the 1980s – and we still get them occasionally – but from then on we never gave them a minute's thought. We had decided we would always remain a family business. Today we are truly grateful we made that decision. After Dolley, most things were really OK, we had enough to live on, we (or rather I) had the enjoyment of the buying trips, and well,

New Aquitaine House
Paddock Road
Reading
Berkshire RG4 0JY

Tel: Reading (0734) 481718
Telex: Dirwin 849197

BORDEAUX DIRECT

Domaine de la Clarière
Sainte Colombe
Castillon-la-Bataille 33350
France

Tel: (57) 40 09 94
Telex: Colombe 550573

Discounted Case Prices for everything.

Price List

April 1983 — Number 73

* Wines straight from the Vineyard
* All these wines are bottled by their growers.

* Carriage is free for all orders over £50 value. (Below £50 add £2.00 per order.
* Notes by Tony Laithwaite.

* All are shipped directly and exclusively by Bordeaux Direct.
* Prices include VAT.

Unless otherwise stated, we make every effort to supply wines in 75cl bottles.   **Standard Conditions Apply.**

Wine	Bottle Code	Bottle Price	Unmixed Case Code	Case Price	Description
HOUSE WINES					
Terra Baixa White	2434	£2.25	C166	£24.50	Pure dry white Catalan — aromatic, fruity and substantial. 70cl.
Terra Baixa Red	3459	£2.25	C167	£24.50	Rich round Catalan red, very full and rewarding. 70cl.
'Chirashko Red' Bulgaria	3430	£2.25	R76	£24.50	'New style' Bulgarian. Lovely mid-weight satisfying red. 70cl.
'Chirashko White' Bulgaria	2418	£2.25	R77	£24.50	'New-style' Bulgarian white, Germanic type 'half-dry', fruity and full flavoured. 70cl.
'La Clariere' Red French Table Wine.	3402	£2.25	R41	£24.50	Far, far better than any other plain French table wine. 70cl.
'La Clariere' White French Table Wine	223	£2.25	R42	£24.50	Clean, dry French white, a true bargain. 70cl.
Chardonnay Provadya Estate 1981 'Balkan Vine'; Bulgaria *NEW*	2472	£2.29	C285	£25.90	Extraordinary value. Shut your eyes and you're in Mâcon; not Provadya. Bulgarian white wine making improves every year. 70cl.
Cabernet Sauvignon 1978 'Balkan Vine' Bulgaria	348	£2.29	C30	£25.90	Full, dark, rich, worth laying-down, but irresistible now! 70cl.
'Alionza' Frizzante di Castelfranco	2437	£2.40	C185	£27.35	Essential dry white drinking from Italy's Emilia Romagna. 72cl.
Dörrenbacher Guttenberg QbA Palatinate Hock 1982 *Litre*	2404	£3.78	T80	£42.99	Full flavoured hock, terrific value. Equivalent to £30.09 per case of 12 x 70cl.

we could always open a bottle... 'quality control', isn't that what they call it? Now, simply, it was a case of finding a way to make Bordeaux Direct and the much larger *Sunday Times* Wine Club work much better.

We faced a whole different set of challenges. How do you cope with going from a damp little cellar to a big mail-order company in a couple of years? We were still in our 20s and, as things had shown, really knew sod all about how to run a business.

TOUR DE FRANCE

Although I did the Bordeaux run for many years, the van (or vans – I wore out two) had given way to a Land Rover which now had to take me further, to many more places.

The Sunday Times Wine Club members seemed more demanding than our gentle, contented Bordeaux Direct customers who were always – and still are – so charmingly devoted to our French friends. Bordeaux Direct always had a large number of reverends on its customer list. What does that say about us? However, the biggest single group by far was always the doctors. Which is interesting, isn't it? The Hospital Consultants and Specialists Association was a big early supporter. We had a very popular Midi wine from the hills of La Clape. Doctors loved sending cases of La Clape to their friends. If you don't get the joke – just ignore.

We soon needed full-time help in France and so set up a small office in Sainte-Colombe. A young lad, Denis Gomme, was to run it, but he got called away on national service. His fiancée, Claudy, held the fort, and he never got his promised job! She was a marvel. Organising myriad French wines, cajoling, beseeching, threatening, whatever it took. Back then, a farmer invited out shooting or *cèpes*-picking saw no reason to be ready for our lorry's arrival. Claudy dealt with that attitude. The cases would be ready. Or else! Those farmers feared and loved her. French bureaucrats didn't love her, but she coped with them too. France, for us, would have been impossible without Claudy.

But the larger the number of customers, the bigger our range had to be. There was a greater demand for more wines. I would set off for France and beyond, relieved of the burden of loading up the van and filling in reams of paperwork, just simply to find new, interesting wines. They had to be delicious of course but by now I well knew that my delicious was almost certainly not everyone's delicious every time. But so as long as the wine had no discernible faults, I would buy anything that interested me, knowing it would at least interest some of my customers.

Some regions produced more 'winners' than others. But I tried them all. I like to brag that I 'bagged' every wine region in France. If you look at the map of France in Hugh's *World Atlas of Wine* you will get an idea of how many there are, and there are actually more than shown. By the mid-1980s I'd 'done', I'd 'bagged' everything within the six corners of the French *hexagone*, from the French Moselle in the far north, round through the gripping Côtes de Toul near Nancy, Allobrogie in the Alps, Bellet above Nice, Banyuls on the Spanish border, Irouléguy deep in Basque country, the Fiefs Vendéens on the Atlantic Coast... and everything in between. Been there, bought the wine.

My perverse nature meant I especially loved finding new wines in hidden corners, down country tracks as far removed from the main routes as I could find. All I wanted was to find producers who cared about their wine and its quality, produced it with passion, and delighted in people drinking it. Simple really.

But customers are mostly quite conservative. In the day, all they ever asked me for when they came into the Arch for the first time was Beaujolais. I, being perverse, would say that I didn't have any. Quite nice Beaujolais did exist but it was rare because the appellation had over-exploited its renown with the Beaujolais Nouveau Wine Race, planted too many vines on marginal land, and produced far too much thin, over-chaptalised, tasteless stuff. I did sell Beaujolais crus which, being richer and stronger, were actually quite good and more genuine. (Today they are amazingly good... so improved.) While mass-produced lean green Beaujolais didn't interest me, the small farmers in the traditional cru villages certainly did. Like Lucien Verger at his Domaine de Chêne high on the hill of Brouilly at Charentay.

The 'Route du Beaujolais' is one of the most delightful wine journeys in the world, as it winds its way through all ten cru appellations. Six communes make up Brouilly, a doughnut-shaped area around the base of Mont Brouilly. Those vineyards on the *mont* itself, the Côte de Brouilly, are blessed with volcanic, granite-based soils and consider themselves very superior to those lower down with their clay/limestone rubbish! Côtes de Brouillys are indeed considered the 'gold top' versions of Brouilly which is characterised by a special light grape-iness. I find a pepperiness too. On one trip, Lucien Verger was pruning vines by the roadside, wasting no time as he waited for my arrival. A big, dark, powerful man who looks frightening when cross (and I once made him cross). He is a *métayer* or sharecropper – not unusual in Beaujolais.

Lucien has 8 hectares of vines in a prime spot halfway up Mont Brouilly with a marvellous view facing full south. Some of his wine is Côte de Brouilly, some Brouilly, but as I tasted freezing-cold young examples from the vats I must confess to having been unable to differentiate. With his cellars being nearly 1,000 feet up, he has problems cold-starting his fermentations. So before proper harvesting, he has to get a little tub of grape juice fermenting away in the warmth of his kitchen; when that is bubbling merrily it is tipped into the first vat as a 'starter' and known as a *pied de cuve*. Each new vat is then 'started' by a bucketful of the one that went before. Like in most Beaujolais, he drops his grapes into the vats from the top, uncrushed – they are semi-macerated. Lucien's cellar is on a slope with two levels of access to facilitate this.

So, perversely, I didn't give the customers what they wanted – as they say you have to – and I probably put off some people. But not too many, because I showed them other wines instead of Beaujolais; maybe a Nouveau Rhône Grenache from a good cellar which had much more gutsy, juicy fruit per bottle. But, as I said before, I believed making money in the wine business was impossible anyway. So it was the enjoyment of the hunt that was my 'payment'. I know many other wine merchants who take this view. We are a mad lot.

I particularly loved hunting down tiny wine regions. *The Big Little Wines of France* was actually the title of a book by an elderly, inspiring American called Basil Woon from Colorado who came to visit me at the Windsor Arch one day. These little regions were so incredibly welcoming, maybe because many had never seen a wine merchant before.

Marcillac was one of the rarities I was looking for up in the Aveyron, which, in spite of its VDQS appellation, I was not sure still existed. But at Valady, a neighbouring village to Marcillac, I found a little wine co-operative. Its

Lucien Verger-Brouilly.

directeur, Monsieur Metge, made me warmly welcome. 'Marcillac wine to Britain? *Quelle idée!*' I found it like Beaujolais in style, though less so in taste – more like blackcurrant and raspberries with a touch of pepper. It's made from the local Fer Servadou or Mansois grape which is a distant relative of the Cabernets. All in all, it is a highly original yet inexpensive wine. We learned that 100 years ago they made 10 million litres but now only 2 to 3 million litres! It was never an export wine like Cahors but more of a local wine. However, phylloxera and the new railway which brought in cheap Midi wines combined to almost kill it in the last century. Since 1965 it had been making something of a comeback, thanks mainly to the fact that traditionally most Parisian bistros are run by people from this area. These *bougnats*, as they are called, like to serve their home wine. Monsieur Metge also gave me the good news that two further wine regions were still alive and hidden in valleys to the north. So I trailed off down narrow lanes past the abbey of Conques. There were steep vineyards everywhere. So where did all this wine go? I emerged on to the top of a vast bare moor, with the high hills of Cantal in the far distance. It was as though I was on the roof of France. Then after a couple of sharp turns I stopped to admire a lovely view: a wine merchant's little El Dorado. There in a crevasse-like wooded valley where two rivers joined (the Lot and the Truyère), the town of Entraygues nestled around its château, surrounded by steep, terraced vineyards such as are virtually never seen in France any more. The owner of the estate I was looking for, Monsieur Viguier, turned out to be startlingly young (19), having been catapulted from agriculture college to running the farm by his father's ill health. But he was pottering in one of the most ancient, cobwebby, dusty old cellars I had ever seen. He farmed 4 hectares, which was more than half the then Entraygues-et-du-Fel VDQS area (although in 1860 the area had covered over 1,000 hectares).

Unfortunately my customers were just not very interested in these unheard-of little wines. But Barbara was quietly resigned to this profitless obsession... for the moment. It wasn't entirely profitless; a few of these unknown wines did catch on and become big sellers at that time. Wines like Côtes du Forez, the Coteaux du Lyonnais, and the Comté Tolosan.

As I have said, I like nothing more than an unknown wine region. Most customers, however, are quite conservative in taste and like names they recognise. Like Côtes du Rhône. One year I was on my way to the Wine Fair of Orange held every January as the first great *concours des vins* (wine competition) of the year. I had dreamed of going for many

Heat-retaining stony vineyard, characteristic of the southern Rhône.

years and longed to escape Britain at the dead of winter for a first snatch of sun. (I still do!) And sunny it was that year, quite warm too. In the sheltered yard in front of the Provençal village house André and Colette, the owners of Château du Trignon, had let us borrow, I could sit on a step in the sun and watch our small, one-year-old son get deliriously happy and drenched in the village fountain. No sign of pneumonia... and only 28 January! I turned up at 8am prompt for the *concours*; I was the first of something like 350 judges, who were divided five to a table. With 70-plus tables, each with about 20 wines, there was a lot of tasting! Away on the count of 10am... give or take half an hour or so... this being southern France, it was *délibération du jury*: rinse, swill, sip, gurgle, 'hmm', splatt –

Monsieur Fayolle draws vine from the barrel with a pipette.
~ at Gervans in the Hermitage district, Rhône Valley.

Monsieur Fayolle drawing a sample.

not a pretty sight! Write something and give a score. I judged at quite a few of these shows, especially the biggest one in Paris on the first Saturday in March. It was an annual treat for Barbara – mimosa time. She could watch the cattle judging while I sipped and spat.

The Fayolles at Gervans near the hill of Hermitage were favourite visits. Hard crushing handshakes from Jules and cries of '*Yvette, Yvette, cherchez les caillettes. Tony est arrivé.*' *Caillettes* are the local delicacy of minced pork and spinach in a square sausage, perfect for rapid consumption. I visited often but mostly only for a short time.

I drove north for about a half-hour until the unmistakable hill of Hermitage, a name legendary for centuries, came into view. At the bottom of the slope, one allotment-size patch belonged to my man Fayolle. Well, it used to be 'my man', now its 'my men' Fayolles, Père Jules having retired and handed over to *Les Fils* – identical twins Jean-Claude and Jean-Paul. Between you and me, I am much relieved, as Jules was a bit of an old beggar to deal with. A peasant of the old school was Jules. Earthy. Likewise his cellar and his wines. His sons still produce 'wines made the old way', but without quite the extremes that Jules favoured.

But he was always honest and made concentrated wines with lots of grapes per bottle. And there never were wines less filtered. His bottles were so encrusted with sediment they scared some customers. But I loved that because he was always meticulous in his cellar, even if it was the oddest collection of old barrels you ever saw. The twins have been to agriculture college, though I still expect to see them up to their waists in the old wood fermenters treading the floating mat of grapeskins. But I know they exercise their heads also, and we already see brighter wine in the bottles. The sons each owned a house in the village, one at the bottom and one at the top amongst the vines. But their father hung on to the family home above the cellars. This proved inconvenient. But, in the autumn of 1980 came 'Le Grand Événement'. At 2am on 20 November Père Fayolle rose from his bed and, following the habit of a lifetime, descended to a very small room by the back door. As the door banged shut, there came a rumbling, a shaking and shuddering, and by the light of the full moon Jules, aghast, in beret and pyjamas, watched half of his house (the old part, uninhabited) slide gracefully down into the cellars below. He dropped what he was doing but it was far too late. Half the barrels in his cellar were gone and a stream of red ran down the road toward the village. Four days later Jules and Yvette left their old home. Jean-Paul and his family moved in. A new era. The cellar is rebuilt already but concrete is not quite the same as those blackened old stones.

Then there are the many wines of the Loire. Vouvray was always special to me. We buy from a lovely family with the brilliant name of Champalou – father, mother and winemaker daughter. Long ago my cousin Ruth, from my childhood farm in Rivington, had told me the story of distant cousin Harry Braithwaite, like my father, an RAF navigator. He was shot down over Vouvray in 1944. A young girl called Madeleine Maillet who worked for the Resistance rushed to the burning plane and hustled away Harry and his mate Fred just as the Germans were arriving. The acres of caves and tunnels under Vouvray are perfect for maturing wine. But also, it seems, for hiding British airmen. Despite numerous searches, Harry and his pal were kept safe until handed over to the advancing Americans. Harry and his family – Ruth too – went back many times after the war... for far more than just the wine. As I go back and back to many many places also for more than just the wines.

Blois has a more famous château and in a dungeon of this landmark I once participated in a strange ritual. Every year, around Easter time, the winegrowers of the then Cheverny VDQS district assembled to taste and vote upon each other's wine for purposes of awarding *les labels*. These were the little numbered stamps you saw reproduced on all VDQS labels. Gone now. They denoted that the stuff was authentic and that it has been tasted by this assembly and found (a) drinkable, (b) typical. Every VDQS area did this; AOC areas did not – it wouldn't be a bad thing if they did. Anyway, there was a gathering of about 50 farmers: good, ruddy-faced, bereted *paysans* grasping in their dinner-plate hands wee little tumblers of the fresh white Cheverny... *de l'Année*. It was none of your frightfully hushed, frightfully pinstripe, frightfully *sérieux* London wine trade tastings. No, this was obviously 'The Big Day in Cheverny'. And not a lot happens in Cheverny, I would say, since Robespierre shut down the big house. They were here today for the party. The noise level was dangerous after five minutes and punctuated by great hoots of laughter and jibes. 'Errgh... this must be Jacko's wine... EH JACKO, cat got in the cellar again?' It must be admitted that Cheverny can be a tart wine. The Romorantin grape from which the wine is made is a little-known local varietal that needs a good deal of sun, otherwise... ouch!

Mobile Still
- Franceuil

The tasting got rowdier while I got more confused. The sample bottles were identified solely by number, so it was a blindfold do. But as the bottles were passed around everywhere, less and less attention seemed to be paid to the numbers. Nobody wrote much, I doubt if some could still write. I was only there as a casual observer with a friend, Pierre Chainier, and so left early, but I still have this one strong mental image. There in the middle of this rustic throng was a painted lady complete with scarlet lips, scarlet hair, rouge, black dress, Bloomsbury Group big black hat and feather boa. Who on earth? 'She used to play piano for Josephine Baker!' After a lifetime of touring the US jazz clubs, she had come back here to retire and grow wine! I felt sure that after we left, Mademoiselle Baker's friend would be dragged to the piano and the Comité de Dégustation would jolly on all night. Everything would be drunk; nothing would be noted down; and everyone would get their *labels*. But that was only my fanciful theory. I am sure the reality was far more *sérieux*...

Later that trip (in 1985) as I was leaving the Cave Coopérative de Francueil at Bléré, I noticed one of those old mobile distilleries steaming away at the back of the cellar. These *distilleries ambulantes* are fascinating things. They were generally run by highly skilled, red-nosed gentlemen who travelled the land with their rusty old steam engines, setting up shop wherever there was anything that could be distilled into something more usefully potent. The right of private individuals to employ these distillers was long ago officially rescinded, and only a few persons of great age retained the privilege of being a *bouilleur de cru*. It was said that some families had been known to keep great-granny going year after year with injections, pills, drip-feeds and so on, just so they could still claim her right to make home-made brandy! However, that day they were working at the co-operative distilling the leftovers: the foul-smelling grapeskin and pulp residue of the winepresses. I often had a job shovelling that stuff; its alternative use is fertiliser and it smells like it! But miracle upon miracle, if it was tipped into one of these boilers, first came this gorgeous smell of plum jam, then after some minutes a bright stream of clear spring water. (Well it *looked* like spring water!) Do stop if ever you see one of these things by the road, they are always happy to let you sip some, still warm from the tap. Perhaps your contortions as the grenade goes off in your mouth amuse them. 'Not bad,' you wheeze, blinded by tears! But I don't think they exist any more.

In recent years, thanks to my family's involvement, I have become increasingly aware of just how sparkling wines are made, but here's something I learned earlier.

During one visit in 1984, I wanted to take my travelling companions to see one of the places that made champagne the great drink that it is (that is, to one of the great houses – 'les grandes marques'). We were invited to Perrier-Jouët whose *palais* (terms like 'offices' or 'works' hardly seem appropriate) is fitted snugly between the Palais Moët & Chandon and the Palais de Venoge on the Avenue de Champagne in Épernay. Frédérique, the appropriately sparkling daughter of the *maître de cave*, gave us the tour. First we saw the miles and miles (ever-expanding) of underground roadways on several levels. Every now and then as they dig, they burst through the Moët (or someone else's) *galerie*. They say that you can cross the town this way in secret, if you know the way.

Then we went for the most fascinating of tastings with 'Fred's' father. It was time for him to *faire sa cuvée* and therefore, a good time to call. We stood very quiet alongside the Perrier-Jouët directors as the big man set out a long row of numbered bottles of the still white wine samples of 1984's crop on the big table in the white tasting room. He then very kindly took us on what was effectively a verbal guided tour of Champagne villages, explaining at length why each tasted the way it did. Cramant was lovely ripe Chardonnay from a prime site village; Chouilly was much less ripe and from a back valley; Ay near Bouzy was a lovely Pinot Noir, the wine slightly tinted by the black skins; Vertheuil, from the Val-de-Marne was a Pinot Meunier wine, dull and bland; Mailly in the north proved stony and tough; Vincelles a dull Meunier; and Bouzy big and magnificent. He thoughtfully tipped different amounts of these wines into a tall calibrated cylinder and we tasted the result. It was better than any single element so far; even the dull Meunier was playing a useful role somewhere in the *assemblage*. Then, he added his 'reserve' wine which was a blend of older vintages kept back down in deep stone vats to give maturity, mellowness and complexity to the new. It certainly did! The result, although a plain, still and slightly cloudy wine, could be identified as a proto-champagne. The imminent second fermentation in the bottle would then add bubbles and extra flavour elements (things like complex amino acids) over two or three years, which make a great champagne.

Lesson in Alsace wine from Monsieur Hauss at Kientzheim-Kaysersberg cooperative. Mural shows the two villages (who've hated each other for centuries).

Provence was a favourite region. Of course it is. Though the wine was hard to sell because people back then did not like to be seen drinking rosé. Today fashion has changed and now it's hard to keep up with demand. I went early because I had a friend there – thanks to the course I took on wine at Bordeaux University in the 1960s! It was nothing very high-powered and the lessons on theory were much less fun than the tastings. So I drifted, as one does, to the back row and met a gangling dissolute youth from Provence by the name of Ott. Rémy Ott and I became good friends but I had no idea just what his home was. It turned out that the Ott family own the largest vine holdings in Provence – three major estates and a head office – each run by one of the four sons of the founder, Marcel Ott. They are a remarkable family and years ahead of other Provençal growers. They had impressive machinery (which they built and maintained themselves as they were good engineers) to tackle this hostile and rugged terrain. On one barren hilltop Rémy showed me their *concasseur*, an iron beast that ate up the dynamited rock fine enough to make soil fit to plant vines. The Otts are wealthy, of course, and their wine (mostly rosé) is easily the most expensive in Provence and, at the same time, probably the best known. You see the distinctive

Ott bottles poking out of ice buckets in all the best places. Clos Mireille is their 'white' estate run by brother Henri. He grows the Ugni Blanc and Sémillon grapes that both do so well in the similarly hot vineyards of Australia. We climbed aboard Henri's old Citroën and he bounced me around the extensive estate. He was planting a new vineyard, using a theodolite – the Otts always do everything perfectly. Space for the vineyards had been cut out of the natural woodland; pine, cork-oak, broom and aromatic herbs. The vines are useful firebreaks against that great enemy of this paradise. The cellar has a well-watered grass roof to keep it cool... and fire-resistant. We went into the beautiful barrel hall with its shiny brass and polished wood and tried the 1983 and the 1982. I detected hints of the sea, iodine, turpentine and eucalyptus trees; it is basically a very classy number – a steely, tough and very big white. As the unusual label suggests, it is also very expensive, but just try it – then visit the estate. After a tasting, you could wander, as I did in the not-too-hot May sunshine, down the track to the beach. Butterflies, buzzing insects and the distant hum of a tractor will be your only companions. Soon you see white sands, a wooded Mediterranean bay with not a building in sight. If this isn't paradise on earth then I don't know where is.

Alsace must be the complete opposite of Provence, very different to the rest of France. My supplier was the donnish Monsieur Hauss, *directeur* of the Cave Co-opérative de Kientzheim-Kaysersberg – twin villages seemingly forever at war with each other: gargoyles on each village's facing ramparts have been sticking their tongues out at each other for centuries.

I always like to enter Alsace from the west over the Vosges mountains via the Bonhomme pass. It is more dramatic and scenic than going in round either end of the mountains. It also drops you right down upon Kaysersberg which is my favourite Alsace village. Alsace is a narrow strip of land squeezed between the Vosges and the Rhine. The vineyards are an extremely narrow strip between the mountain pines and the valley cabbage fields (for this is the home of *choucroute*).

One year, it was snowing particularly heavily as I approached across dreary Lorraine, so there was the added thrill – with badly worn tyre treads – of 'Would I make it?' I did, albeit very slowly. Winding down round and round through all those dark pines, I saw happy skiers pass us; it must have been the first decent snowfall for them that year. I continued down through the upland villages and pastures past the little distillery, owned by Monsieur Miclo, from whom I bought occasionally. (He has another on Tahiti and a range of white alcohols that runs from bilberry, cherry and Williams pear to mango, pineapple and passion fruit!)

Soon the Kaysersberg castle loomed up in the dusk on the left and I drove right into a Christmas-card scene. The narrow cobbled streets, the overhanging, timber-framed houses with steep snow-covered roofs, the bright shop windows and the frozen fountain... magical. Alsace is the only wine region I actually prefer to visit in the winter.

Great times. For me. While I was off 'pootling' it was all the harder for Barbara back home keeping the Company going on her own. Not straightforward. Our first forklift, a second-hand job, caught fire the first day so Barbara had her first court case. She won. We had about 30 people now. The office was full and Portakabins started sprouting up in the warehouse, which was run by the son of Mother's cousin. All my small family helped. Mother herself would turn up in school holidays with another teacher friend coerced into helping out. Our first dog, Jasper, a pointer, slept all day, guarding my desk. One time Geoffrey Roberts, the great Californian wine specialist, bypassed reception with characteristic Old Etonian insouciance, marched straight into my apparently empty office... then had to be rescued from my incensed hound.

MARRIAGE

One night, down by the water near Windsor bridge after we'd been to our favourite Italian restaurant (where we always used to go when we had got in some money), I proposed to Barbara.

She didn't reply. So of course I just assumed that was it. Then, weeks later, she rang me early one morning and said: 'The answer's "Yes",' and of course, barely awake, I went and said, 'Yes what?' I will never be allowed to forget that.

We didn't immediately live together or, as they used to say back then, cohabit. The 1960s may have swung for many but the Scottish Presbyterian world of Barbara's parents hadn't changed. She lived in London; I in my flat in Windsor. Her parents were fine, though, about us living in sin once we bought a house together. Couldn't possibly waste money paying for three properties. Morality maybe comes second to financial probity in Scotland. Our wedding was in 1975 in the village of Burrelton, just north of Perth. It was a biggish do, as a lot of winegrowers came. Barbara's many cousins also attended. Hugh and Judy Johnson came. Barbara nearly bottled it on the morning of the wedding, and had to be given a large brandy by her dad and be pushed into the car. I wasn't so certain either. But with all those Scottish cousins, there was no way out for me. There was a pause though. She got to the church and Dave Lowther, my best man, rushed out waving wildly. They couldn't get the organ to work. The Bride had to hang around outside while they found and dusted off the old harmonium. Lots of giggling during the hymns with a little old lady peddling away frantically alongside us, trying to keep the dusty bellows going. We also had a bagpipe player. Compulsory up there. The reception was in Perth with the bloody Scots trying all day to chuck the Englishman into the Tay.

We spent our wedding night in a sleeper on the train to London. Our carriage was filled with winegrowers so we didn't really get to bed. They all loved Scotland, they all loved whisky, and they liked to party. The next day we got a train to Paris – evading the winegrowers. One blowout meal and a few drinks took all of our money for the entire honeymoon. Paris! We managed to get on to Bordeaux and honeymooned on nothing at La Clarière, the Cassins' vineyard, where we had use of a little house. It was our shipping office really, but with rooms in the attic.

People think we make a good team because we are opposites – she, the sensible organiser; me, the mad, optimistic dreamer – and they are not wrong. But we actually have a lot in common too. I can be quite practical and sensible. I might have odd ideas but I can often make them work. I am not really an optimist, more a pessimist. Because I spend a lot of time watching out for approaching dangers. I'm careful, I don't even get drunk... because it's risky. I never bet. And I certainly never 'bet the farm' in business. I'll take risks only as long as I think that we will survive when it all goes horribly wrong.

While I might have been daft 'Nod' Laithwaite, Barbara was more than a bit wacky herself. She claims she just believed in taking shortcuts, but she did blow up those Durham University laboratories. Caused a lot of damage. Twice. So she cannot really be classed as a truly sensible person. Only up to a point. That was and still is crucial to our working relationship. Any time I had one of my odd ideas and wanted to take a wild jump into the unknown, she might throw me a ton of questions but she would usually jump with me if I insisted. She likes order, she believes in hard work, but every now and then Barbara does a 'Sod it! Why not? Just do it.'

So it was a surreal moment, 50 years after leaving university, when we two were sat on the stage in Durham Cathedral before an audience of hundreds of earnest, newly minted graduates, and got awarded honorary doctorates. 'Fookin' Laithwaite, man! Of all people... fookin Laithwaite!' as our Geordie mate Maccers memorably put it, shaking his head in disbelief.

Barbara and I have always had Plan B, which was that if all goes tits up we were going to move up to the Lakes where my parents now lived, find a cottage, become gardeners, cleaners... or something like that. Not a bad life at all. Both our sets of parents backed us, so they would have made sure we didn't starve. Crucial. And kind of shows that we didn't rate our talents that highly. We thought it all was going quite nicely, well... the aim was a 'good life' rather than pots of money. We knew plenty of people in the Lake District and other nice parts of the world, who seemed very happy. Mostly of course, we were influenced by the happy folk in France, small wine producers who worked extremely hard and didn't make a lot of money but would never dream of doing anything else.

But we've never needed Plan B. Well, not yet. I suppose a lot of what drove both of us in the business is that we didn't want to be laughed at any more, we didn't want our friends saying 'Poor Laithwaites'. When Barbara and I came together, Barbara had no great interest in wine. She always preferred a G&T and that lasted until ten years ago when she planted her own vineyard. Now she's as obsessed as any winegrower I know.

As for me, I had no interest in business management. I liked to set things up, I liked to shape the Company. But I just cannot cope with the day-to-day running of things.

Our first home was a small house in Fulmer, Bucks – near Pinewood Studios – with a tiny garden. We got chickens and planted vegetables. We subscribed to *Farmers Weekly*. Barbara also acquired two retired racehorses which we kept in our garage. Barbara had always wanted a horse, and retired racehorses are very cheap, just tricky to ride as I painfully learned. We were so in debt after buying the house that we agreed our first married year we would be meat-free at home because we couldn't afford it. We were so busy we didn't miss it really. The business grew steadily but didn't take any profit as we always ploughed back all surplus into advertising for more customers. We thought the best thing to invest in was customers. Happy, loyal customers. Better than stocks and shares which we didn't understand and which therefore seemed risky. We had acquired a business adviser who helped us a lot in this. Bill Symonds was a City banker working for my dad's company's bank and living proof they are not all monsters. At my dad's request, he came and chatted to us a bit. His first advice was never to go anywhere near his chums in the City of London. We'd be eaten alive, he said. He didn't say it was because we were naive innocents. But that was what we understood. Anyway, we've followed his advice ever since.

A month before our wedding we had taken what seems today like a risky adventure. It was. We chartered the cruise ship *Ithaca* in Athens and took 500 Wine Club members on a week's cruise round the Greek islands and the Dalmatian coast visiting wineries and restaurants. A young chap called David Walker organised this superbly well. He coped when a sudden gale blew up and the ship had to up-anchor and quickly move away from the lee shore at Split. He had tried to get everyone back on board, women first of course, and there were glorious sights as our somewhat mature, well-dressed, Wine Club lady members, who had just finished a big wine tasting, flung themselves heedlessly from the heaving, plunging tenders into the arms of Greek sailors. Made you proud to be British, it did!

But the other half of us got left on shore for the night. Say what you like about the horrors of Communist regimes, surely only they could at an hour's notice find a completely empty but fully staffed hotel able to accommodate and feed 250 people. I shared a room with a snoring Monsieur Cassin.

The Marques *in Bordeaux in front of the Pont de Pierre.*

WILD ADVENTURES

Then, a month after our wedding in an even more bonkers adventure, I sailed away again, this time in an ancient brigantine called the *Marques*.

Barbara wondered if she'd ever see me again as she waved goodbye from the quay of Charlestown harbour in Cornwall, with a wild and wacky Cornish crew en route to Bordeaux. The plan was to load her up with cases of wine and sail it all back to Britain, thus recreating the great Bordeaux trade which for hundreds of years was, they say, the greatest trade the world had ever seen, when great fleets – hundreds of little ships called 'cogs' about the size of our *Marques* – would bring back the new Bordeaux vintage to slake the throats of the ever thirsty

British – the 'GBs' or *gueules de bois* (wooden throats), as they still call us in Bordeaux. Two thousand cases were skilfully packed into her hold by Bordeaux dockers so well that, when we hit a storm mid-Channel, nothing moved and possibly their weight as ballast saved our lives. Because some years later the poor old *Marques* hit another storm near Bermuda, but this time without any cargo. She capsized and sank with all hands. Hugh Johnson and I will never forget our night being hurled around the fo'c'sle swigging bottles of old Marcel Ragnaud's cognac as we awaited our watery end. Pursued by towering waves, we made it into the safety of Torbay, as many a ship had over the centuries, miles off-course, sails shredded, deck cargo of barrels all vanished overboard... but not a single bottle broken.

Another wild adventure at this time was going behind the Iron Curtain to Bulgaria with a college friend, Pat Carter, now Lord Carter. It wasn't easy to get there; we flew in what looked suspiciously like a bomber. It had gun turrets. Tea was served from an old blackened kettle on a gas ring. Pat went his way looking for a supply of cheap tractors and I went to 5 Lavele Street, Sofia. That was the only place to buy wine in Bulgaria. Literally the only place. Bulgarian wine was a state monopoly. I sat in the waiting room for several days. A charming young man called Margot Todorov was pleasant, brought tea and spoke English. But finally I got a '*Niet*' and returned home empty-handed. However, some time later there came a call from a man who said he represented one of the famous cola firms. They had, it seems, just put a load of their stuff into Bulgaria and been paid off, as was quite common back then in such countries, with a barter deal. They had a few thousand bottles of Cabernet Sauvignon and wondered if I'd like it. I tried a few bottles at the Bulgarian Embassy and it was truly wonderful. Rich, dark, round, fruity, soft... it ticked all the boxes. And it was amazingly cheap – way below what such a wine would cost to make in France. So of course I took it all, and then more, and then truckloads. For a year or so it was basically all we sold, because the customers enthusiastically agreed with me. It was soon coming in by shiploads. The Bulgarians wanted me to become their sole agent but I wanted to keep my independence. So who should step in but my friend Pat who abandoned tractors, bought an old London wine company, and took the job on. All the big retailers then started buying Bulgarian and the inevitable happened. Quality dropped. The well of good Cabernet ran dry. So we stopped buying it. Shame. Then everybody stopped buying it. Then the Berlin Wall came down, good in so many ways but not for wine. We keep trying to find what we once had in Bulgaria but I doubt we will.

Our Bulgarian winemaker friends in Sukhindol open an ancient pre-revolutionary bottle from their secret cache kept hidden in the winery (right) from the authorities.

It was the Wine Club that powered these big adventures but I still had to look after little old Bordeaux Direct. I still had to find local customers in simpler ways. I was given a very large old barrel by Jean Demolombe, my main Midi supplier. Empty. He just put it on the back of a lorry load of wine because I'd so admired the old things, which were gradually being replaced with concrete or stainless steel vats. I had the bright idea of cutting a door in it, installing seats and putting it on wheels. I attached nice Bordeaux Direct signs and towed my barrel caravan to local fairs, notably Windsor Horse Show. It weighed 2 tons. People liked it. Mobile wine tasting! Trouble was, it was incredibly heavy and after rain the thing sank into the ground and became totally non-mobile. Idea abandoned.

We lived in Fulmer until 1980 and enjoyed the delights of Slough and our munitions shed just downwind of the Mars factory. Working in an atmosphere of chocolate must have affected our choice of wines I suppose, but things went well nonetheless.

BULGARIAN CABERNET →

'BALKAN VINE'

❋

THIS WAS THE VERY FIRST BOTTLED WINE TO COME OUT OF BULGARIA, MAYBE OF ALL THE BALKAN COUNTRIES, AND WAS AN ASTONISHING SUCCESS.

It wasn't just our top seller; it was responsible for over half our sales in the late 1970s. It certainly helped that its price bore no relation to its cost of production. Bulgaria's Communist regime never bothered with details like profitability, they just desperately wanted foreign currency. But I believe the wine's success was also due to large, sunny vineyards of good Cabernet Sauvignon, and as we could see, Merlot (it was really a classic Bordeaux-style blend, though they wouldn't admit that). And also large wineries put in by French entrepreneurs in the 1930s. Being taken over by the state in 1945 presumably ruined the Frenchmen but their investment came good for us. It was like we had discovered good Californian vineyards in Europe. Even the most traditional of customers didn't baulk at wine from a country they had barely heard of, once they tried it and saw the price. Sadly for the talented winemakers we knew there, the regime got greedy and, to sell more and more, let the wine quality go down and down until we had to drop it.

❋

There was of course the period in those difficult 1970s of 'the three-day week', at the height of the Unions v. Government wars. All over the country offices and factories had their power turned off by British Electric or whatever it was called, for all but three days a week. But my luck held, for our place, while not quite on Slough Trading Estate, was nonetheless coupled up with the estate's own private power station. So our phones, lights and heating were able to go on working full time. As did we. Very full time. While others couldn't. Barbara and I didn't have any holidays or days off, barring Christmas Day, but then we didn't really want any. There was just one day: Uxbridge Day! Don't know why but one day we just stopped... took a day off and we went... to Uxbridge. Of all places! Well it was the nearest town but we'd never visited. We walked around, shopped, had lunch, shopped some more, got all romantic with flowers and went home. It was magic. We have no idea why it was just so good, but still, our private term for a great day is 'Uxbridge Day'.

It seemed like I travelled all the time. I tried to get everywhere there was wine, I tried to take all my customers to where there was wine, and I tried to get all my wine suppliers to come and meet my customers. Having done all parts of France I covered Europe. But I needed help. I needed guides. I had Hugh Johnson, of course: I could tap into his encyclopaedic knowledge. We enjoyed great trips together. He'd take me to grand cathedrals of wine like the Gymnasium in Trier for exquisite Mosels served in elegant Römer glassware. Then I'd take him up some ravine in the Minervois to stain his teeth with young purple Carignan out of a paper cup. We shared great times.

The best wasn't a buying trip but a customer trip. Perhaps the best way to learn about wine and wine people is by taking customers around the vineyards, being a tour guide. I first did this when I worked in Bordeaux in 1969, occasionally hiring myself out as an English-speaking guide to the CIVB, who look after promoting Bordeaux wine. My first job was taking round a party of British journalists... a baptism by fire, that was! Their prodigious wine consumption had the result of me getting my first – and so far, only – newspaper headline: 'Ex-Eton Tea-Boy in the Vineyards'. No, I didn't go to Eton, but I had worked on building sites in Eton.

CALIFORNIA DREAMIN'

We advertised a wine trip to California in spring 1976, hoping to get a bus-load of people as normal, but I guess the price, the lack of familiarity with the wines, and the long distance were a bit much, so we ended up only 16 of us.

We timed it right. (Luck.) In May, Steven Spurrier held the legendary France v. California wine tasting in Paris, 'The Judgement of Paris' – now a 'major motion picture', *Bottle Shock*, with Alan Rickman playing Steven – where, for the first time France's total dominance in fine wine received a knock from the American upstarts. The top French experts, tasting blind, rated the best Californian wines higher than the finest of France. The 'Upstart Crow' wines, previously dismissed as simple stuff, were revealed to have all the finesse of a Mouton or Meursault.

I read Steven's autobiography and couldn't put it down because he and I were almost exact contemporaries, but we came across each other only rarely. He tells a tale of starting out wealthy and ending up, well, less wealthy. But as I've said before, wine people – real wine people, obsessed with the whole world of wine – don't do it for the money, they do it for the sheer pleasure. In that respect Steven did very, very well. While I was working from a wet railway arch, an old Slough munitions shed, and trading estates in Reading, he was enjoying his house in Provence or living on a barge on the Seine by Notre-Dame. On lifestyle Steven wins hands down... and you only get one life to style. And that one tasting in Paris means he will never be forgotten. I could be jealous about that.

So Californian wine in the 1970s was already news. But you didn't yet see Californian bottles anywhere on UK shop shelves. People in the wine trade were talking about it a lot because it was in California that so much of the modernisation of wine happened. You could say the New Wine Age we live in began in the 1960s in California. The research, the discovering of new ways to do things, the improvements – so much of that was done at the University of California in Davis. There was good research going on in all European wine countries, and in Australia, but it was quiet stuff. California was not quiet. Is it ever? It shouted loud and it challenged. 'The Judgement of Paris' in Steven's little wine shop was considered a scandal in France and the result was hushed up, and ignored. Not in California it wasn't.

Oh no! By the time we flew PanAm to San Francisco in October 1976 the wine people there talked of little else. When we landed, instead of a bus, we hired two of those big old American station-wagons. Eight people in each and all the luggage roped on to the roof racks. We were shown round the brand new Wine Museum by its boss and afterwards got red carpet treatment at the California Wine Institute. It is amazing the carpet that gets rolled out, just through having Hugh with you.

Then the convoy set off for the vineyards. We were a mixed bunch. There was a young lawyer, a young British couple from Holland, a retired Indian Army officer and his memsahib... very, very different people but all fascinating and all getting on amazingly well. And there was me, Hugh and Judy Johnson, and the resourceful Bill Brenchley who organised the whole thing.

We went up to the Napa Valley to the Mondavi winery where Bob Mondavi met us and did his version of the Paris thing by opening a bottle of Château Latour for us to compare with his Cabernet. Some said it was the Californian climate, some reckoned it was his strength of personality, but anyway, everyone did prefer the Mondavi wine.

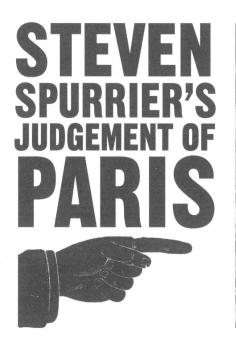

STEVEN SPURRIER'S JUDGEMENT OF PARIS

At Schramsberg, the now absolutely iconic sparkling wine of California – then just beginning – we enjoyed a tasting and picnic under the trees with Jack Davis and his wife. Then we went to a winery looking like an all-white Spanish monastery, that had just opened perched on top of a hill, which you went up to in cable cars: Sterling Vineyard. How could someone dare do that? This was something you were never going to see in Europe, where wineries were either nicely old or new and ugly.

That evening we went round to Heitz Cellar after hours and met Joe Heitz, a slightly tetchy gravel-voiced old fella; his Martha's Vineyard label had triumphed in Paris. He was generous, but clearly didn't suffer fools. This fool kept very quiet.

Then the Beringer Estate laid on a picnic for us in the warm night air. We then went down the Russian Valley to SIMI and its woman winemaker – which was a first for me! We had lunch at Souverain, where we still buy, though it's now known as the Francis Ford Coppola winery.

We drove south of San Francisco to the Paul Masson winery and Mirassou and to the Monterey Vineyard and Dick Peterson who was a great friend of Hugh's and showed the range of wines that impressed me most on the whole tour, and which I arranged to buy. We climbed up in the hills to a half-built Chalone – another winner in Paris, with, amazingly, one of the first wines they ever made – where the semi-naked, whippet-thin, ultra-fit owner Dick Graff impressed us all, especially the ladies.

The trip ended with lunch on his lawn with the great Ernest Gallo. Me, sitting, babbling next to the biggest wine producer in the whole world. 'Did you do it by taking over other wine companies and clever deals and stuff like that?' And this big, laconic American chewed on his steak and slowly replied, 'No son, we just started a long time ago and every year, we just grew a bit.' I am sure it never was that simple but that was a revelation for me, and an inspiration. It's what our business has done ever since: we started (also long ago now), and we just try to grow a bit every year.

We went to see the grapes arriving. I've seen plenty in wineries over the years but I have never seen one like this. Great rows of trucks lined in military formations. At the grape arrival dock they had monster machines that just grabbed each grape lorry – the whole lorry! Turned it upside down, shook it a bit so all the grapes came out into the receiving bins. I remember thinking those truck drivers had best be getting out of their lorries a bit sharpish.

Then we saw where the wines were made. These were the days before Gallo started making their varietal wines. Back then they basically made a red wine called Hearty Burgundy which was a massive, massive seller. And a *shablee* – Chablis (the US has never worried overmuch about borrowing French appellation names). Hugh believed Hearty Burgundy was the best 'everyday' wine in the world back then... far better than the *vins ordinaires* of France. I agreed. They made basic wines superbly well. And kept the costs down by sheer engineering. They said they had a factory where the grapes went in at one door while, through another, sand went into furnaces and got turned into glass bottles. Somewhere in the middle the two came together and out at the far end came hot-bottled wine. It just boggled your imagination. It was all very California Dreamin'.

Having Hugh as a guide was unbelievable luck but I had other guides. I owe so much to my guides like Dubernet and Andrée Ferrandiz in the Midi. In Germany I had Bob Mendelssohn and David Hallgarten to show me round. In Italy I had Renato Trestini and Burton Anderson, in Spain Tony Barrero. In Madeira David Pamment. In Australia I had David Thomas and in New Zealand, Terry Dunleavy... in Chile Hector Rossi. The only place I didn't go was Argentina, what with the war back then... and its wine at that time being, basically, terrible. How things change. I didn't buy much through UK merchants. Only did that when I had no option. It was just that I always found it far better to talk directly to my producers.

In 1978 we were celebrating the fifth anniversary of *The Sunday Times* Wine Club with a dinner and wine cabaret at the old Quaglino's. I remember Andrew Lloyd Webber was in the audience. Harry Evans gave a very funny speech, concluded dramatically when he said he would have to leave immediately, go back to *The Sunday Times* and completely, maybe permanently, shut down the newspaper. As he walked out there was silence, followed by a standing ovation. We all knew trouble had been brewing between Rupert Murdoch and the print unions. We now saw it up close. For many months until the surprise reopening in 'Fortress Wapping' the only sight of *The Sunday Times* was our adverts in other papers. I was always impressed that *The Observer* let us run *Sunday Times* wine ads. Decent of them.

149

BUBBLING OVER

THE ROARING EIGHTIES

The Roaring Eighties seriously kicked off in 1980 – what a year that was! A new government had come in, and a very different decade lay ahead. A wine company called Majestic was founded.

Meanwhile, Barbara and I produced our first child: a future winemaker, of course. We also bought a vineyard in France, which significantly altered the whole direction of our business, and hosted our first London Vintage Festival, which continues to this day to bring together winemakers and those who love what they make at one great happy, noisy annual get-together... probably the best wine party on the planet. We also moved both our home and our Company HQ over to near Reading where we've remained ever since. We opened our first shop and began our adventures Down Under, which again was something else that altered the course our Company took thereafter. It all just happened. Nothing was planned. We must have been out of our minds. I guess we probably were, most of the wine... I mean most of the *time*.

Even with the success of *The Sunday Times* Wine Club, we hadn't seemed able to lift ourselves out of a hand-to-mouth existence. But with the change of government came reduction in business tax and a change in our fortunes began to seem possible. I have been called one of Thatcher's Children, which I wasn't. I was one of Wilson's rather fewer children. But now, it seemed in 1980, if we made profits we would not have to pay so much tax. But, as it turned out, throughout most of the Thatcher years we didn't make any profits. So no change there, then. There were two reasons for that: my continued desire that we should always put having fun before profit, and the need to meet the challenge of what supermarkets were now doing to the wine business. Supermarkets as we know them today only really got started in the 1960s and it was a while before they got round to getting licences to sell wine. Imagine how scary it felt with these giants moving into our territory. To us it seemed that if we wanted to survive them we'd have to grow. Maybe not to their size but at least we had to try to be in the same league. So we concentrated on growing, not profits. We did, eventually, get to be bigger in wine than Waitrose, but never got close to the really big supermarket groups. If, approaching the end of any year, we looked like making a profit, we would spend money on another customer-recruiting campaign and that would remove any likelihood of profit. It meant we wouldn't bank any money, but we thought of it as banking customers instead. That seemed a better idea. They don't tax you on customers. It meant of course that we didn't get rich but we were having a good time doing what we loved and – most of the time – feeling a bit safer. Well, at least I was. Barbara had a slightly different view. Going on buying trips and leading customer tours were, for me, probably as good as any holidays. Everyone assumed my trips were holidays anyway. Always, whenever I returned from a trip, my lot would – completely innocently I'm sure – ask if I'd had a good holiday. And I've lost count of the number of times customers have offered to come on my trips to carry my bags.

So wine merchants are envied. Why? They don't, traditionally, make much money. This is, I believe, because as with me, money is not their great goal. Their/our great goal is the approval of fellow wine merchants and wine writers. What interests us – passionately – is to win the award for the best wine list, or to discover a great wine no one else knows about. That's what rings our bell. Not profits.

So my typical wine merchant's desire to show off by discovering and offering wines no one else had offered before, helped keep profits down – well, non-existent – for 20 years. And perhaps would have for 50 years if things had worked out differently.

Today we research everything. We have 2,000 customers on what we call our 'hub' panel and all new wines and ideas are run before them. They tell us what to do... mostly. In my early days it never occurred to me to do anything like that. If I heard about or tasted something I liked I went after it. Simple. But quite often costly. Anyway, the profits had to wait.

We finally outgrew our Slough warehouse and had to move west all the way to Caversham, Reading, to find a larger place that was suitable. Small industrial units were like gold dust in those days – another reason, maybe, why start-ups were rare. We found a unit on a tiny industrial estate that had previously been Zanussi's UK warehouse. So it went from washing machines to wine. We were happy there and started to grow faster. Over 19 years in Paddock Road we gradually expanded our footprint, taking over the unit on our left, then the one on our right, then the one over the yard. This meant the yard itself became an important part of our operations. As well as trucks, forklifts and sandwich vans it became a meeting area. Very healthy the outdoors, apparently. Jo Denis, my favourite artist, whose husband Ian did most of our commercial design work in those days, painted us a lovely Lowryesque triptych which, bending the buildings to fit, faithfully

Jo Denis's view of Paddock Road, Caversham. Quite a few are still with us.

captured all the faces, and the lovely atmosphere. It's way better than any photos. I love it for its memories. Names I can't always remember but I know all those faces.

We struggled to fit everyone in, no matter how we expanded. We built offices on mezzanines, put in Portakabins, and converted toilets into offices to cram everyone in. I had a prime corner office at first, but by the end found myself in a room at the back of the most remote warehouse. It was quiet and lacked any windows but that meant I could cover the walls with lists of ideas, and charts and drawings for future mailings. People tended to stay away from The Madman's Cave.

Henry, Tom and a bored Will. Henry's a winemaker, Tom a wine merchant. Will became a brewer.

THE FAMILY

The year 1980 was extremely eventful as Barbara and I moved into parenthood with the arrival of our first son, Henry Laithwaite.

Will and Tom followed in quick succession – Barbara being efficient as always. Amazing really, as I was travelling all over the world fairly continuously and also complicating my Managing Director/wife's life with Wine Treks, Wine Plans and any other ideas that caught my fancy. I admit I did rather take my wife for granted. However, I certainly realised just how much I needed Barbara in 1983 when, two months after Tom was born, she suffered a brain haemorrhage. She was only 37. It was our first confrontation with serious ill health. We had two horses at that time and Barbara looked after them as well as everything else. Early one morning she was bending over to scrape their hooves when she felt this incredible pain in her head. When she came back to the house, screaming, I could tell it was really bad because normally she's a real stoic.

At A&E at the Royal Berkshire Hospital in Reading they finally diagnosed it as a haemorrhage and had her taken to the John Radcliffe in Oxford. Three small boys. We feared the worst. But... that luck again; Barbara was one of only 2 per cent of people with that condition to just simply recover. After a while. What a day when the X-rays showed it was getting better! She was in hospital for a couple of weeks and then was supposed to be kept at home. No way was that happening – she went straight back to work.

They were good boys, ours. Not a lot of trouble; being so close in age they entertained themselves. We just needed to chuck 'em a ball. We were working all the time. To get to know them better I'd take them one at a time on my Wine Treks. Wineries didn't impress them a lot but the food did. Those trips – all part of a cunning plan! – must have worked as none of them has ever seriously considered a career outside wine, except for Will... and he chose beer.

LA CLARIÈRE VINEYARD

Also in 1980 we moved into wine production by buying a vineyard in Bordeaux.

Monsieur Cassin, my teacher and mentor, wasn't finished with me yet. Early one morning in summer 1979, he phoned from Bordeaux, very angry, to tell me that I was going buy his family vineyard: La Clarière. His nephew Jacques, in Saint-Émilion, had just told him he'd rather Monsieur did not leave La Clarière to him in his will 'because it's in Castillon not Saint-Émilion'! Jacques was not stupid. He was then at a *grande école* in Paris – and he went on to run EDF, the French electricity supplier. Anyway he was already going to inherit his share of the family's nice estate close by but – significantly – just over the border in Saint-Émilion. This estate today, under its new name of Château Valandraud, is most certainly making handsome money, selling wine at well over £200 a bottle. That daft border makes a big difference. Jacques knew La Clarière was a loss-making affair. Côtes de Castillon prices were at the bottom of the range. Even worse, Monsieur sent his grapes to the Castillon co-op which was notorious for paying its members very, very late, if at all. Forcefully Monsieur told me that now I was going to buy the vineyard (on easy terms – he knew we had no cash) and somehow make a good wine and prove the little estate could be profitable. And that would show Jacques the error of his ways. Quite a challenge but I had to accept, otherwise he'd have exploded. And anyway, I was a sucker for new adventures and he knew that.

Harvesting at La Clarière. Monsieur, me Labrut, Old Marthe, and small helpers including our vigneron *Olivier and his brother Pascal (now running the cellars at Château Lafleur Petrus).*

He said he'd give me a very fair price (there was never any question of him *giving* it to me) and he also said he would bring together the 40 or so vineyard *parcelles* spread over three villages which comprised his and Madame's estate. This was the way of it, back then, with French landholdings. The Napoleonic Code decreed that children should inherit equal shares. None of that old primogeniture stuff. So farms got sliced and diced and sliced again with every generation.

When I take people to see vineyards, they just see great fields of vines, no walls or fences, so they assume it all belongs to one person. But walk along the rows, and almost invisible – often totally invisible because they have become hidden underground – are markers that indicate some rows belong to Thomas, a few to Richard and a couple to old Harriet. And they can get all mixed up. We have a friend and supplier in Pauillac whose rows of vines are still madly intermingled with those of her neighbour Château Mouton Rothschild. Bottles from this row £40, bottles from the next £400, the next £40. It is crazy. Monsieur did his rationalising, wheeling and dealing, and ended up getting it down to just five *parcelles*... or six really, as an old devil of a neighbour held out for a ludicrous sum for his two rows which ran down the middle of our Roc de Maugras plot and we baulked at that. That silly strip of land is still there today. He said it was valuable building land. For a house 2 metres wide?

I asked that we could pull out of the co-op and build a winery of our own, ostensibly so we could make a much better wine, but really so we could have a lot more fun. We did. Monsieur also thought it a good idea to add my name to the vineyard, an idea pinched from the Rothschilds. It became Château La Clarière Laithwaite. He uprooted and replanted the entire vineyard with the latest clones available. And found me a guy to be our farmer: Guy Delage. But who was to make the wine? I wanted to, but didn't know how. I had, however, watched lots of winemaking happening over 15 years and one particular local wine producer stood out well above the others and generously came to my rescue. Peter Vinding-Diers was a very great Dane born in Stockholm's royal palace, who became a very good winemaker, first in South Africa and Australia, then in Bordeaux running two famous estates. He offered to show me how to do it at Château Rahoul in the Graves district. I spent a harvest or two watching what he did and copied everything. He introduced things I'd never seen in years of vineyard travelling. Like he harvested his grapes into small baskets to keep them whole and undamaged. Common now, but unheard of then. While living in Africa the Cassins had given over their vineyard to a neighbour Monsieur Godineau to look after as a *fermier* or sharecropper. He was still in charge when I first turned up. He ran the land like it was his own and took half the crop in payment. He did all the wrong things, things that did nothing for Castillon's reputation. At my first vintage I watched him in the vineyard filling the wooden tubs in which grapes were transported to the winery, right up to the brim, then jumping in with his muddy boots and stomping it all down to get in as much as he could. So the grape juice was oxidising and starting to ferment with any yeast or bacteria that was around and the whole thing was surrounded by wasps. And this stuff was going to make wine? It wasn't just Godineau, they all did it. If a grapeskin is broken, the juice starts going brown like a cut apple does – and if left too long that dulls the wine. Tipping grapes into big containers split most of the grapes. Peter's small baskets kept them whole. He also passed the bunches along a wooden sorting table where anything that didn't look good was removed and thrown back on the vineyard as compost. Fermenting tanks were also regularly 'plunged', as we called it. A new idea, then, in Bordeaux. The action is like punting on the river, except the pole has a large foot on it and is shoved through the great dense 'cap' of floating grapeskins to break it up and reimmerse the skins in the fermenting wine. It's like stirring tea leaves in the pot. The more you stir, the more colour and flavour you get. But also more tannins. You have to get it just

Opposite: *Château La Clarière today.*

right. It is seriously hard work, and really makes flabby office workers' muscles ache. I had not seen any of this done elsewhere in Bordeaux. When we copied everything he did, we were mocked in our village. Farmers driving past our winery would shake their heads and tap their foreheads, saying, as Asterix did: '*Ils sont fous, ces Anglais!*'

Peter's fermented wine went into expensive new oak barrels at several hundred pounds each. So now, ours did too. The upshot was that after our first disaster vintage of 1984 over which I will gloss, we produced a 1985 that won us our very first gold medal at the Concours National des Vins in Mâcon, the biggest wine competition in Burgundy. This was somehow achieved by me and a team of locals plus the odd holidaying Brit, harvesting, sorting, crushing and putting into tanks. But my secret was that, every evening after work, I would drive all the way south, crossing the Dordogne and Garonne to Peter's place in the Graves district with my samples, my weights and temperature readings. While Susie Vinding-Diers prepared lovely suppers I would get my instructions for the next day. Back and forth I went night after night. But it worked and eventually we had enough wine for 24,000 bottles and it was a wine that stood head and shoulders above anything else then made in Castillon. That's not an empty boast. I have been known to make empty boasts, but this is not one of them. It was simple logic. If you take all the trouble with your winemaking that we had, new oak barrels and all, you will, as long as you have good healthy vines planted densely on a limestone ridge in poor, well-drained soil, as we did, get a really good wine.

At that time no one else in the Castillon district was taking this amount of trouble making wine, or running up our sort of costs. Why? Because back then, there was absolutely no incentive for them to do so. The price of Castillon wine per hectolitre (in those days almost all the wine producers around us did not sell in bottles, only in bulk) was fixed on La Place de Bordeaux – the wine 'stock exchange'. The price was published every week in *Sud Ouest*, the regional newspaper. And that price was low. Very low. Basically a price at which if any producer wished to make enough to live on, they just could not afford to do all the expensive stuff we were doing – certainly not new barrels at £500 a go. So Castillon growers kept their costs low. Some boosted their yields, illegally, way above the appellation maximum limit, harvesting early and fermenting hot and quick. It's easy to pump more wine out of your vines. You prune very long to produce more bunches and you overfertilise. This means your grapes usually won't fully ripen, so you add a few sacks of sugar to your tanks. In those days the railway yard at Castillon and every other town in Bordeaux was a mountain of sugar sacks every September. The appellation sets an upper limit of 6,000 litres a hectare but it's not hard with a young vineyard to push yields over 10,000 litres. People even had hidden tanks in abandoned buildings around the village. You'd walk past some derelict place and wonder why it was making gloop, gloop noises in the night. The wine books said Castillon only produced 'good quaffing wines'. And that was true. Because at that time there was no earthly point anyone trying to make anything better than the sort of cheap claret that gets gulped down every day without any fuss. Did they know how to make a better wine? Mmm, no, most small farmers didn't. Some did, but the system was against them. Appellation Contrôlée protected great wines but it also condemned potentially excellent winemakers in low-rated areas to being unable to produce their best. Unless they happened to have a few thousand faithful customers already like I did and which was my great opportunity.

At La Clarière we were able to break the mould. We were able to produce what Monsieur wanted: a wine he could pour for Jacques, shouting '*Et voilà*... I told you Castillon could be just as good as your *fameux* Saint-Émilion, *Sacre bleu, Nom d'un chien!*'

But as usual I hadn't quite thought it all through. There was enough of this excellent wine for 2,000 cases – proper, traditional, wooden cases – but I found that wine doesn't just sell because it's nice, particularly an unknown wine from a barely known region, and what with all those new barrels and other costs, is more expensive than any other Castillon wine. We'd made what was, then, a very different sort of Castillon. Our neighbouring vineyards did, in fact, ask that our wine be declared *hors de concours* in the local wine show competition, as we were not, they felt, playing in the same league – not playing fair.

THE CONFRÈRES

So how to sell it?

We did have tens of thousands of customers. But they were not about to buy 2,000 cases of an unknown relatively pricey wine – every year! It was not going to happen. I began to think this adventure had been

One of the first harvests at Château La Clarière, with Guy Delage, the Cassins and team.

too rash. Then I remembered how we'd got out of a previous problem when we'd written a letter to the customers, explained the problem and asked for help, and offered a little incentive. So I wrote and said, if anyone placed an early order before we bottled the wine, I would basically give them the wine 'at cost' with a big discount on what would be the wine's usual price, I'd guarantee they'd always be first in line for cases in future vintages and, as thanks, I'd also put their name up on the cellar wall as a founding Confrère de La Clarière Laithwaite and we'd register the Confrères de La Clarière as the wine's producers on the label and on the box. This plan worked again and we got almost 2,000 Confrères. For 2,000 cases. Problem solved at least for the 1985 vintage. But the next vintage? When you make your own wine you can't just turn the tap off. You can't just stop buying as merchants can. It just keeps coming. The 1986 turned out to be really good. Two golds! And, luckily again, virtually every Confrère agreed to take their second case. They really liked it. Next year, 1987, was not a vintage with a great reputation, but we sorted extra hard, threw away lots more dodgy bunches and made a very respectable wine indeed. It got three medals this time and again the Confrères didn't hesitate. They plunged in and it all went. And so it went on with barely a glitch. It still goes on today, every vintage no matter whether the vintage is pronounced by the experts as 'Great' or not. The Confrères always take their case. We always win at least a medal a year, usually gold, and the Confrères are now saving over £100 a case on what the surplus wine normally sells for in Britain and around the world.

Maybe I should explain here about what constitutes a good vintage and what is a bad one. Up until the 1960s a bad vintage meant very, very bad. Disastrous. Today it only means the wines may be a bit lighter than usual. In the 1960s you only had to look to see a bad vintage. I saw a couple. You could probably have seen them from space. Bordeaux was covered in a dense fog, a very unusual fog, a fog of spores from the grey and black rot – pourriture – that was consuming the grapes. A damp and warm summer brought *mildiou* and botrytis. To combat it there was just Bordeaux Mixture – copper sulphate coming out of feeble backpack sprayers. It didn't protect much at all when rot really set in. People were

Ready for loading at La Clarière.

Barrel hall at Le Chai au Quai, Castillon.

harvesting empty grape skins, their insides all eaten out. I remember my teacher Professor Peynaud telling us that the 'modern' vineyard – thousands of near-identical plants, crammed close together for 50 years or so – was, ecologically speaking, a 'disaster waiting to happen'.

Today, there are very efficient sprayers or atomisers which can put anti-fungal treatment right into the heart of the bunches if done at the right time. Sure, this stuff must be used carefully, so there are controls and penalties. But there are sprays of stuff that is so safe it is 'food grade'. There is also hourly information on what might be attacking vineyards available on the Web, and most growers these days have been to wine college. So basically everything has got better and the Great Rots are things of the past.

Wine writers and critics still play up the differences in vintage quality because, well, that's what they do, that's their job. It's fun and it keeps the customers interested. Which is vital. We producers play down the differences because we need to sell our wine every year, but also because we know the basic difference now is between rich vintages which will keep well – and indeed need to be kept a while before they gentle down – and lighter vintages which are nice to drink when young, and usually cheaper. La Clarière has been happy to release every vintage bar one (2013), and that was my decision and one much criticised by my winemaker since the wine did actually end up winning a silver medal and so cannot have been all that bad.

New methods keep improving every vintage. Today we have an apparatus that uses a bath of juice at the correct specific gravity to float away all but perfectly ripe grapes from our wine. Other estates use similar methods. If every vintage is made only with perfect grapes then vintages will all tend to taste quite similar. The difference will be that in some cool years there will be more unripe fruit jettisoned than in sunnier years. I often wonder what old Godineau would say if he could see today's growers throwing away grapes! We've come a long way.

We won at least one medal in France's Concours National every year but we only got really successful in competitions when in 1994 Jean-Marc Sauboua became our winemaker. He is the winemaking equivalent of a Michelin star chef. I was happy with any medal. Jean-Marc wants only gold medals. He has well over 100. He also trained Henry, my eldest (whose winemaking began aged 15 with the basket of overripe pineapples he won in the village fete), who now also wants – and mostly gets – only golds. It would have been an unprecedented six Paris golds in a row for La Clarière but for a silver in 2009! But that was still enough to win us the *prix d'excellence* for the Bordeaux Region. And we won it twice, and as a result of that I, who didn't actually make any of those wines, was given the great honour of being appointed a *chevalier du mérite agricole*. That's another Napoleonic thing. The Revolution and the Emperor did away with all the old noble titles and he created his Agricultural Knights instead. I wear the little green and yellow ribbon in my buttonhole on every possible occasion. It's very tiny, so I generally have to point it out to British people. I am such a show-off, even though in France it's known somewhat disparagingly as wearing *le poireau* (the leek)!

Our success with La Clarière changed the course of the Company, encouraging me further down a track I was keen on: winemaking. We certainly weren't going to give up buying wine from others, but in some areas winemaking would give us an advantage. We had pursued rapid growth as a way to defend ourselves from the threat of giant supermarkets. But there was another threat. We were also competing against other wine merchants, most of whom had been around for centuries and for that historic reason were greatly respected. We were just young upstarts. I worried we were not taken seriously and I thought

Harvest time lunch break with Jean-Marc Sauboua.

a way to get treated more seriously would be to explain ourselves as the wine merchants who mostly lived in their vineyards, rather than in London. We reckoned we already spent much more time travelling the vineyards than the others. But actually owning vineyards and wineries was, I thought, unique.

So we started thinking about extending our winemaking a bit further. I got keen on the idea of making a white equivalent of our red La Clarière. A 'big' Bordeaux dry white, fermented in new oak barrels. We grew no white grape vines so in 1986 I persuaded a co-operative winery across the river in the Entre-Deux-Mers to let my buy some of their juice and allow Peter Vinding-Diers into their winery to ferment it for me in 40 new oak casks. No co-operative had ever, to my knowledge, fermented white wine in new barrels. That was what the top châteaux in the Graves did, around Pessac and Léognan. Co-ops just did normal fermentation in concrete tanks. But I thought that if I could get their perfectly good but inexpensive Sémillon grapes, add a top winemaker and the best barrels, I could produce something pretty similar to a top Pessac-Léognan for far less. We did – well, more accurately, Peter did – and it all sold out.

This despite the president of that cellar, a tall, proud, crusty old gent, stamping around all the time, incensed that foreigners were being allowed to mess around in 'his' cellar.

THE FLYING WINEMAKERS

That same year I was sitting on the floor alone in my winery at harvest time, trying to get a bucket of yeast and juice to start fermenting.

It was being stubborn and I was cross. Suddenly there was a strange whirring sound and a flash of light and in walked The Doctor! Well, maybe not quite, but that was the way Dr Tony Jordan should have arrived. I'd met Tony on my first trip to Australia. He had been the head of a famous wine college and taught many of the country's winemakers. Now Dr Tony, along with Brian Crozer of Petaluma fame, ran a big wine consultancy. He looked at my efforts with the yeast, firmly took the bucket away, got the thing going, then showed me how to launch my tanks properly. Well, he was a doctor after all. He explained he was just over on holiday and, looking around, had decided he'd like to come back next year and make some proper white wine in Bordeaux. Australia makes its wines in March. So he'd come over in September, his quiet time. He really wanted to make white wine, because he'd seen so much uninspiring stuff. So had we all. I showed him what we'd done with Peter in the co-operative and said I would try and find another cellar that would welcome him. Preferably one without a crusty old president.

Dr Tony went back to Australia and I started looking for a white wine cellar. I found one not in Bordeaux but just upriver, across the border in the Dordogne *département*. Saint-Vivien is, like Saint-Émilion and Sainte-Colombe, on the crest of the ridge of limestone that forms the northern boundary of the Dordogne river valley. So it is very good vine-growing land and in Monsieur Goubault it had a delightfully cheery, unstuffy and welcoming co-operative president. He was happy to have us. So was his consultant: Professor Pascal Ribéreau-Gayon, Émile Peynaud's successor as head of Bordeaux University's wine department, and the son of that *département*'s great founder Jean Ribéreau-Gayon. So far so very good. The wine didn't have to be a Bordeaux. No reason why it couldn't be a Montravel. And after all, my first really successful

ESULÉ
FROM
REDHEADS STUDIO

✳

WHEN, AFTER THE HARVEST, THE FLYING WINEMAKERS RETURNED HOME TO AUSTRALIA TO THEIR DAY JOBS, OFTEN AS JUNIORS IN BIG WINE OPERATIONS, THEY MISSED WHAT THEY'D SEEN IN FRANCE, SPAIN, ITALY.

Small winegrowers making their own wines. They'd also enjoyed doing their own thing under minimal control. So when we provided them with a low-cost drop-in centre for winemakers with no supervision at all, they decided it was going to be like a recording studio and they were there to cut wine 'hits'. So they had to have the labels like record covers. Some were horrific to my eyes but I rather liked this one. Esulé. No idea what's going on here but the wine is a rich Cabernet. So they say. (It's still a bit anarchic there, though much less than it was, and characterful enough recently to have scored 95 points from Australia's top judge and eight gold medals.) Production is tiny. Esulé, along with the other wines in the studio RedHeads, has helped refresh an over-corporate Australian industry where 'never in history has so much wine been made by so few'. Shed winemaking, shedism, is now almost common, and lets many small winemakers and growers into the world's markets. And customers love the fun of it, as much as the wines. This label is now in the Museum of Modern Art, San Francisco.

✳

dry white, Château de Panisseau, had come from the Dordogne. And that too had been made by a foreigner: Madame Becker from Alsace! So all told, things looked rosy.

But then, bugger it, Dr Tony only went and took a job with Moët & Chandon, first to build and then run its big new Australian venture – a sparkling winery in the Yarra Valley – and so could no longer come over. But we didn't give up and he found a bright young graduate called Nigel Sneyd (today, a respected Master of Wine, who directs Gallo's international winemaking) and sent him over instead. Nigel could only come for a month – the length of his holidays – and Dr Tony was not prepared for him to leave unbottled white wine behind. So we had to work fast. We chose our own concrete tanks in the co-op and, before Nigel arrived, spent days scrubbing them shiny clean. Australian winemakers taught by Dr Tony demand pristine cleanliness. Everything, even handrails and stairs, must be immaculate. This was not, back then, the southern French tradition. I was taught by the French that wine was naturally antiseptic, so you didn't have to wear out any scrubbing brushes. They weren't entirely wrong, but too much reliance on wine's natural antiseptic qualities is risky. A quick hose down is not quite enough. Nigel arrived and immediately phoned home. The nightly call to Dr Tony was how this wine was to be made. The harvest had begun and tractors and trailers were beginning to queue for the receiving bays. Nigel went down the line, peering at every load, looking for clean, healthy-looking fruit. He'd then chew a grape or two and like the man from Del Monte maybe give a nod and hand the tractor driver his reward: a little sachet of white powder. This was metabisulphite of sulphur, not cocaine. It was to be sprinkled over the grapes to ward off any nasties trying to attack the fresh-picked and therefore vulnerable grapes. (Sulphur has been essential to winemaking since the Etruscans.) Only the best trailer loads got the sachet and, after the initial surprise had worn off, you'd see growers grinning their heads off when they were among the 'chosen' ones. We didn't pay them any more but now there was prestige to be had. One of the problems of wine co-ops back then was that co-op members were paid by grape tonnage multiplied by the sugar content of their grapes. Riper grapes earned more, but there was no motivation to produce healthier, tastier grapes. These days, in most co-op wineries that has been addressed but we could see at Saint-Vivien that the good growers enjoyed having their superior work finally recognised.

We didn't use the pipework that normally conveyed crushed grapes to the tanks, as we'd looked inside those pipes and hadn't liked what we saw. We bought our own new flexible hoses. We also brought in our own refrigeration unit. The ability to chill down tanks is vital in modern winemaking. Only after the introduction of refrigeration were hot countries like Australia able to produce the fruity wines for which today they are renowned. Before refrigeration most hot country wines had a cooked or stewed taste. Australia is much hotter than Bordeaux and the fruit flavours could easily be boiled off in uncontrollably hot fermentations. In Bordeaux and surrounding areas like the Dordogne, cold autumn weather would usually help avoid that, but was not of course guaranteed every year. All these changes we brought in improved our white wine, a wine that tasted quite unlike anything that cellar had ever produced before. But there was one final thing Dr Tony, Nigel and we, the back-up skivvies, did that truly amazed the wine world of Bordeaux. Nigel had only a month with us, and Dr Tony believed if he left our two tanks of this delicate, fresh dry white behind in a co-op with loads of other wines, white and red, being fermented all around it, then something or somebody would come along to mess it up. He was dead right, as we found out the hard way a year or so later.

A wine, particularly a delicate dry white, is a very vulnerable thing and is only 'safe' when securely tucked into its bottle. Nigel was instructed to bottle this wine, our Montravel which we called 'La Chapelle' before he left. The authorities, of course, said *'Impossible! Non, non. Absolument non!'* In France there are always *les formalités* and vast amounts of paperwork relating to wine. No one had ever bottled a wine in under six months in the South-West. But somehow old Goubault and his influential friend Professor Pascal got us special dispensation, albeit granted very reluctantly.

Anne Linder and Claudy Gomme, who ran our French office, called in our usual bottling truck. (We had plenty of experience bottling our own wines by then. We were among the first to use the new idea of renting mobile bottling machines for wines we bought so as to avoid the risks involved in moving wine by tanker.)

This produced a sight that remains lodged firmly – rather proudly – in my mind. An unremarkable wine co-operative, with tractors and trailers queuing with 1987 vintage grapes down one side, while on the other side a big truck was loading cartons of a finished 1987 wine. All done

SEC SEC SEC MONTRAVEL

BY THE FLYING WINEMAKERS

✺

WE ORGANISED THE GREATEST CULTURE CLASH IN WINE.

It was our idea to fly over young Australian winemakers and put them into sleepy old French wine village cellars we believed could do better. The results were immediate and revolutionary. And quickly copied by virtually every major British wine retailer. France has winemakers as good as any but... the French classification system hampers them. Young Aussie winemakers just didn't accept being told that they could not make a great wine because some *fonctionnaire* in Paris had decreed that the village they'd adopted wasn't in a 'great wine' region. Two fingers to that. This wine, made in a co-op in the Dordogne, won wine of the show in Mâcon, a very important show (in 1988 I think it was). I doubt those Burgundians even knew the Dordogne made wine. They do now, and ever since the Dordogne has never doubted it could make terrific wines.

and dusted in four weeks. Possibly a world record. Certainly a record for Bordeaux and surrounding regions. The wine was just delicious. It wasn't a big vintage that year, lots of grapes but not as ripe as other years. But the wine proved very popular because of the shock customers got, tasting its quite unexpected zingy, slightly spritzy, fruitiness. The next year we got the now famous Martin Shaw of Shaw + Smith, who make the best Sauvignon Blanc in Australia, to come over with another now great winemaker, the Kiwi John Belsham, and they made an even better wine. We entered it in the Concours National in Mâcon. It won the trophy. It was Wine of the Show... from the Dordogne! Which had never had a success like that before. *Ça alors!*

Back then, for really fresh fruity inexpensive dry whites, there were not all that many reliable places to go in southern France... southern Europe even. Certainly not the Midi. Just Alsace, Burgundy and the Loire in the cooler north. But now you could add to the list the Dordogne.

The Dr Tony Jordan/Nigel/Martin/John team and of course Anne, Claudy and all rushing around doing the cleaning and other tasks had just proved something remarkable.

It opened up so many possibilities, not just around Bordeaux but also in the vast – but hot – Midi. Clean, refrigerated winemaking would soon change the wine map considerably.

Over the next few years Anne and I brought over whole teams of Flying Aussie Winemakers, putting them into four cellars in Bordeaux, two in Languedoc-Roussillon, one in Spain, one in southern Italy, one on the Italian/Yugoslav border and others I've forgotten. They caused a big stir everywhere except in Burgundy where our preferred co-op winery in Mancey baulked at the idea of Aussies, but still came and studied what we were doing and then did it themselves. That worked rather well too. In the Rhône we got a retired French winemaker to be our 'Flyer' at the Chusclan co-operative. Old André Roux, my greatest winemaking friend, a wise guru, and in his time the winner of an unrivalled number of competition golds, 'flew' across the Rhône in his 'DS' daily and made wines the co-op could never have managed themselves... as they cheerfully admitted. A series of athletic young winemakers were hired to help him and do the running up and down the stairs in that big winery. We went further afield and even put young Martin Shaw into the huge

Flying Winemakers All Stars: Martin Shaw, President Goubault and John Belsham.

Canepa winery in Chile where he made not just one but a dozen superb varietals. We got ticked off by a wine writer for starting a movement which would globalise winemaking and lead to a narrowing in the wine spectrum and in some ways she had a point. Looking back now, you can see some regional idiosyncrasies have indeed been lost. But the upside is that standards of winemaking have risen everywhere and the range of wines now available to consumers in Britain and America is vastly greater than the range 30 years ago. As retailers, we can only offer such a range if the customers are happy to buy it. But they are only happy to buy it if it falls within certain norms, if it isn't too weird. Strange and unusual wines please sommeliers but few actual consumers.

The wines our Flyers made impressed everyone, particularly our competitors. It only took a couple of years before every supermarket in Britain had wines made by Aussie winemakers in Europe, making fruit-rich wines where only dull dry wines – usually called 'Old Git' wines – had been made previously. The globalisation of winemaking would have happened anyway soon enough – I mean everything's been globalised now – but the Flying Winemakers just happened at the right time and provided the spark. Flying Winemakers, by the way, was a name that came out of a very heavy evening in L'Envers du Décor, the Saint-Émilion wine bar, as some of us remembered an Aussie radio show from our childhood: *The Flying Doctor*... 'Calling Wallamboola Base... over... Doc we need help!' We registered it as a trademark, but it became impossible to protect, because everybody started using the term. Still, it got me a mention in *The Oxford Companion to Wine*. Thank you, Jancis.

The Flyers were entertaining. They were not all Aussie larrikins, it just seemed like they were. One managed to 'park' his hire car halfway up a tree off a hairpin bend, and one got arrested for breaking into his own winery. It was fiesta day in Murchante, Navarra, and of course everything in town was shut down. In a winery where fermentations are in full flow they need regular chilling lest they boil over. That Flyer then had to be smuggled out of Spain across the Pyrenees in a car boot. There was also the one who started an affair with the daughter of his winery's owner, ignoring the warnings that she was betrothed to the son of a well-known mafioso. We had to get him off home very fast too. But those boys and girls made lovely wines for us. It wasn't so much their skills, but their energy and 'can do' attitude which really fired up the wineries they worked in. If the appellation system and the textbooks say you are second or third grade it's demoralising. You are a keen young winemaker fresh from college, you get a job in some backwoods winery determined to show what you can do. But your best efforts are only ever classed as second or third rate and always will be, no matter what. So eventually you stop trying because you can't win. Then along comes this young Aussie, looks at your grapes, chews a few, says: 'Jeez mate' (that really is how they talk) 'these are bloody good, better than I get given at home, we can make a great wine here.' The Flyer crashes around the place, working all hours, pumping wine and partying the nights away, and makes a wine that wins medals and sells very well in Britain. Very important wine people, wine professors and their like, pay visits to wineries they would never have considered visiting. The Flying Winemaker period 1987 to 2005 was very exciting for me. At their peak, our Flyers made a quarter of all the wines we sold.

Aussie winemakers just love to tell you exactly how they make such good wine. French winemakers, on the other hand, had a long tradition of implying that it's all down to the Hand of God and the precious piece of His earth that they just happen to own. The French said, 'If you don't like it, there's something wrong with you.' Aussies rocked up and said, 'How can we make it more to your liking?' What was funny was that back then the Aussies themselves didn't seem to know just how far ahead of the game they were. There was one time an Australian radio 'shock jock' phoned me live on air, mocking me and my idea that Aussie Flying

Opposite top: The original RedHeads studio, complete with sofa and pinball machine.

Opposite bottom: Plunging and crushing grapes at RedHeads' second cellar.

Winemakers had anything to teach the French. He couldn't believe it. He called my Winemakers 'tall poppies', which is a big insult in Australia. Tony Jordan was hurt by that. But I couldn't believe this radio ignoramus was so unaware. Our conversation didn't go far.

Today it's different. We are still Direct Wines: the notoriously invasive merchants who like to get seriously stuck into our suppliers' vineyards and cellars, checking everything, tasting every tank and barrel. We enjoy being a nuisance still, but we no longer bring in our Australians because there is now no need. Winemaking across Europe, even as far as darkest Moldova, has caught up. Today we can issue a *carnet des charges*, a specification, in the certain knowledge that the excellent cellars we select will produce what we want.

But the Flyers were not finished with us yet.

REDHEADS

Several of the young Flying Winemakers we employed in Europe through the 1980s and 1990s told us of the frustration they felt going back to their humdrum jobs in big Australian wineries after more or less doing their own thing for us in Europe.

The Australian wine industry had been severely 'rationalised' in the 1980s and 1990s. One by one, family wineries got bought by bigger wineries who then got bought by even bigger ones. Bankers and finance people, not so much wine people. Certainly not winemakers. Winemakers didn't like this one bit. One of them, a regular 'Flyer' – Justin 'Jutty' Lane – showed us the four barrels of vivid Shiraz he had fermented in his garage in the McLaren Vale region, south of Adelaide. They were very good indeed. Such concentrated flavours. Justin was a good winemaker but he told me it was really down to him getting his hands on 'top fruit'. He had a winegrower mate who had four rows at the top of his vineyard that the irrigation system didn't quite reach. (Almost all Aussie vineyards are irrigated by drip-feed systems.) The mate was under contract to a big winery but he let Jutty fill the back of his 'ute' with what few grapes survived up there. Grapes from vines that

are on the point of dying through lack of water are the very best grapes that Australia does. And the big winery was never going to miss a few, were they? His mate would get a couple of cases of the wine made from his grapes, as payment. That was something he'd never had before and something to be proud of. Usually his grapes disappeared into a huge blend, never to be seen again. This gave us an idea: why not find Jutty a bigger garage? He took me to see another friend who'd already done just that. Phil Christiansen had been made redundant by a big winery and, with no money and no prospect of a job, had set up his own winery on a shoestring in a semi-derelict old shed in McLaren Vale. I was so impressed! I'd always loved sheds since my days at Grandfather's shed. I am a confirmed 'sheddist'. I just loved how 'Philbo', this no-nonsense quiet Aussie, had lined the place with cheap foil roof insulation, bought rainwater tanks as fermenters, used a milk-cooling unit and reels of garden hose for refrigeration, renovated old pumps and cleaned up discarded old barrels. With this set-up he made remarkable wines... from top fruit. So we went driving around McLaren Vale looking for a shed. After two days we had run out of time and were sitting, dejected, over coffee, the only customers in a sort of café called RedHeads, discussing our failure, when the proprietor, who must have been listening, came over and said, 'You could have this place if you want; me and the wife have had enough. We've bought a camper van and we're off to the Outback.' They do that, Australians.

So we bought the RedHeads Café. We kept the sign out front because it sounded right for a winery, a red winery. Jutty, Philbo, the grape grower Nat 'Natski' McMurtrie, the winemaker Adam 'Hoops' Hooper and others replaced the tables and chairs with rainwater tub fermenters and made a copy of Philbo's place plus a pinball machine and powerful sound system. And they kept the long wooden bar. Word went out and a dozen winemakers signed up to use the 'facilities' to make, not wines for us, but the wines they themselves wanted to make. We just said we would like to have first refusal on any we liked. That was the deal. Don't give the crazies any orders. No point. No chance they'd obey. Just tap into their frustrated creative passions. It mostly worked extremely well. At first. We got a handful of very impressive wines. Our ever-enthusiastic customers signed up as they had before, with Château La Clarière, to place advance orders for these wines before they were bottled. Justin, who has a generous 'gift of the gab', went travelling, spread the word wider and found new customers in the US, Denmark and I forget where

Would you entrust a winery to this lot? But it worked... mostly.

else. I went over to see the place as often as I could. I'd stay upstairs at the winery. Harvest was a riot. Literally. The massive bar was a long, rough slice of tree and all night long 'mates' would drop in for a cold beer out of the wine cooler and to watch the guys working their tubs of blood-red grapes, long into the night. I would bail out early. Lying in bed upstairs listening to the thudding rock music and pumps going hard, the yells and laughter below, I realised this was more fun than I'd had in a decade. It rejuvenated old me. It also really turned on young Henry who slaved there as a 'barrel monkey'. It even converted our Tom, previously adamant that wine was the most boring thing ever. We Laithwaites owe it a lot. I also think we did good for the Aussie wine industry, our customers and ourselves.

Not that it all went smoothly. In fact it didn't go smoothly at all. A bunch of 'creative' young Aussies, with me – another 'creative' – supposedly in charge. Disaster time. They went wild. True, that was their image, which appealed to many customers. But while image is all very well, you do need at least one sensible person to ensure the madness doesn't get totally out of hand, or you end up with chaos, ruin and no wine. Any sane company faced with what RedHeads became after a few years would have canned it. But mostly, I think because my nice kind people saw how much it meant to me, my lot managed to save it. Rachel Robinson is a very clever direct marketer, the cleverest I've ever met, but sorting out a chaotic winery was not really what she signed up for. She originally joined us to set up our Laithwaite's Wine People wine club in Australia, based in Sydney, not to sort out RedHeads. But she did, she paid off the debts, sold the RedHeads building to one of the winemakers and moved the whole operation just down the road to a shiny, brand-new shed, purpose-built by Steve Grimley, perhaps McLaren Vale's most successful young wine entrepreneur. A rigorously organised guy himself, the anarchic RedHead image nonetheless appealed to Steve. And changed him somewhat. Like he decided to have rare-breed pigs in the scrub at the back of the shed so as to be able to serve visitors fine ham and *saucisson* with the wines. Steve, who is amazing at finding us lots of wine bargains, ran RedHeads for several years until it was judged healthy enough for us to take over again. Whereupon we moved it over to the next region, the Barossa. Not just for the change of scenery, but because RedHeads had more or less fulfilled its aims in McLaren Vale. Almost all the winemakers who made up the original team had by now set up their own wineries, in their own sheds, and we could buy from them. We

now needed new talents. So we rented a shed in the Barossa, then two years later another, then we got space in the old Illaparra barrel hall on Murray Street, Tanunda, which was a return to where Doug Lehmann had bottled for me the first Australian wines I'd bought in the 1980s. Dan Graham became chief RedHeads winemaker. He basically ran the show with Rachel and Cousin Iain who, after 20 years buying for the UK's most successful 'on-sales' merchant Bibendum, had returned to us, the company he started with, to run all our winemaking operations. They took RedHeads in a different direction. A smarter direction, I felt. They moved the emphasis away from winemakers. There are already plenty of great winemakers around whom the entire wine universe is said to turn. We now saw no pressing need to create more. But there are also quieter winemakers prepared to admit that, in fact, 'great wine is made in the vineyard'. It's the grapes, stupid, 'just get fully ripe grapes and do as little as possible'. Most of us now accept this, and that the winemakers' job is basically just not to mess things up. So the emphasis at RedHeads today has changed and is no longer Young God winemakers but 'the

forgotten men and women of Australian wine' – the grape-growers. Forgotten? Well, yes, you drive through the Barossa today, you see vast buildings. 'What's a car factory doing in a wine region?' you ask. 'And is that an oil refinery all lit up over there?' No, it's Wolf Blass or Penfolds or Jacob's Creek – the huge corporations that produce most of Australia's wine. Most of the vineyards around them, however, still belong to hard-working farming families who have been there for generations, and it is upon their hard work in the vineyards they cherish that the reputations of the big names are built. It's the grape-growers who produce the fruit (grapes here are always referred to as simply 'fruit') that wins the medals and 'improves' the big blends. The 'Mission' of RedHeads was, and still is, to let customers taste the fact that great Australian wines don't have to have famous labels or high prices.

As I said, every two years RedHeads seems to have to move to a new, bigger shed. It was a wandering winery. But in January 2018 we bought 8 hectares of prime Shiraz at the heart of Barossa and began to build the perfect cellar. It will be an unusual cellar, because it must continue doing the small, tiny-batch fermentations which have made RedHeads' name. Not big fermenting tanks. RedHeads is anti-corporatist and must continue to think small. We all just want to do 'small' better. It's always been very exciting... now getting even more exciting. And still rejuvenating for me.

RedHeads sparked off another of my daydreams.

LE CHAI AU QUAI

I got it into my head that it would be fun (that obsession again) to take over the splendid old riverside wine *négociant* premises in Castillon-la-Bataille where I'd worked long ago.

I'd heard they were empty and I wanted to revamp them and turn them into something exciting. 'Yes, but what?' my Board asked me, reminding me that most merchant cellars in Bordeaux had closed. I floundered. They didn't look happy. The idea began to look like a non-starter. But my ever-loyal wife spoke up for me, reminding the Board that in the past she hadn't always grasped quite why her husband wanted to do a project, and that quite often even he didn't know exactly what he wanted to do it for, but that she had usually found saying 'Yes' paid off. Eventually. That swung it: they said 'Yes' and Direct Wines took on Le Chai au Quai, which stands on the quayside of the Dordogne. This rather magnificent structure had been built in 1850 by three enterprising sisters. There would have been some sort of wine building on the quayside for centuries, between the great town wall and the river. But the sisters built something quite magnificent and what I've always loved is that they had the names of everyone who worked on the building inscribed on the hallway walls. Masons, carpenters etc. Everyone except themselves. They must have been very nice ladies to do that. They would have had a stream of local winegrowers arriving on carts, bringing barrels of young wine to the receiving bay – it's still there – up on top of what's left of the town wall. The wine would then be poured through a pipe system down to great blending tanks below, then on into barrels stacked high, to age and mature, before being rolled out front on to the quay and into barges to be taken downriver to Bordeaux and from there to the waiting world.

It was *négociants* like this who created the fame of Bordeaux. But today they have almost all gone. Now is the age of the winegrowers, the châteaux. Customers want 'famous châteaux', not anonymous blends. So, in that case, why did I want this great blending palace? The Board was right to ask. All I can say is that I had these sepia images of masses of barrels piled six high stuck in my head. But not as before, all containing the same big blend. No, in my imagination I saw lots of different wines from different regions, of different grapes, made in different ways. Great towering walls of different flavours and colours. I then imagined a long zinc workbench under the great windows that overlooked the river. And on the bench my great winemakers Jean-Marc Sauboua and Mark Hoddy would work like top chefs work in their kitchens. This would in fact be a 'wine kitchen', where new creations would emerge gloriously... some of this, a touch of that... a sprinkle of the other. More oak? More time? Some of the world's most talented noses would create masterpieces. Not standard blends at all, but highly individual little wonders to delight our customers. And inform them. Sauvignon Gris? Who's heard of that? Grenache Gris, anyone? Put some big deep black Midi Syrah together with a fresh pale but aromatic Gascon Cabernet. Why not? They do it in California and Australia, so why not in France? Well, it's against the law for starters. Yes, you can do such a blend. But French law said you could not tell customers what it was if it was a strange brew. Put the names on the label and you would be prosecuted. But some time ago

Not much has changed in Le Chai over the past hundred or so years.

we found a way that satisfied our trusting customers. So if we put out a wine with labels that just said 'GG' or 'Le C au Chai' they might give them a try if we explained to them (just not on the label) what they contained. They did give them a try. Not in huge numbers, it's true. But enough did. And they came back for more. We set up regular mixed-case deliveries of our latest creations to fans we called 'Keyholders'. Over the years they've bought some pretty weird things from us but they still like us. Also, like RedHeads, my Chai dream included helping to bring forward small-scale, forgotten winemakers and grape-growers. Like Jean-Charles Duran in Maury. For ages his family had produced meagre amounts of wine from ancient old Grenache bush vines on steep stony slopes in the windswept Agly Valley above Perpignan – the hottest place in France. But it had become increasingly hard. He works on his own now. Parents too old, wife having to work in a shop to bring in money, and his son sent off to be a Paris fireman. Why does he carry on? Simple, he believes his vineyards are special. So do we. We want him to go on. So we buy all his new wine and age it in Le Chai because he has neither the space nor money to do that himself. Mark, our Chai winemaker, is his big mate and looks after this wine like it were his own. We bottle it under the 'Vent de Folie' label, Jean-Charles is delighted, we are delighted, and our customers are delighted.

Those are the dream reasons for having Le Chai. I couldn't explain them at the beginning but I see it now. We all do. And even the French government has seen fit to help. It does now allow us to blend wines from different regions, and say what it is on the label, just like the Australians do, under the new catch-all appellation Vin de France. *Merci*. We must have been doing the right thing.

We got proof of a sort one summer, when an Englishwoman just passing along the quayside called into Le Chai. Shown around and given a tasting, she suddenly said to me: 'I always thought Laithwaite's wine was just like Tesco. It isn't, is it?' It meant a lot to me, that.

Le Chai is a great visit. Like a sweetshop for grown-ups; so many flavours, unlike your normal Bordeaux château which only has one wine.

Mind you, if you want to see a good château, we can do that too. We take visitors up to our Château La Clarière which is now very different to how it started. It is no longer in Monsieur's converted barn, but in a fourteenth-century fortified farmhouse reached by a great long drive through vineyards with terraced vineyards climbing up behind. We don't live there. No one lives there, but there is a great welcome and there will soon be accommodation for Confrères – the vineyard's special and loyal supporters – who like to come and taste how things are going at 'their' château. Currently I consider that I share La Clarière with 5,000 Confrères and love sharing it. One of my favourite things these days is joining in showing them round.

Barbara and I, when in France, live happily a couple of hundred yards down the road in the house we bought from Monsieur Berthoumeyroux, the fishmonger, which has a lovely view of the château – particularly from the bath. I gaze at it for hours. (I spend hours in my bath. It's where I write, though I don't have a secretary taking dictation like Churchill. I write on my phone.) We acquired 20 hectares with the château and have been bringing the vineyards up to the highest standards, which takes time. We've also now begun to improve the winery. We don't actually want to take our wine up into the price stratosphere set by many of our neighbours. I do understand why people will happily pay hundreds of pounds for wines from just along the ridge from us. But I get more fun, like old Henri Bourlon did, from pouring people a glass of our very inexpensive wine and a glass from one of the pricey Saint-Émilion châteaux and seeing which they prefer. If they don't see the labels it'll most likely be our cru. I do so love doing that. With my La Clarière I'm your total wine show-off.

FIZZ BRITANNIA

After Australia and France, we then started our wine adventures in England.

When we moved Direct Wines from Caversham to its new premises in Theale in 1988, we planted a little vineyard on the great pile of rubble which remained from the previous building. We shaped it into a mini *côte*, covered it in soil, and planted 1,000 vines in steep south-facing rows with roses at the ends and a few fruit trees alongside. We just thought it would look pretty, and more appropriate than the usual trading estate shrubs. It did. But it must have puzzled commuters on the railway that ran beside it. But then we picked the grapes and sent them down to be turned into fizz by the Roberts family of Ridgeview in Ditchling (from whom we had bought a very nice English sparkling wine, SouthRidge, since 1993). When the Theale wine came back finished, we went 'Wow!'

This was amazing. To think that little old England could actually, unbelievably, make a very classy – and internationally competitive – wine. Just as long as it had bubbles in it.

Theale vineyard's first bottling came seventh in a sort of world championship of sparkling wine called 'Effervescents du Monde' held annually in France. Award-winning bubbles from a pile of rubble!

That was just a trial run, really, for something even more exciting. In 2003 Barbara decided she didn't have enough to do, and that she would like to enjoy some of the fun part of wine. (The bit I had reserved for me.) It so happened that our Henry had a soulmate at school called Ben Postlethwaite. Barbara and Cherry Postlethwaite would meet at the school gate. Ben and Hen, as they were known, were the perfect combination on football fields – their ball-addled brains apparently fused together. Whereas Barbara the businesswoman and Doctor Cherry the artist who'd lived amongst vineyards near Modena, when her husband Harvey had run Ferrari Racing, couldn't be more different. In 1999 Cherry was tragically widowed. Shortly after, she wistfully told Barbara how she and Harvey had planned to plant an English vineyard and had bought the stony field next to their house a couple of miles from where we live in south Oxfordshire. The dream had died with Harvey. So, of course Barbara said, 'Why don't we...' And they did. They went on winemaking courses and started planting. Wyfold Vineyard was the result. Maybe they thought it would be a bit of a laugh. A hobby. But that's not how wine works. And it's not how my wife works either. Wyfold showed immediate promise. It actually won the first competition it entered, a strange-sounding event called 'The Judgement of Parsons Green' which pitted all the top English sparklers against each other plus a group of champagnes for reference. This was supposed to be the Fizz version of the famous 'Judgement of Paris' mentioned earlier where some Californian wine upstarts had beaten France's finest crus in a tasting held by Steven Spurrier. Steven himself was, I believe, on the Parsons Green panel with a lot of MWs. And they voted Wyfold the best. That changed everything. Driving obsession time now. For Barbara, normal. Ever since she took over as our Managing Director she has driven everything very hard. She now wanted that pole position again. Wyfold has won a lot of medals. No way is it a hobby any more. Barbara, indeed, was incandescent when some bloke at HM Customs wrote and told her he considered 2 hectares to be a hobby. I only ever before heard her swear like that when she was in labour and the anaesthetist turned up late saying sorry, he'd been watching the rugby. If she could, she'd have that HMRC guy out in Wyfold in the snow pruning for six hours. Thinking of starting a vineyard? I wouldn't if I were you.

Henry did, though. Having done holiday jobs in various vineyards and wineries since he was 16, been a Flying Winemaker, been a 'barrel monkey' at RedHeads, had a winery of sorts in Sheffield for the love of his lady, and then a much more successful one in Bordeaux, Henry, with Kaye, finally found his own stony hillside above Marlow, Bucks (that noted centre of gastronomy). Their hillside was even more stony than Wyfold. Extreme stones. Flints so big and sharp they constantly destroyed his tyres and machinery. Vineyards require constant harrowing to keep down weeds. And so it got its name: 'The Kaye-I'm-going-round-with-the-*Harrow*-today-*and*-I-just-bloody-*Hope*-it-survives Vineyard'. Edited down a bit, it works as a name. Those two are resolutely independent and I have learned to respect that and leave them be. It's all their own work. And, by God, I'm so proud of them. I'm proud of all my sons. They always respectfully listen to their dad. No, they don't. Not in the least! But they are, actually, what I'm most proud of. Anyway, my genes must be in them somewhere. Henry and Kaye winning another gold or the trophy for Best English Sparkling Rosé... again!... makes me much prouder than when I used to win the occasional medal myself. And they've given us two grandchildren as well, who seem to like to join in on the bottling line. The third winemaking generation is already here!

In 2011 we planted our fourth UK vineyard in Windsor Great Park, on land leased from the Royal Farms. This we consider the greatest honour. I grew up in Windsor and, as a boy, roamed all over the Great Park. So when our Windsor shop and Anne Linder started a conversation with one of its customers from the Castle, Sir Michael Hobbs, which led to us being offered a choice of sites for a vineyard, I was able to choose one behind the Copper Horse, that huge statue of George III, 'Farmer George', on horseback that stands at the end of the famous Long Walk. It's a lovely spot in a private part of the park that I'd never got into before. Sheltered by a copse of big old trees to the north, a gentle slope runs south and west down to The Great Pond. We took soil samples and sent them via a champagne-grower friend to be analysed in Champagne (being vague about just where in Champagne

Barbara leaf-stripping at Wyfold.

they came from), and they passed the test. Only later did we find out our vineyard is next to what are still called The Vineries, where until the 1950s grapes were grown – but for eating, not wine. I was able to reassure Her Majesty that the Royal Archives revealed that during the reign of Henry II there was a vineyard at Windsor Castle, on what is now a patch of grass just to the right of the main gate. Perhaps that is not so surprising – the king was, after all, married to Eleanor of Aquitaine! What we do know for sure is that our site is now producing a very excellent English sparkling wine that seems to be much appreciated up at the Castle. Sources tell us it has already been poured for a few European heads of state. How I would have loved to have seen their faces when told what it was!

THE VINTAGE FESTIVAL

There was another way we came up with to show off our closeness to the vineyards when, in 1980, we moved into 'showtime' by hosting the first London Vintage Festival.

I had done plenty of wine tastings in people's homes and at the Arch, and with *The Sunday Times* Wine Club we'd started doing bigger tastings all round the country from the Shetland Isles to the Scillies. But another one

*Promo material for the
Vintage Festival.*

of those early morning ideas arrived: wouldn't it impress customers –
and be fun for us – to get all our wine producers together in London to
meet and chat and get a load of customers along to meet them and enjoy
their wines? '*Du producteur aux consommateur*' as I wrote on my van,
couldn't get any direct-er than this: growers from all parts of the wine
world actually talking to each other and to our customers. We get around
100 wine producers to meet around 5,000 wine-lovers. I knew others had
had a stab at doing wine fairs, but they always seemed to fizzle out after
a year or two. I wasn't exactly sure why, but having gone to a couple I
reckoned it might be due to customers getting totally blitzed and falling
over a lot. This would not impress the winegrowers. So they wouldn't
bother to come again. But I believed I had customers who might behave
more rationally. We would make it an all-ticket affair and aim it at just
our good customers. There were still a few incidents at first. The worst
was me getting into a fist-fight with the booze-inflamed hall manager I
had inadvertently interrupted working hard on staff relations with an

attractive cloakroom attendant. We'd spilled wine on his new carpets too. The next year we changed halls to the wood-floored Royal Horticultural Halls, and all has gone smoothly ever since. The festival – these days in the Old Billingsgate Hall on the Thames – now breaks even and the friendships formed with winemakers keep a lot of customers loyal to their new friends' wine as well as our Wine Club and our Company. Growers have always said they love our customers because they are 'so interested'. I have only ever missed one session of our London event, simply because I don't ever want to miss any of that show. That's well over 100 parties... err 'sessions'. Some winegrowers like Carlos and Anna Bujanda, and Paolo and Anna Rita Masi, have been coming for over 30 years now – it's their annual treat too. They enjoy London and seeing customers who have become real friends.

On the first morning of the festival we used to invite wine writers, merchants and experts to taste all the wines and award medals. The idea was that the winning wine on each of 12 tables would go into a mixed case: *The Sunday Times* Dozen'. The bottles were all masked and the results often surprising when 'unknowns' beat the famous. (Which was my cunning plan.) We got the odd keen customer along to help. Ronnie Corbett was one, Ken Livingstone another. All sorts! I regret that we discontinued *The Sunday Times* Dozen tasting some time ago. But it has now been superseded and surpassed by the much larger *Decanter* and *Wine* Challenge tastings.

THE WINE TREKS

The 'Wine Trek' idea came to me one stormy evening at La Clarière in 1984 as I watched a fleet of massive thunderhead clouds sailing up the valley, all lit up inside with flickering bolts of lightning like that scene from *Close Encounters of the Third Kind*.

'This portends something' was my thought. Next day I was setting off on another buying trip up the Dordogne and beyond. I resolved that this time I would take proper notes and then write a log of the trip, detailing where I went, who I met and what I decided to buy. This I would send to my customers with the offer of a mixed case of the wines purchased en route so they could retrace my trek via their wine glasses. It worked in one way: people liked reading about my treks and they were left in no doubt that I really did spend my life trawling vineyards around the world. But sales were not great. Well, in truth, they were appalling. Few people wanted a mixed case of wines they'd never heard of from wine regions they'd never heard of but I ignored that small detail and persisted for many years round France then all over. Well, it was fun for all, so why not?

MADEIRA

Thanks to the booming Wine Club I now had to explore the entire world of wine.

All of it. Lucky old me. Every wine country and every type of wine. As an example of a unique style, here's a note about going to Madeira for the first time. In 1982, I guess, as Barbara came along on this one, heavily pregnant with Will. I remember I had a great time in the cellars of the Madeira Wine Company. At that time they still had bottles from the nineteenth century for sale... at reasonable prices!

> *We drove to the wine district at Câmara de Lobos, the biggest pocket of winegrowing on the island, and saw terracing disappearing up into the clouds. The taxi groaned steadily upwards from a highly aromatic fishing port, to the first level of vineyards, where it is warm enough for banana groves as well as vineyards producing the very grapes needed for the sweet Malmsey Madeira. Heading further upwards we enter into a better class of housing – smart villas apparently for those who've done well in America and returned. The air is clearer and cooler, the views nicer. This is the Bual level. Not as sweet as Malmsey. Up higher, the affluence and temperature decrease somewhat. The bus routes stop here. Level three is where you see the levadas, Madeira's amazing system of little irrigation canals that wind around the hills, offer gentle walks to older hikers and water to the thousands of bedspread-sized terraces clinging to the rock walls, growing orchids, fruits and vegetables. Virtually anything from anywhere will grow on Madeira provided the Evaderas agree to blow their trumpets and divert you your two hours' worth of water per week from the gushing little canals. This*

Tipping the grapes (Alionza)
Castelfranco '85

is Verdelho level. Yet higher it's positively cold and depressingly poor. Two small children warm themselves by a burning cardboard box. Urchins beg. Not nice. Men work in strange spaniel-eared pointy woolly caps, standing on baskets to prune the vines on pergolas 5 feet above the earth. The ground itself is needed for growing vegetables. They don't waste space on steep Madeira. In autumn those self-same baskets are full of lovely white grapes and stacked by the roadside to be taken to the lagars. This is the Sercial level, the driest of Madeira's and the one I like best. Still sunny but, 1,000 metres up, cold, windy, misty and wet, it feels distinctly North European.

VALTELLINA

I've never lost my passion for the 'less well known'. Here's a place in the Alpine foothills of Valtellina in the South Tyrol where I went with my guide, the American wine writer Burton Anderson.

The following morning we attacked a fiercely steep hairpin climb to 6,000 feet to cross, at alarming speed, the high Alpine valleys between us and Valtellina (I don't think we paid any attention to the contours when we planned the itinerary!). Cuckoo-clock houses, forests and cows with bells and, so they say, crazy, inbred locals. No vines.

Passing the last of the ski-lifts, which look so pathetic in summer, we first glimpsed, far off and far below, some of the most extraordinary vineyards of Europe. Nothing had prepared me for the sheer verticality of Maroggia, Inferno, Valgella, Sassella and Grumello: the five zones of a wall of vine-hung rock towering up at least 500 feet.

The quickest way to locate the best winegrower in any area is to go to the best restaurant, be ever so nice, tip heavily and ask the patron his advice in such a way he will not just send you to the place that gives him the biggest kickback. Today, after heroic efforts with the incredibly heavy local cuisine, we got a good tip and went off to hunt down two brothers. We found one on a roof. But he came down and took us below to a very impressive collection of old casks. And even more impressive old bottles. He dug out a 1945 covered in an amazing fungoid overcoat. Valtellina reds impress me because a) they are made from Nebbiolo (here called Chiavennasca)... the great grape of Barolo, b) they are grown on these amazing cliffs where they harvest by ladder! and c) they give the wine away! Ridiculously cheap prices compared to Barolo.

NAVARRA

Treks were not just about wine. In Navarra

Barrero the Basque and I found the road blocked when we first turned up at Cintruénigo. Crowds of people. Fiesta. Man said the cellar would inevitably be shut, Director would even more inevitably be in his favourite bar. Preparing for festivities. Went to bar. Groups of florid gentlemen, obviously well lunched, were well into some competitive Spanish singing... who could project most distress loudest for longest without drawing breath. Two early-round losers were giving close inspection to the cracks in the lino. Could not find the Director and the Barrero became agitated... 'Bloody Spaniards' (he's a Basque). OK, we'll leave the car and walk there. Crowds quite dense in the town centre. Lots of smart white outfits with red bandanas and berets... Basque uniform... confusing. Very solidly constructed, these barricades... and every road systematically blocked off. 'Barrero, why are we walking so fast and why the defences?'

'The Bulls,' he says.

'The Bulls? You mean like Pamplona?'

'Sure. Doanworry.' (His favourite expression.) 'Bulls here are no so fierce. Walk quickly and we be OK. Nearly there. Anyway they send up a warning grenade when the bulls come.'

At that precise moment there was a loud bang!

Barrero sprinted. He's a big lad, eats well, but he reached and shot right up the nearest 6-foot barricade in seconds. I followed. From our perch we then blushed to see little old ladies calmly finishing their chats before hobbling into their doorways. Boys, girls and men of all ages stood their ground. There was competition to stand where the street was narrowest. Then there was shouting and movement. Just before the dark shapes arrived people shinned up drainpipes, swung from balconies or crammed into corners. But then the bulls. Poor things. For bulls, read cows. And very bored, scrawny, knackered-looking ones at that. Though they did have big horns. And used them. And one big bull did appear as a very funny-ha-ha surprise when we'd all got back down. Never did get to the cellar that time.

One day a customer sent me her publisher son, who took my trek letters away and turned them into a book. You can still find *Laithwaite's Great Wine Trek Part One* in secondhand book shops. Usually £1. I've never stopped visiting vineyards but so far Part Two hasn't emerged.

THE WINE TOURS

Throughout the 1980s we continued with the wine tours, another way of demonstrating our unique vineyard links.

I loved leading tours. I still lead them twice a year, but now they are for our staff as we insist everyone in the Company gets taken to the source of it all, the vineyards. I especially liked the early wine trips because they got me to places I might otherwise not have got to. Plus posh hotels, top restaurants, the Orient Express, the Star Clipper, sort of thing. Plus it was like a travelling drinks party. You meet people, some you know already, many you don't, but you always seem to get along. Because you have a common bond: wine, the world's great social lubricant. Strangers at the beginning, sworn lifelong buddies by the end of the week. So maybe it turns out otherwise, but it's great at the time. *The Sunday Times* is a name that opens every door and Hugh Johnson is a name that opens every cellar door. You just need a good organiser. Bill Brenchley, David Walker and 'The Blasters' (Arblaster & Clarke), we've – that's my customers and me – been spoilt by them all.

There was a special trip for the Wine Club's tenth birthday in 1983. We flew a Boeing 737 of Club members plus Hugh Johnson and Frank Giles, the editor, to Bergerac and held a huge party in the great Château de Monbazillac. At that time Bergerac didn't have an airport, just an airfield for private planes. The town got excited... in different ways. On the one hand someone went round daubing '*Non aux Boeings*' on walls; on the other Monsieur le Maire and his Conseil, plus the Town Band, all turned out for us. They, Barbara, our three very small boys and I stood waiting as the plane flew in, circled, circled, and kept on circling above. Worrying! But it wasn't anything technical. Just the Members up there refusing to rush their last glasses of champagne. It was a great party that started up in the air.

Talking of champagne! Our most popular trip was The Champagne Bus. This wasn't surprising as the moment they left Victoria Coach Station, passengers would be enjoying their first flute of champagne. Two days later, as it arrived back, they were finishing their final one. In between they'd been over the Channel, across France, down a few champagne caves for tastings and lunches by flaming torchlight, and dined in style. On the first trip I found myself next to a chap who turned out to be the

CEO of a very large company. I said I thought he wasn't classic coach-tripper type. He replied that spending three days being told what to do every moment, with the accompaniment of plenty of champagne, was just heaven for him.

THE SHOPS

Also at this time, we started opening more wine shops. Our own shops this time, not franchises.

Had things taken a different turn I suppose we could have ended up like Majestic or Oddbins with hundreds of shops. Did we have a choice? Logically yes, but it has always seemed to me that it's the Company itself that has decided which way we would go. Not me. I mean I do come up with ideas. But it's the Company – staff and customers – who decide which ones we finally follow. We had our shop in the Windsor Arch, and we sent out our mail order stuff. Then along came *The Sunday Times* Wine Club so mail order really took off and the idea of shops, while not forgotten – I'd never let that happen – became a sideshow, in numbers anyway. But I've always loved shops. But by that I mean shops that might now be called old-fashioned. I like small shops. I don't like to shop in big supermarkets. Nothing personal, chaps, but it's just the way my heart

A Jo Denis painting of a typical shop.

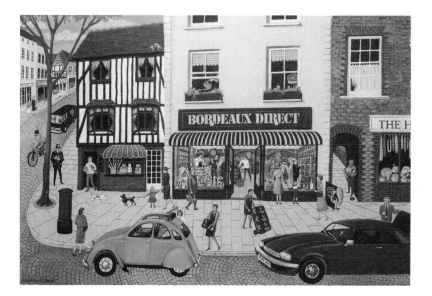

sinks when Barbara gives me a shopping list. It's just a chore! That's wrong, shopping should be a treat. Even everyday shopping. As a boy, I used to love the old grocer's where they gave you a cheery hello and a bit of banter and a slice of ham to taste or if you were a child a broken biscuit. And these days, all those tantalising smells have gone. When I was at Durham Uni there were two free treats I gave myself. One was the town's wonderful covered market on a Saturday morning; the other, on a cold, dark winter's evening, was to go into the grocer's with the steamed-up windows on Framwellgate Hill and walk slowly round, inhaling aromas of freshly ground coffee, cheeses, bread, cakes, and bacon being sliced. It wasn't necessary to buy anything. Just to inhale.

Do you see what I mean? You probably don't if you are young because there are no smells today, everything is wrapped. Anyway all this stuff was in my head and I wanted to open shops inspired by it.

So they were and still are small in size and number but they smell of wine. Though I'm not now allowed to put sawdust on the floor any more. Our railway arch in Borough Market is big, but the others are small. No prime high-street sites for us. At first we made our own fittings, often recycling wooden wine boxes. I think we still use some wine bins that I

Tasting at 'The Arch' Borough Market store in London. Underneath the railway arches, again.

made myself. But the shops' key feature was, and still is, the staff. They must be lovely people. I learned to worry less about their wine knowledge and more about their sociability. The girl with a first-class degree in French who insisted on correcting her customers' pronunciation of wine names didn't last long. But another – from the same shop – who used her holidays to go and visit our producers so she could excitedly tell customers all about them first hand – well, she's still with us.

We got pushed out of our original railway arch in Windsor. A shame. But we set up around the corner in what had been Mrs Battersby's sweetshop when I was a schoolboy. She sold 'penny drinks'. We can't quite manage that but we do give free samples. Our shops encircle London, with one near Birmingham, one near Manchester and one in Nottingham. I keep up my habit of doing one of my commentated tastings in every shop every year, a 'pour and bore'. Son Tom and I sometimes do a double act. So I'm glad we don't have 200 shops!

Our shops may not have those old grocery smells but we do have our 50-year tradition of the tasting table. Sip, chat and relax. Rush round all your other shops but in ours... slooooow down. Your heart should lift as you pass our portals. Mine does. And you don't even have to lift your case to the car: we still do old-fashioned service.

CELLARMASTERS

A rather unlikely thing also started in 1980.

Back in that exciting and rather crazy decade, for some daft reason I helped an Aussie called David Thomas clone our business model down in Australia, thus creating what became our biggest competitor: Cellarmasters. Doesn't sound like such a clever business idea. This has been mentioned to me. But actually, over time, it proved to be a very good thing.

I had got a letter from David in 1980 while he was working at Tasmania House, saying he'd like to meet to discuss him setting up something like Bordeaux Direct or *The Sunday Times* Wine Club in Australia. I found him working at the reception desk in the small building. We immediately got on well. Seems he'd had a business in Tasmania, sold it, was now

BLACK STUMP

❋

BLACK STUMP DURIF SYRAH IS OUR BIGGEST-SELLING WINE EVER.

When we started doing Australian wines we were very fortunate to be rather ignorant. We did not know that Australians themselves considered wines from the Riverland to be inferior. We would blind try samples from all over Oz and reckoned some Riverland wines were terrific. Riverland is the wine name for the vast Murray–Murrumbidgee irrigation area created in the 1950s in what had been desert. When that region was first planted with vines they had been simply flood-irrigated. This resulted in huge crops of tasteless grapes and wines, which had given the area their poor reputation. This had stuck, as reputations do, despite the good producers there having long since installed drip irrigation such as is found almost everywhere else in Australia. And the resulting wines with much less water in them could be as good as anywhere and won the awards to prove it. We and our customers realised this before most Australians did. Durif is a grape variety that also gets sniffed at. Again, we didn't know. It's been our best seller for years now. Unknown grape, unknown region... might indicate my customers are as perverse as I am. No, it's just bloody good wine.

helping his government out in London and 'doing Europe', while looking for a new business to get into. Wine appealed and he'd looked at various wine companies and thought we had the style he liked best. He was always against 'stuffy' old wine merchanting so he came to me for advice. I didn't realise it then, but this was the start of a big switch for me.

David asked if I'd explain how we worked and offered me shares in his start-up. I turned them down, saying I'd rather he just bought all his European wine through me. This was possibly my most stupid business decision of all, because it turned out that Australians back then did not want or need any European wines. He went off and started Cellarmasters in 1982, partnering with American Express. It went OK, but not great. It was just David and his powerhouse wife Barb and a couple of friends when I first visited them in Sydney. He had plenty time to take me on a tour of wineries from Melbourne's Yarra across to Adelaide.

But then, just as things were going wrong for us in the UK, his business hit a vein of gold. He did an offer to customers of Westpac bank and it went stratospheric – three times better than anything they'd ever done before. It was just a slip of paper in the bank's monthly statement. The same sort of 'continuity' offer we did: a mixed quarterly case of nice wines. He built on that success, doubled his business in three months and suddenly he was Australia's largest wine retailer. Direct marketing is a mysterious art. I admit I was extremely jealous.

Then I became very worried as Cellarmasters built on this success and grew and grew, beyond Australia into the US, Europe and even the UK! David and I had exchanged lots of ideas at first but I reckon he gave me as many as I gave him. Then he had a heart attack and had to pull back. The man he handed over to, Terry Davis, a tall ex-Olympic rower, was different. He very much wanted to acquire our business which was, in 1988, having a shaky patch and so he piled on the pressure. But that was actually good for us. Nothing motivates like fear. They were stressful times but we now had this real threat that made us dig in and raise our game considerably. Can't have the Aussies beating us, can we? They grew fast but eventually we grew faster. Cellarmasters today is still the dominant direct supplier of wine in Australia but is now part of Woolworths, the biggest overall wine retailer (they sell over half the wine in Australia) and is no longer trading overseas. I think the No. 2 in Australian direct sales might now be 'Laithwaite's Wine People'. More of

David Thomas.

that later. But David and I have always stayed great mates. We FaceTime each other and are co-chairmen of our own mutual admiration society. He was in the news recently when he gave a huge chunk of his fortune, $40 million, to help save the Great Barrier Reef. He's a good bloke is David.

David coined the title 'Wine Plans' for the 'continuity offers' that we jointly evolved over our period of working together. Continuity is a direct marketing staple. Remember book clubs that sent you a book every month – are they still around? – and today there are people who will send you boxes of chocolates, nuts or razors – and even underpants I'm told – on the same basis once you have signed up.

It started for us when I noticed that as our customers' confidence in us grew, many of them, presumably busy or maybe just reckless, began to say, 'Oh, I don't know what I really want... just send me some wine.'

So I did, and then I offered to do this for others. I said I'd pick my wine of the season in spring, summer, autumn and winter and the obviously named 'Quatre Saisons' was launched, and took off well. Quite well. My first (winter) wine was a big Madiran, my second a pretty Jurançon for the spring. I so loved my little wine regions of France and now I was able to place what were, for those little estates, really huge orders, and so get much lower prices... which the customers appreciated. I wish I'd continued with that programme. However, I didn't, because it then dawned on us that, really, we ought to do this with our signature offering, the mixed dozens, because they were what customers mostly bought. So we did. In Australia David did too and we both experienced the enormous sales which took us both to the sort of size we are today. David rocketed there in a matter of months. We proceeded more sedately. I think David hit the million-bottle mark first. But we got to the million cases first. Wine Plans – where a customer asks us to send a case of wine every three months – were our secret weapon. Secret, that is, until Terry Davis showed Marks & Spencer how to do them and then all the other supermarkets followed. But that's how it is supposed to go in business! We do remain, though, the most successful at it.

TRAGEDY

It would be wrong to see this decade running entirely smoothly and serenely. There were problems and disasters all the time but my mind has managed to erase most.

But I can't forget the time when David Wright, our lawyer who had become a Non-Executive Director, informed the Board that he believed we might be trading insolvently. Luckily the loo was just next door as that completely unexpected announcement had such an alarming effect on me. In truth I was entirely to blame. I wasn't in the habit of testing my offers to customers which is what every textbook on mail order says you absolutely have to do or risk disaster. They are right, and I proved it. I must have thought I was so clever. My offers always worked, and I believed my creativity had to be given free rein. Every month my customers were mailed a pack of leaflets and a selection of wines that were completely different to what they'd got the month before. Every mailing was different in layout, format... even paper. And this worked... right up until this time when one didn't. One such failure we could cope with. But then the next month's offer also failed, and that started pushing us over the edge. Except it didn't quite. The legendary Laithwaite luck lived on. It turned out we were just about OK and I made bloody sure the next offering contained only wines that had all worked well before and, thankfully, did again. With one mailing, we were free! Ade Bentham (we met him earlier in the book) who didn't like me calling him Captain Careful, started to take over more of the work on mailings. I didn't want any more brown trouser moments.

But one came anyway. Due to Bloody Computers! We'd been computerised since Barbara started in 1972. One IBM system followed on another, nice machines, few problems except when the guy who had modified all our programs suddenly left us. He'd made no notes of what he'd done. So we didn't know how to run the things. We had to get a new machine and we got sold – it sounded so good at the time – this all-singing, all-dancing big new thing called Mailbrain. They called it a 'turn-key' system. As the sales patter went, 'You just turn it on and it does what you want'. We innocents believed this and bought this very expensive big box. And we turned the key. It started processing our orders so we keyed in the customers' orders and cheques. But then, the money didn't come out again, so it didn't go to the bank. So the bank rang up and said: 'Where's our money? You are way overdrawn.' And we said, 'It's in the machine' and unsurprisingly they said that was no earthly good to them. So that Friday afternoon at close of play, this cheerful bank chappie called and said: 'Look, if you don't get us our money by Monday we will have to foreclose on you. Sorreee!'

Prepare the brown trousers! I could get nothing from the Mailbrain office. It was shut. Desperation time. Then I remembered that the installer they had sent to us kept a horse somewhere near Newbury. This was before we all had mobile phones so I got in the car and drove round the pastures of West Berkshire asking for her. I eventually and miraculously found her and almost literally dragged her off her horse into my car and back to Caversham. I wish I could remember her name but this great woman rose to the challenge and spent the weekend toiling in our office, still in her jodhpurs. Finally, as the clock ticked down like in the finale of a Bond film she got the machine to start coughing up the money.

We learned a lesson. There is no such simple thing as a 'turn-key system'. If you buy a fancy system you must also hire a clever person or two who understand the thing and can master it. Or it will eat your money and you too.

I really should have heeded my mum's words. She worried a lot, did my mum, and was fond of warning that 'Life is always waiting around the corner... with a great big stick.'

There was one catastrophe which was far, far bigger than the rest. My friend and dear colleague Tim Bleach, our first employee, just out of

ALTA TIERRA
CHILEAN SYRAH

✳

IT IS HARD TO BELIEVE TODAY THAT IN THE EARLY 1990S WE WERE THE ONLY COMPANY IMPORTING SERIOUS AMOUNTS OF WINE FROM CHILE.

Thanks to Hugh Johnson, we had discovered the Los Vascos Estate, founded on classic Médoc estate lines by Vascos (Basques), the Eyzaguirre family, and long before it was acquired by the Rothschilds. It was this wine that showed us the way forward. We sent the great Australian winemaker Martin Shaw as a 'Flyer' to work with a family company called Canepa in their brand new stainless steel winery. What he produced stunned everybody. He used new oak barrels from Burgundy instead of the traditional huge Rauli wood foudres. Chile has always grown fantastic grapes but given more sophisticated handling... wow! Martin produced eight different varietals and they blew people's socks off. That's how we started in Chile, but I have chosen a more recent find: our great counterintuitive wine from Chile, Alta Tierra Syrah. For wine with more fruit character, you'd assume it would be a good idea to look to the southern, cooler parts of Chile. But weirdly, we found the best wine far to the north, on the edge of the Atacama Desert. How on earth?! Well, it's to do with high altitude, with super-clear air and the cold Humboldt Current. It almost never rains in the Elqui Valley, irrigation is from channels built by the Inca, and the – literally – blinding sunlight creates phenomenal rates of photosynthesis which result in super-intense flavours.

school, was a key part of our still small team. We shared the office, the wine-buying and so much else. Big, beardy Tim, the 'Neanderthal' as Bob Mendelssohn, our German supplier, affectionately called him, had decided, in the early summer of 1988, to do another big buying trip like we both did all the time. He flew to Bordeaux, hired a car and drove over to and around the Midi, then south over the border into the Barcelona area, then west to Rioja and finally down to a new area for us: the Ribera del Duero. He was then going to drive on to Madrid, drop off the car and fly home. It was a normal sort of trip, a lot of driving but covering a useful range of winegrowers in a short time.

But at Bordeaux they didn't give him the proper car. I had always been a bit worried about accidents (wine and driving are not a good mix of course) and insisted we should pay a bit extra and always get a really solid car, but Avis didn't have one, so they gave him a little one... and him, such a big bloke. His trip complete, he headed towards Madrid. It had been a successful trip and he would have been happy to be heading back home. He stopped to fill up with petrol... and then drove out on to the wrong side of the road. It was early in the morning, he'd have been perfectly alert but that wrong-side-of-the-road-abroad thing happens a lot. We've all done it. He was in that small car in the days before airbags and he hit a Mercedes head-on.

He was taken to hospital in Madrid. I flew out with his wife Josianne. We went with plans to fly him home, but the sight that greeted us at the hospital forced a rethink. He was all wires and tubes and drips, but seemed cheerful enough, and had nice nurses. It was an immaculate, friendly hospital and all seemed better than we feared, so I left him there with Josianne, and he was fine with that. Three days later Barbara and I were visiting family up in Glasgow and when we arrived they said: 'We've had a call, it's bad news.' The hospital had decided to get him up, as he was on the mend. They got him out of bed but there was a blood clot. It went straight to his heart and he just dropped dead. He wouldn't have known what hit him. It was devastating for Josianne of course, but also his delightful mother and sister and all of us who worked with him. He was such a very likeable bloke. God, the laughs we had had.

HEART ATTACK

It was summer 1988. I went daily to console Josianne but she gradually turned on me because she said we should have flown him home.

I can understand it now. Not then. She really went for me – I found that almost more distressing than losing Tim. The upshot was I started getting chest pains. I remember driving to Bordeaux and back with my chest aching all the way and I had Henry – aged eight – with me. Then the pains got really bad. The doctor, at first, thought it might just be bad indigestion – he knew my lifestyle. But eventually he sent me to see a specialist who said: 'You've had a "silent" heart attack, the left side of your heart is dead. If I were you, I would sell your business, retire and take lots of walking holidays. I recommend the Pyrenees this time of year.' I said: 'But that's almost what I do anyway.' I wasn't going to sell my Company. No way! But I was scared stiff. I was in my early 40s and had been working with not many days off for over 20 years but hadn't saved any money. I loved my work so much, but I was now scared literally almost to death. I began to walk around on eggshells. With a wife and three little boys, I couldn't die! It kind of changed my personality. I thought it had to change. Clearly I couldn't continue leaping about, being the alpha male all the time, I had to become quieter and keep my blood pressure down. So I pulled back. Calmed down. Beta male. Walked the dog a lot. Stayed home more. Barbara soldiered on and actually started making us serious money, probably because she no longer had to cope with me having a bright new idea every day. And I discovered we did have a good little team. I was quite miffed how they well they did without me. I was at home a lot, looking after my dog and my chickens. Barbara started calling me the 'chicken farmer'. She didn't much like the way I had changed. On the other hand she was obviously very worried, and certainly didn't want to be left on her own with the business and the boys still at junior school.

That same year I also lost two other important people: Jean Demolombe, my great friend at Château Pech Redon in the Midi and a terrific finder of wines from all over the Midi, and the lovely Romy Signorini who found me most of my Italian wines. What had happened to Lucky Laithwaite? I kept asking myself, 'What have I done?'

But looking back I'd say our 'health episodes' were almost inevitable. Our turnover was now around £15 million. We had maybe 50 people in

Ade Bentham. Our man in the US – originally recruited to work under the Windsor arches.

Caversham plus the French operation and several shops. I travelled all the time, bought the wine, wrote all our literature, took the photos, set up the shops, did wine tours and tastings around Britain. Yes, I loved it all but it was mad. Barbara ran the Company and the family – as we'd never successfully hired a nanny. So basically we still ran everything ourselves like we had since the beginning. We were what in the US they call a Mom and Pop operation. But a rather big and complex one.

So suddenly I felt vulnerable. My heart required five pills a day – it still does – and was checked up on regularly. But at least I was on the cardiologist's radar. That's the good thing with heart problems – 'they' keep a check on you. And there's a lot they can do now to prevent further attacks. The people who die of heart attacks tend to be the ones who are not being monitored. So much progress has been made in my lifetime. I can remember my father saying that virtually his entire sales division at British Aluminium had heart attacks. Hearts were a huge problem back then. I eventually returned to work, but went slower and never back to the non-stop way of working that I had in the first years of the business.

It was the non-stop excitement that kept me going in those early years. But that level of excitement and pumping adrenalin was apparently now dangerous. I did soon start working more or less normally again, but

I would stay at home writing, and not travel so much. I did, as they say, spend more time with my family. That was really the silver lining. I did get to enjoy my boys growing up. I took them to school throughout their years there and came home early every day to pick them up. Without the heart attack I might not have seen them growing up as so many dads don't. Those three were a lot of fun. Annoying, but great fun. Still are, actually.

I had an office, and my title was Chairman. In theory I was still in charge of marketing. I already had Ade Bentham to help me do the writing; I picked him because he was the funniest writer we ever had... genuinely very funny. I came to realise later that despite the jokes he was also a very clever guy. But it was the jokes that got him the job. He now runs our American operation and he's still as funny. They love him over there. It was good working with Ade. We worked together on the mailings and batted stuff backwards and forwards between us. Hilarious times like it had been with Tim. We sold more wine because of what we conjured up in our joke-filled sessions. We were much more effective writing together than I had ever been on my own. And it was a lot more fun – 20 years after we started! Barbara was very much more in charge and for the first time ever we – she – actually made proper profits, in 1989 and 1990.

THE NEW VINTAGE

HANDING OVER

Barbara and I had finally realised, after her brain haemorrhage and my heart attack, that before something really did us in, we might be better off – maybe live longer – if we got someone else to run the Company. Maybe a whole team.

Le Chai au Quai façade by night and day.

We didn't know if that would work. I, like most entrepreneurs, was convinced that only I really knew how to run things. But the other option of selling the business did not appeal at all. That would be the end of life as we knew it. So we went looking for our team. We decided they would be handsomely paid but, after the Dolley scare, would never own shares and never handle my letters to customers. We realised the CEO, CFO, COO, and all the other acronyms you must learn, would hold the key positions in our multimillion-pound company. They would be the people who ran it. Not us. Now, turning over £15 million, we had a rather big and complex operation. So we started looking for people who would continue to take the Company in the right direction – our direction. In 1991 we handed over the running of what Barbara had finally – after 20 years – turned into a profitable business, to a full management team, with Greg Hodder taking over Barbara's role and Ade Bentham and Anne Linder taking over most – but not all – of my buying and marketing role. This produced a long period of good and profitable growth in a booming UK market. In a decade we went from £15 million to £100 million. Puffing and wheezing, repeatedly checking I still had a pulse, I tried to keep up. But from now on I had to accept I would never again be able to do exactly what I wanted with the Company. I accepted I had to learn to persuade and cajole rather than just give orders. Maybe I even welcomed this. I had come to realise I wasn't infallible. I also realised that, in fact, it was fun working with a talented team and we somehow managed to get a great one. They stayed together for 14 years and grew the Company extremely effectively.

Anne was definitely not Greg's favourite. He basically tried for years to sideline her, just didn't take to her, thought she was crazy. She is a bit crazy, but then, if you think about what she did, she had to be. Anne will never forget her first buying trip. It was to Yugoslavia. She was on holiday when I had my heart 'do', got recalled immediately and despatched, in my place, to Yugoslavia. All these old guys with big moustaches in a smoke-filled room, astonished to see a young girl turn up in my place. A girl? Frowns all round. Not friendly at all. She battled on through the tasting and the deal-making. Then there was a knock at the door and a completely new team of big moustaches filed in while the original lot left. No eye contact between them. Not a word. It was a foretaste of the war soon to come, but she knew nothing of that.

Getting into Czechoslovakia, just as the Berlin Wall was coming down in 1989, was interesting for Anne, when a local junior school teacher Vladimír Moškvan was the only English-speaker we could find. He helped Anne find wines from Znojmo (Moravěnka) and Saldorf (Archioni) and also the Primátor beer which we still sell in great volumes.

Anne also ran Flying Winemakers from beginning to end, sending Martin Shaw to Chile and Canepa and then Tarapacá with Claudio Cilveti and lovely old Hector Rossi.

She then put Martin into Vipava, Yugoslavia (now in Slovenia), to make our Alpi Juliani wines. When the civil war actually broke out, she had to conclude the deal in the army barracks opposite the winery. There was then a memorable goulash in a vineyard hut in Villány, Hungary, with Éva Keresztury and Ede Tiffán... to the sound of artillery, not that far away. Anne, Ade and I got hysterical and wrote my obituary crying with laughter, too much Villanyi Burgundi (local Pinot Noir) and too much paprika. Then apparently we ran into gun runners in the dead of night in the countryside.

I was sound asleep at that point but it seems our cars were flagged down by some shadowy figures near the frontier. Our driver got out... then rapidly got back in again and we sped off fast. We were not the convoy they were expecting – we didn't have the guns!

Anne's been robbed, threatened with a knife and meat cleaver, beaten and tied to a tree in Moldova. No, that last bit was just the lorry driver. We lost the lorry and the wine. Wine-buying is not always a cushy life.

In 1992 Anne helped create the first Farnese wines with three chaps in a single room above a chemist's in Pescara. Those three 'boys' went on to build one of the most successful Italian wine companies and moved from over the chemist's to a beautifully restored medieval turreted castle.

She remembers a lot of work in Spain, discovering, digging out and renovating a deep old cellar full of great earthenware *tinajas*, the Finca Muñoz – it's far from boring, our life!

In 1997 we discovered a powerful, fiery red in a cellar just across from the fire station in Cariñena. 'Fireman' in Spanish is *el bombero*. So guess what we called that wine. There just isn't room to tell all the stories!

Alex Fraser, an Anglophile Australian, became Marketing Director. I had thought he'd help produce mailings for me but no, it turned out he was a pure direct marketer; a 'numbers man', though very keen on wine – *very* keen. There was also big David Hamilton who Barbara recruited as Finance Director, mostly because with his thick shock of hair he reminded her of her dad – just twice as tall. Like Harry he was a strict Scottish 'Ne'er a borrower nor a lender be'-type accountant. David also took on Personnel (known now as Human Resources) where he happily dished out the traditional old British response to All People Problems: 'Oh pull yourself together, man!' In Philip Diamond we finally got a proper IT person – like he actually understood the computer. We didn't understand him, but still, things worked better. Ade didn't realise how scared of dying I was. So he thought it was a brave decision to invest in senior management. 'We were an odd bunch,' he remembers; 'Greg brought his Primrose Hill aesthetic, powerful drive and fierce temper ("red mists" as they were known). Alex was smart, lovable and chaotic; David was shrewd, patient and sensible; Philip was Philip. I was starting to figure out how to persuade customers to part with money.'

Ade became Wine Director, covering both buying and selling because we knew from experience it was unwise to separate the two. You get a lot of fights if you do.

On the subject of fights...

PILLASTRO PRIMITIVO

❋

SOUTHERN ITALIAN WINES WERE, FOR SO MANY YEARS, LARGELY OFF LIMITS FOR REASONS WE COULD NEVER UNDERSTAND AND WERE TOO NERVOUS TO ASK ABOUT.

But today they dominate Italian sales. Customers love all that richness, warmth and bold, ripe fruit. Pillastro comes from Puglia, in Italy's deep south, best known for big, smoky wines mostly made from the local varieties Primitivo and Negroamaro. Made by Angelo Maci, one of the leading figures in the Southern Italian quality revolution of the last two decades, and whose cellar Cantine Due Palme has twice been named Italy's Winery of the Year. Angelo made this wine purely from Primitivo, which produces rich, powerful reds with plenty of ripe fruit. But its real secret is a period of oak ageing, something previously little heard of in Puglia, which lifts what was a rustic sort of wine into an altogether classier league. At this moment in time Southern Italy, including Sicily and Sardinia, is probably our most exciting source of new European wines. But of course, this may – probably will – change. Many people are worrying about the effect of climate change on warm climate wines. While that is a logical thought, it does not yet appear to have any effect on sales of their wines.

❋

CHIEF EXECUTIVES

In the Company's 50 years we have had five Chief
Executives, all much brighter than me, but none with my
odd, sideways-thinking – lateral – brain.

Faced with any problem or opportunity, my brain doesn't see the logical
next step, but tends to take me off in unexpected directions. It's perverse
and drives people mad. Results can be ludicrous but sometimes it works
quite well. I regard it as a blessing. Not sure anyone else does. Barbara,
the first Managing Director, coped with it for a long 20 years. The hardest
years. No one's ever matched that. Then came Greg who notched up 14
years, then Oliver Garland who moved up from being David's successor
as Finance Director to MD but who unfortunately didn't stay long. Nice
bloke, Olly, and very brainy. But the life of a CEO where tricky stuff of all
sorts just comes at you constantly from all directions isn't for everyone,
even the most cerebral. After him, Simon McMurtrie, who we brought in
to accelerate our moves into overseas territories, stepped smartly into
the CEO job as a quick emergency replacement and did seven years.
Finally came David Thatcher who has done six years so far and promises
us a few more. Each has been very different in their style, personality
and in their relationship with us. It is not an easy relationship for either
them or us. Quite tricky really. Fighting is quite normal, I'd say. We want
our Chief Executives to take charge and make the Company perform
better than we could. And then we complicate things by expressing our
wishes somewhat vaguely as 'Make it beautiful'. But then Barbara and
I do come from the 1960s. 'Peace and Love, man!' We know the sort of
company we want. We know when it feels right. But this may not be the
same thing as maximising Company performance. The CEO wants to
be praised and rewarded for his or her talents in increasing turnover
and profits but he or she is doing it for a family business – a business we
see very much as 'ours'. We brought it into the world, and it carries our
name. So, inevitably, there is conflict.

We found Greg Hodder when he was Marketing Director of the kitchen
company Smallbone. It had been extremely successful with its big, full-
colour ads in all the glossies. He was responsible for all that, and he had
in fact helped set up the company with founder Charlie Smallbone. It was
very clever marketing that I much admired. It was beautiful and subtly

conveyed the impression – without actually saying it – that the company had been around for centuries when in fact it had only just started, but with that perfect name, it just sounded old.

The remit we gave Greg was 'Polish the Rough Diamond'. We thought we already had a terrific company with a few unique ways of introducing people to wine and earning their loyalty. It just didn't run smoothly. He and a full team of directors should sort that, we thought. Barbara said she would pull out after a few weeks of joint work and she did, she really did. Greg has always said he hadn't believed at the time that she really would pull out and leave her 'baby' to him, but she did. I didn't pull out because that wasn't part of the deal. I wasn't going to retire. Just sit back a bit from the coalface, maybe. I wouldn't, from then on, be carrying the full load. As long as I kept the team's support I could 'direct' the marketing and buying but I wouldn't be responsible for bringing the sales in, and wouldn't have to cope with all the daily hassles. At first it all worked quite well. Then it got difficult... for me and for Greg. As, while we wanted it 'polished', we didn't want our Company to change too much, but of course it did. The 1990s saw our image change. There was also that new thing called the World Wide Web, and we started, very slowly, becoming an online wine merchant. Our newspaper advertising now showed the same few wines – always at close to half price – while the number of wines we actually listed rocketed up from being in the hundreds to the thousands. I was not quite sure why. I had made a point of always knowing every wine we sold, as well as its producer and vineyard. But in the mid-1990s I found I could no longer keep up with so many new wines and had to rely on a growing team of buyers. Barbara and I stayed as Co-Chairmen on the Board and tried to follow things as closely, while not being involved so much. So began a period when, as we were less involved in 'the everyday', we hoped, standing back, to see a wider view of our whole business. So we'd be able to make more sense of what we were doing and evolve a few good strategies. Inevitably the Company did, in fact, change a lot and it grew very big. We had, some time before, put in place a profit-share scheme for the whole Company. This was particularly effective for Greg and his senior team. So of course they went all-out for profits. This was a bit of a change from my time. But hugely effective. I might bleat that we were losing our way a bit, losing cherished wine suppliers, and that hammering relentlessly at our £39.99 a case recruitment advertising, while it got us very well known, did change our image from 'great wine sleuths, discovering many new wines, wine regions and even wine countries' to now being the 'cheap and cheerful online wine supermarket'. But when sales are surging up, profits too, and the entire Company is looking forward every year to ever-bigger profit-shares then, well, I was wasting my breath. We changed.

So there, I had my moans. Plenty of them. But that was just on the personal front, for the business was going well... very well. There were, I think, two reasons for that, apart from us just being good wine merchants.

WINE PLANS

First, those Wine Plans: more and more customers really liked to be offered an 'effortless way to wine' where we just sent them mixed cases of wine four times a year.

Sales rocketed. Then our new Marketing Director pointed out that book clubs (where he had worked) recruited their customers by offering heavily discounted books upfront and that we could do something similar. We did, and sales then really went off the scale. Responses were in their thousands. So we were able to take full-page ads in the Sunday papers. In the colour magazines mostly, but also in the main paper. Full pages! Bit of a step up from going round Maidenhead with leaflets!

Then, realising that there were, of course, more people who liked to choose their own wines but might nevertheless like a spot of advice and maybe even a free taste, we introduced an alternative scheme with the name 'Premiere'. Customers did have to pay a subscription, but then they could order whatever they wanted and every time would get a couple of free bottles to try. When just two orders had been placed the customer had got back their subscription... so the sample bottles from then on were effectively free. It, too, was a successful scheme. It's still going and better than ever as we have got cleverer at sampling Premiere customers only with the wines which we and our software have worked out will be to their taste. Everyone's taste is different.

Secondly, we had realised that *The Sunday Times* had been such a success because so many people could see us. They gave us lots of space. But also, crucially, there was this confidence thing – if *The Sunday Times* said it was

more inside

When we started allowing customers to ask us to choose a wine for them and just send it, that proved extremely successful. But we had to choose right!

OK, it probably was. It wasn't then like it is today; back then people were not at all confident about wine so they had to be reassured. They didn't trust their own palates. So the thought occurred to us that if the reassurance of *The Sunday Times* name was so successful and gave us such a good profile, why shouldn't there be more links with other prestige companies? Back in the 1980s, Barbara and I had been to see Barclaycard and made them a wine club proposition. They were really interested when we showed them a spreadsheet on our new personal computer – an 'Apricot' the size and weight of a suitcase full of bricks with a tiny green screen. And would you believe it? The marketing division of Barclaycard – a bank – had never seen a live spreadsheet before. They were so impressed! We did a deal that worked very well. When Greg arrived he quickly spotted that 'continuity' Wine Plans and Third-Party Wine Clubs were our main USPs. So he focused (not something I could ever manage) on this breakthrough and seriously ramped up sales. What Greg saw when he came was that when you put adverts in all the papers with a case of wine at half price, people will sign up: 'Yes, I'll take a case every quarter.' He saw that as the key to it and he really, really just kept pushing that button and tweaking the model. The numbers went up and up. I was concerned that there would be a limit to the number of customers interested. But there didn't seem to be. While the 1970s and 1980s had seen a gradual and steady growth, the 1990s under Greg's leadership saw sales begin to rocket. When we handed over to him it was £15 million turnover. He quickly got it up to £50 million, and we thought 'Cor!' He then got it up to £100 million. 'Cor blimey!' When it went over £200 million and kept heading higher, we were deprived of speech. It revolutionised everything. Our whole lives. About then *The Sunday Times* started doing its Rich List and I was on the first one. I remember well that moment when our boys burst into the kitchen; 'Dad, Dad, James says you're in the Rich List!' and I thought 'Oh no!... no more are you going to be sweating over homework now!' This, thanks to the very paper without which we wouldn't be anywhere near the Rich List. Thanks. My simple idea of Bordeaux Direct had now become a size way beyond anything I had ever imagined.

There was a catch. Which was that to keep the big numbers coming in we kept our prices low. But the Chancellor kept putting up the rate of duty on wine, VAT, social security... everything. To the taxman's repeated disbelief, we have never gone in for any kind of tax avoidance. There are times when I think we might be daft, but my father had – literally – beaten his strict morality into me, and Barbara is so very Presbyterian. Carriage costs also increased and the price of wine from the producers of course increased. The result was that the wines we were known for became too expensive to fit in our mixed cases. Amazingly, but almost certainly wrongly, we didn't increase the price of our recruitment cases for about 20 years. The wines were good but maybe not quite as interesting as they had been. To me anyway. We still sold many of our traditional wines but they no longer appeared in our advertising, so, as I said, our image changed.

THE STRATEGY MEETINGS

I took the Board off together once a year on some memorable trips, what we called Strategy Meetings, in lovely wine country locations which I thought might spark more inspired ideas and thoughts than just sitting round a table in the office in dull old Caversham.

At the Strategies I would try to launch us in bold new directions.

At the first, near Bordeaux, I wanted to encourage greater realisation of the importance of showmanship, the entertainment aspect of wine. I wanted the Board to just look at what those great Bordeaux châteaux do! If that isn't 'theatre' I don't know what is. All that flair and pizzazz. Nobody but nobody knows how to market wine better than top Bordeaux wine people.

*As wine warehouses go,
our Gloucester cellars
are pretty big.*

They actually invented the whole 'fine wine' game, and they still play it better than anyone. Who else gets pages of copy devoted to their wine every year on the day they decide to let people have a little taste of it for the first time? Who else then sells wine in such huge volumes for such vast amounts, even when nobody actually gets their hands on it for another year and even then are told not to drink it because it's still unfinished, so must wait another three years? Is there any other product in the world that gets away with stuff like that? People do howl and complain, but the *grands* châteaux just do their collective Gallic shrug and put their prices up yet again. This feat I thought deserved closer study by my lot. But I suppose it's difficult to see how how the workings of Château Lafite relate to how to run our Company. I think I failed with that one. It is possible to dismiss it all by pointing out those châteaux took 200 years to build their brands.

However, Ade did at this time start introducing many more of the great wines which are usually called fine wines on to our list. I've always been a bit dubious about that term, implying as it does that most wines are not 'fine'. I dispute that. Every wine we sell is made with finely honed skills and tender, loving care. Anyway, the amount of wine in the so-called 'Fine' category that we sell still grows steadily almost every year. We have a climate-controlled storage facility in our Distribution Centre where we store such wines for our customers. At any one time we will have over £50 million worth of their wine stored there. I find that astonishing. One chap arrives by helicopter to collect his occasional cases.

At the second Strategy, in Alsace, I suggested we debate 'The £1 Billion'. Standing back from the business, out of the heat of the kitchen, I had time to come up with crazy deep thoughts like this. I don't think I seriously thought we should aim at sales of £1 billion but I just wanted my lot to see that if they raised their eyes from the daily struggle, they would see that there was a huge global market out there and that there was no shortage of good wine to be found and sold. So there was no real limit to how high we could go. Mad dreams can actually happen. In Florence, another year, I asked for us to create a 'workshop' – I believed the whole firm needed to be more skilled, to become craftsmen. Florence just makes you think that way.

In Seville I wanted them to stop being so cautious and slow – to jump into a few new things. There hadn't been any really new things introduced recently – Greg was certainly 'polishing the diamond', but maybe we could find more rough diamonds? We were seeing success – big growth, big profits – but it was distorting our image and I feared we would pay for this later on. I also began to feel that with Greg and me it was becoming a question of 'This firm ain't big enough for the both of us'.

Our growth could suggest it was easy. But there were plenty of struggles. Keeping the business growing by 20–30 per cent p.a. (a target Barbara had established early on) was getting harder and harder as the numbers just grew bigger and bigger. We tried to start up in France and Germany, but pulled out each time, basically because our home market was just so good.

But at one of the last Strategies, in Madeira, we made the momentous decision to start working in the US. Why this obsession with going overseas? It seemed to Barbara and me that all our eggs were in one basket, the UK basket, and while it was at that time a good basket with wine sales growing fast – well, you never knew what was round the corner, waiting to whack you with a big stick. What actually happened was we all discussed where we'd expand to and all agreed it would be Europe, which, as I said, we had tried a bit. Then, at lunch Greg and I got together and just the two us decided that was all wrong and we'd go to the US instead. Today I am very glad we made that call. Unpopular though it was that day.

A MOTLEY CREW

Many, including us, have wondered just how come we've managed to sell so much wine – it does run to £ billions, against competition from massive supermarkets and wine merchants with reputations going back hundreds of years.

We appear to succeed when logic says we should not. We once asked Wine Intelligence, our industry's think tank, to take a look at our prospects. They came back and said we had none; nothing they could see anyway. So what is it we do? Jancis Robinson mentions my 'whimsical charm and lateral thinking... operating outside the wine trade mainstream' which doesn't really seem enough to justify our results. And Jancis possesses the most incisive brain in wine. If she can't work us out, who can?

I remember at one of our more formal parties blurting out in a speech, 'I mean, just look at us, a motley crew, and yet they say we are the most successful wine merchants on the planet!' (One paper had said exactly that.) Mad planet, then.

Maybe it was due to no one (including me) really understanding exactly how we market wine, but the one problem that part of the new team had was marketing. Marketing folk came and went rather rapidly, but a core of talented, committed, hard-working, fun-loving people stayed the course and created whatever it is that is seen as the Laithwaite house 'culture': Anne, Martin, Sarah, John and Nikki Kemp, Dan Snook, Helene, Tina, Sophie, Jean-Marc, Fiona and many others. They were the alternative wine trade, down-to-earth, self-deprecating, distinctly uncorporate but highly commercial and deceptively ambitious. It was a work-hard, play-hard business. Parties were frequent (they started with pizza parties at the Red Cow), liaisons (even marriages) were made and unmade, ambulances were not uncommon – not least for Alex who would tumble off his bike regularly, navigating home after another evening with his spreadsheets and a bottle of red. He and his mangled bike feature prominently in the triptych that Jo Denis painted of Caversham days.

Heart-watching old me didn't join in all Direct Wine's parties like I had before. But I didn't just sit around at home thinking deep thoughts. Barbara certainly didn't – for her it's a physical impossibility to sit still. Barbara just has to be working or she gets very unhappy. I can just happily sit and stare... but not if I see someone threatening to overtake us, then I fly into a frenzy, dodgy ticker or no. I am very competitive. Over the years we have faced a whole string of bright, young challenger companies – at least one a year – but mostly not very good. Selling wine seems, on the surface, quite easy, so many give it a try without too much thought. And like with Hollywood, people with money from less interesting industries get involved to add some after-dinner party conversation to their portfolio. Rarely works.

I had to chill down. I started doing yoga thanks to the wife of a local GP who thought it would keep my blood pressure down. And our own doctor, who is also a great friend, suggested a little stress-free break would be good too. In his mind this meant no airports and minimal driving. So Doctor John, Lindsay, Barbara and I went to Canterbury for a few days one February and listened to choral evensong in the vast, darkened cathedral, which is a marvellous uplifting and soothing experience even if you are not particularly God-fearing. During the day we wandered around the cathedral, the museums, secondhand bookshops and tea rooms. We ate well and enjoyed it so much that the next year we went to York... and then the next year to Chester. It became our annual winter calming treat. And it has never stopped. After 30 years or so we've 'bagged' almost every cathedral and cathedral town there is. We recommend it. It really is very calming and inspiring.

I still did plenty of actual work stuff. I slipped out of buying and selling but carried on working, in niches that fitted me, and on activities the others didn't quite 'get'.

My main interest lay in trying to direct undirectable young Australians in our increasingly ambitious Flying Winemakers programme. Then making sure what they produced was well packaged and marketed. So I spent a lot of the 1990s being driven round our own winemaking sites in Europe, kept away from the wheel, and mollycoddled by Anne, who was convinced that with the slightest stress, I was going to die on her. Flying Winemaker or Own Production wines peaked at over 20 per cent of our turnover, which meant we had become a major league wine producer even though we then had no wineries of our own, barring little La Clarière.

I don't think it was really planned, but at this time we acquired some other companies. Averys' German owners asked us if we were interested and as I had known Ronald Avery and liked John. We agreed to buy them, and promised we would give them back their buying independence. We also bought another company called Warehouse Wines which had been set up in Preston by a charismatic young entrepreneur called Jay Wright. Then Richard Branson offered us a struggling Virgin Wines for free. This had been set up by Rowan Gormley. A customer who had met Rowan wrote and said I really should meet him as he reckoned we were very alike. I met him and yes, we were alike: two lateral-thinking creatives. He's more of a serial entrepreneur though, setting up Virgin Money and other businesses, while I can only do wine. South African Rowan had long been keen on Wine Clubs. His first was called Orgasmic

Wine, his second Virgin Wine and his third is Naked Wine, now part of Majestic. I always thought he got the names in the wrong order. Anyway Virgin had not gone well so we were offered it for nothing. We showed Rowan how to do things our way, how to turn it round and he did. It worked well, and quite independently for many years. Then there was a big falling out, often mentioned by Rowan – which our new CEO at the time, Simon, saw in a very different light. They just didn't trust each other, those two. Simple as that. It happens. And so Rowan left and we moved the young Jay Wright and his Warehouse Wines in to take over a merged Virgin/Warehouse company.

Bordeaux Direct actually disappeared when it became 'Laithwaite's WINE'. Not before time, as many still persisted in thinking we only sold Bordeaux wines when patently we didn't. We now sold wine from 27 countries... and counting.

Basically, Greg didn't invent new stuff, but he certainly did what we had asked him to: he polished our rough diamond. Plus he grew it enormously. With his favourite word, 'focus', he made our people just stick to the key things that made such a huge difference... and he put it round – *sotto voce* – 'Bin all memos from Tony about any bright new idea'. I could never have focused like that. Me, I still focus on the new idea I'll have woken up with that morning. Sort of like a 'one-night-stand businessman', me.

As wine warehouses go, the Wyfold barn is rather small. Barbara, Henry, Kaye and co labelling and packing Wyfold.

Our Windsor wine shop.

One area that did not appeal to Greg was the Laithwaite shops. He didn't see them as a useful contribution to the Company which he wanted 100 per cent focused on the success of mail order. Their viability was questionable. He wanted to close them down, and I was horrified. So I spent a lot of time struggling to save our shops. I no longer saw our dozen or so shops as a nascent nationwide chain. But I did see them as the best exponents of proper wine merchanting. They guarded a precious jewel: the sublime art of keeping good customers happy and keen. Someday, somehow, I wanted all our customers to be looked after this way; meanwhile the shops had to keep those skills alive.

The shops were copies of our Windsor Arch; they were where the close personal customer/wine merchant relationships were warmest. My shop people, as far as I was concerned, kept the pure essence of our business growing healthily and strongly. Only problem was... they lost money. Not a lot. If you did the numbers in a slightly different way – my way – they broke even. I had to ask – beg, in fact – to get them saved. And they were. The deal was: 'Shops, OK, we'll keep them, but you must look after them and they are not getting any more money.' So the shops survived, under their leader – a lifelong, dyed-in-the-wool retailer called John Knapp, who I always thought of as 'Sgt Major Knapp'. To him, I imagined, I was wet-behind-the-ears 2nd Lieutenant Laithwaite whom he had to obey, but at the same time keep out of trouble. Together, we had to find ways of our shops surviving in their own division, without handouts from the main mail order company. We managed it. While John instilled sound retailer disciplines and was the finest motivator of young people I ever met, I encouraged constant creative development. We had always kept details of our customers and their preferences on index cards. John got a young programmer to convert this into a programme on the new PCs. Amazingly, he did, for just a few hundred quid – at a time when we were already spending hundreds of thousands on our mainframe. So while I did what I could to ensure our shops people acted like individual entrepreneurs and took decisions of their own, John drilled them into a well-disciplined force. Sounds like a recipe for conflict but John and I enjoyed going round the shops together and stubbornly made it work. They had a lot of libberty, did our shops... just as long as they phoned in good sales to John every Saturday night.

One way of keeping the Company culture intact was our parties. The organised ones rather than the local pub riots. We held a lot. We still do. A summer party – now done healthily with games at a local cricket ground – and a Christmas party. Some legendary parties have gone down in Company folklore, not necessarily for the right reasons. But mix a few hundred young people together with wine and rock 'n' roll and what can you expect? Of course that's all changed now. Older and wiser. No more kangaroo outfits, no more large chaps leaping from giant cakes (note: we've always been strong on gender equality). We even have speeches now, though I discourage that.

Barbara and I didn't totally give up trying to influence things. And I still enjoyed parts of it. People have said that with the money now pouring in, this would have been the time any normal people in our position would have sold up and headed for Barbados. But I don't think this crossed my mind. (I'm not so sure about Barbara's.) After all, convinced from the outset that this business would never make money – and for 20 years it hadn't – I had set it up to be just a very enjoyable business for me. True, it was no longer quite so enjoyable as I wasn't allowed to do exactly what I wanted any more, but touring vineyards was still as pleasant an existence as anything else I could envisage. And selling out seemed to have many drawbacks. We had extracted £1 million when we handed over in 1991. Just in case everything fell apart. We had invested it in stocks and shares... and promptly lost half of it. Better, it seemed to me, to have your money tied up in something that you understand and can more or less control than put your money in stocks and shares which you don't understand and do not control at all. Bill Symonds had told us to beware of the City. He was right! We remember visiting our friend Sacha Margeritoff who ran a similar business to ours in Germany. He had just sold his business and assured me it was all perfectly wonderful. But as we talked, I saw he couldn't stop himself constantly, nervously, checking share prices on his screen. 'My buyers would like to buy you too,' he said. 'Just think, you'd have lots of money and could continue doing what you love. Just once a month you'd have to come over and report to our group of German bankers.' Sacha never did understand why we turned that idea down. We did go to Barbados. Thought it very nice, but got bored after a week. Rum and Coke only gets you so far!

But I still felt that the atmosphere of the Company was changing and despite the growing profits, I didn't like it. Despite all the success, the 1990s were my least happy decade. My philosophy was still 'Make it fun, make it exciting'. That way, though work might be hard, it doesn't seem hard. And playing, well... any excuse for a party or drinks, and along the way plenty of jokes. I see the people I work with as friends. It is our culture that goes back to the first Arch with us all crammed into our packing-case office. And I always reckon if I hear laughter, things can't be too bad. But Greg's harder attitude changed the atmosphere within the Company and not necessarily for the best. And I, post-heart attack, wasn't the man I had been. I was a bit of a wuss. I didn't stand up for our principles. But it's a strong culture, is ours, and it survived. Maybe went underground a bit. The core of people who had been 20, 30 or more years with us, remembered pre-Greg times. That core, old hands like Ade and Anne, was very important. Greg depended an awful lot on Ade because he himself knew little about wine and wasn't actually all that interested.

We finally outgrew our Caversham trading estate and moved to the other side of Reading, to Theale and a custom-built warehouse with offices. It was grand but it wasn't the same as before. Some soul went. It felt dangerously 'Corporate'. It was so quiet when we moved in. Just keyboards being tapped. Unnerving for those who were used to the rackety, noisy old place. The decibels went up when our Wine Advisors moved in. Nice to hear noise and laughter again but they were on a different floor, which was logical, but not, I thought, a good idea. Because it meant we had two floors: the noisy floor and the silent one. If ever one of our Wine Advisors had to go to the floor above and walk the long central aisle, they referred to it as 'the walk of death'. I understood that. But couldn't do much about it. One brave, very athletic girl, on the day she left, went up to the top floor, sprinted down the aisle and did a long series of backflips, all the way down, like Jake Blues in *The Blues Brothers* film. That showed 'em.

I managed to negotiate a small office for myself in an annexe to the tasting room which had – as it should have – a central position in the office.

There was some good and clever wine marketing along the way, lest we forget. Four Seasons (starting as Quatre Saisons), Wine Options (with Barclaycard), other business partnerships, new wine plan schemes, Premiere/Charter Plus, targeted offers, the launch of Outbound, the Fine Wine Service (it became one of the biggest in the country), wine storage, dozens of strong wine brands, Flying Winemakers.

The uneasy relationship between Greg and myself was getting worse. There was a bit of a disconnect and there was a bit of unpleasantness. It is obviously a built-in thing when you delegate the running of your business to someone else. He was interested in the relatively short term even though we built in some long-term incentives over three years. But that's just three years whereas our family view is there isn't an end to it. It's going to go on for 50 years... or, well, who knows?

Grape selection at McPherson's harvest in Australia.

I disagreed with quite a lot of what he did. I wanted to do new things and my interpretation of that was I wanted to keep up to date because markets change. The market is not a static thing, it's very alive. So it's not just changing the wines, it's adapting to what other people are doing, what your competitors are doing, and what the public is doing. It wasn't just us that was zooming up in the 1990s, the supermarkets were too. Wine consumption went up massively. And the range of wines widened. At the beginning of the 1990s we were, for example, the only people taking Chilean wine seriously and then three years later everybody was doing it. The same thing had happened with the Bulgarian wine: we were the only people, then everybody got on the bandwagon. Australian wine came in in the 1980s and in the 1990s Argentinian wine came on line. In the late 1990s New Zealand came along and all these and more joined what had been just Bordeaux, Burgundy, Champagne, Rhône, Loire, Germany, Chianti and Rioja. Now suddenly there was tons more choice.

We may have led the way in finding new wines and selling them in new ways. Traditional off-licences may have been closing all over the place, but we still had competition everywhere. The supermarkets were doing a better and better job because basically they made wine much more easily available. Most people now put a bottle or two in the trolley when they are coming out of Tesco's but with us you generally have to buy a dozen bottles. We did nevertheless get a few million people to try our cases; they may not all have stayed as customers but they tried us and then it was 'I like this stuff, but I will get it from the supermarket'. We were quite good for the nervous beginner, but once they got over their nervousness they would often go off to the supermarket, which was cheaper and, as far as many people believed, just as good. But a sizeable proportion of people didn't think they were just as good and thought buying from us remained the best way. Thank God. We do pay a bit more for our wine so we do have to ask the customers to pay a bit more but that's the position we have to be in; we can't be down there with the supermarkets, our place is a bit above, and giving proper old-fashioned service too.

It seems odd to look back and think I started with just one wine but then I suppose our success had helped create the market that was now offering such competition. I used to argue with Greg a lot. I didn't want to start fights. Might have killed me – my heart, not Greg. Anyway, what could I say when every year we sold more wine and made more money? That knocked my argument for six. I wanted us to start selling abroad because I worried that the UK was likely to get harder as a market. Greg let me do a start-up. We called it Vinisphere, and launched it in France, then did a bit in Germany... and then he went and canned it all. He reckoned there was no point. If we spent the money in France we would get a few more customers but if we spent it in the UK we would get a lot more customers. I was saying we had to think ahead, we had to think to the future. The UK wouldn't always be such a good market. I am so glad that sometime later when our recruiting costs did escalate in the UK we did decide to go to the USA.

Barbara used to worry about me because she thought I was not supposed to get wound up too much on account of my heart. But Greg and I did get wound up. Our problem was not good for the effect it had on the team, especially Ade and Anne. They were people I had found, brought along, relied upon and were actually now close friends. They were really torn; they were not in a great position. Ade was Greg's favourite, his blue-eyed boy. Ade understood me but he also understood Greg so he had to steer a middle course. There were some bad moments and in the end it got to the point where we decided to get a 'marriage guidance counsellor' to try and find a way we could carry on working together. If we were in the same room we couldn't look at each other... just like a failed marriage. He found a wise woman, a lecturer at the LSE, who came and would take us out, rent a room in some pub, and there force us to look at each other. Then we each had to say why we were unhappy and try to reconcile. It allowed us to patch it up and work but in the end we finally agreed that enough was enough, and Greg left with a very large 'thank you' from us... but why not? Greg had done great stuff.

Greg and Direct Wines parted company in 2005 after 14 years. I know he thought I'd renege on our generous settlement, and was surprised when I didn't. He then joined the shirt company Charles Tyrwhitt, but in 2015 became a non-executive director of Majestic Wine. Now chairman. Mmm! Yes, we are now competitors – well, that's good for the customers isn't it?

I couldn't argue against the success, but would it always go on being successful? In the end the reason Greg left was because I felt we really had to finally accept that the market had changed. Everybody now delivered wine. Most also did wine plans. We were no longer unique.

Customers had much more confidence in their own palates and were more adventurous. But maybe it was mainly because I had got back what we 1960s people refer to as my 'mojo'. It happened unexpectedly.

THE NEW CENTURY

It was lifting that bloody great iron millennium beacon into place that did it. I shouldn't have tried that, because before I knew it I was in hospital.

My quadruple heart bypass came thanks to our village New Millennium party, in the big tent on the village green... 12 years after my heart attack. There are four arteries that feed the heart muscles, and they can 'fur up' with the excess chloresterol found in all my favourite foods. Being unable to refrain from steaks, sausages and cheese, my arteries had had to be sort of 'dyno-rodded' at various times through the 1990s, to prise them open again. But that only partially helps, it seems.

I could feel something bigger had gone now. They did the exploration thing where they inject a dye into you so they can see the state of your arteries. 'Ah!' the cheery chap said, excitedly, looking at the screen, 'you've a good one this time, right by the aorta. We call it the "widow-maker", you need the full bypass... like now. Ready?' Having no time to panic is certainly the best way. It was a bit painful when I came round, but almost immediately I knew I had got more energy; and the blood was moving happily around again.

The operation turned out to be a crucial time in my relationship with Greg. He came to visit me in hospital and I said I felt I'd been semi-retired for a decade, and not enjoyed it. I told him 'I really want to do stuff again now'. I think that was the beginning of the end with him and me. I was out of action for a couple of months but by the summer I was fine. Laughing was the only problem; with ribs just stitched back together with wire, you worry you could just explode open like Monty Python's Monsieur Creosote. Therefore there was to be no laughing. So I started doing things more seriously. At first, anyway.

Then I started 'Tough Developments'. This was a nursery company within a company, for new ventures. Because Greg still resisted most of

HUNTER'S
SAUVIGNON BLANC MARLBOROUGH

✳

TODAY MARLBOROUGH SAUVIGNON IS CONSIDERED MAINSTREAM.

Not in the 1980s, it wasn't. It seems like yesterday, there was me landing in the region's only real town, Blenheim, in something like a flying box-van, to be left alone in a field beside a bus shelter. Lots of sheep. No people. It was my second visit. Hadn't been too impressed first time... here or in any NZ wine region. Then, one grey day in London, a wine hit my palate as nothing had before. I'd been buying Sauvignon Blanc for years. Pungent little grape. But this one exploded. There might have been a bang. Or trumpets? To announce the arrival of an entire new wine nation. Thanks to the man who roared up to that bus shelter and rescued me. Ernie Hunter produced the Marlborough Sauvignon which first demonstrated that New Zealand could do world-class wines. Tragically he didn't live long enough to see his country install itself at the top of world's ranking for average wine price. Where it has remained ever since. He didn't make his Sauvignon. His wife Jane was the viticulturalist, and Dr Tony Jordan oversaw the winemaking. But beaming, gift-of-the-gab Irish Ernie was the overwhelming force of nature who made it all happen. He died so soon after but in his few years shook up the wine world so much I was asked to write his obituary for *The Telegraph* in faraway London. The Australian David Hohnen then planted the block next door and in creating the Cloudy Bay brand carried on brilliantly where Ernie had left off and New Zealand wine has never looked back.

✳

HUNTER'S

Jane Hunter

Winemaker : Gary Duke

Harvest Date : March & April 2014

Estate Bottled : Family Owned

2014
SAUVIGNON BLANC
MARLBOROUGH

my dafter new ideas, as was his right. But I was quite within my rights to take some of our profits or potential profits to set new ideas going. Other people in this position buy yachts. Or racehorses. I preferred to set up a Beer Club. Then a Sherry Club. Then a wine bar. Then a food company called Estate Bottled Foods. Then RedHeads. They all sort of worked but, apart from RedHeads, didn't quite. Once again I was taught that lesson about not spreading yourself too thin.

THE CANCER

In 2005, Barbara was diagnosed with cancer.

The doctor in Reading found a tumour in her colon, thought it was probably benign, but operated successfully it seemed. As she was recuperating after the operation, he burst in late at night and said: 'It's cancer!' She was there on her own, while I was having a celebratory dinner with friends and they had to rush me back to the hospital. She had to recover from the operation then start treatment. So we carried on, and went to France as normal in August with the warning that, if anything appeared a bit dodgy, we were to go to the hospital. One morning it did appear dodgy. So we called the ambulance and rushed her into hospital in Libourne. The guys there were very good, they booked her straight in and X-rayed her and said the gut lining had burst, the stitching had come out, and peritonitis had set in – chronic peritonitis! They would have to operate immediately but unfortunately the guy who would normally do it was on holiday; that's France in August! This young guy said he was a general surgeon and he would have a go. It was either that... or... well, it just had to be done. They whipped her off and Dennis and Claudy from the French office sat with me until late that night. It took a long time. She seemed OK, but he said he had to give her a bag, a colostomy. She was then put into intensive care. Every day I would go and see her, the usual crowd of friends who were staying with us would come in too. She was there for three or four weeks, the hospital was very good. I think maybe better than we would have got here in the UK. I mean, the trolley comes round with bottles of *wine* in Libourne hospital! She lost masses of weight but did eventually come out and came home. I can't remember how it happened but we ended up going up to the Royal Marsden and the guy up there was wonderful. David Cunningham just gave us so much hope, and was so inspiring. He and his whole team were so positive. It is a very good hospital, as everyone knows. We went every month for the chemo. We'd make a day of it, and go out for a nice lunch, then she would have all this stuff dripped into her as we chatted. It was actually a nice atmosphere at the Marsden, quite amazing in the circumstances. After many weeks the results came through that it was all OK. But she had to have the colostomy dealt with and through the Marsden we were sent to the Basingstoke and North Hampshire Hospital and we met up with Bill Heald who was very senior in that sort of thing. He was sort of semi-retired from doing the surgery but liked to take on challenging cases and Barbara was a challenge apparently. So he did the operation and successfully reversed it. It is the mental thing with these people, it is so much to do with how they give you confidence. Or don't. Some might be quite talented but just don't give you much confidence, and you must always keep your optimism. Throughout the whole thing our relationship changed. Normally she is in charge and she tells me what to do. For a period I was in charge and I told her what to do – I quite liked that, actually. The Marsden carried on checking for three years and then finally in 2012/13 they said 'all clear' which was lovely... really lovely. Barbara has since helped other acquaintances of ours who have had the bag thing. It is something people are really embarrassed about. She was somebody they could talk to about it. It is a thing you just have to get your head round. Anyway the Laithwaite luck held. The brain haemorrhage could have done for her and logically the cancer should have; it wasn't good odds but the luck held.

STILL TRAVELLING... MOLDOVA

And the wine travels and treks still went on, further and further afield.

Even after 30 years we still found new countries to go to for exciting wines. In 2001 we sent Jean-Marc to help make us wines in Moldova. Moldova, when he finally found where it was, turned out to have the cleanest fruit ever. So I rented a plane to get more of us over there. Most people don't even know where Moldova is. Squashed between Romania and Ukraine, it's on the western edge of the Russian Steppes and is the poorest country in Europe. As we landed, the view suggested that its entire industrial economy might have collapsed, for ruined factories were strewn everywhere. As we circled to land at Chişinău, the capital, it truly looked like the bomb had fallen here. The thought occurred: just how far is Chernobyl? But this is the place that produced the wines of the Tsars – served with fine champagne alongside.

But the air was crystal-clear, and there was, apparently, no pollution. While I thought the city was not very pretty, the countryside was delightful. Like what rural England might have been a hundred years ago. The roads were empty, except for flocks of geese everywhere, and tethered goats and cows. Horse and cart seemed to be the main rural form of transport. Mind you, we, on the other hand, travelled everywhere in a convoy of 4×4s with some large, bulky men in suits, earpieces and dark glasses. Slightly worrying.

But there was lots of lovely dark rich-looking soil and agriculture seemed to be doing well, in a pre-war sort of way. All very organic! Organic was all over the place and got all over you. The silver lining to economic collapse was that they had no chemicals and certainly no GM. They couldn't afford them. Moldovans might be poor but they could eat and drink well. As we found. They clearly wanted to impress, and did. So generously. They also have this thing about proposing little toasts to everyone throughout the meal. And every time they make sure you drain your glass of wine, brandy, vodka, all three, whatever, who cares any more? Where am I? Then they want to dance. It's tough, eating and drinking in Moldova.

Moldovan ladies.

But the agriculture was in good nick compared to what I remember from my visits to Communist Bulgaria in the 1970s. Back then, driving around, I saw great teams of people just sitting around in the barren and empty fields, presumably because that's what they were told to do by the State Farms. Here, when the Berlin Wall fell, they split up the State Farms into individual smallholdings. Alas, these mostly failed. After a lifetime being told what to do every day it must have been hard, suddenly, to become self-sufficient farmers. So they put the big farms back together as co-operatives, which seemed to be working. Well, the wine co-op we saw did. Old and primitive but clean and proud of their work. I think it's something to do with being left alone to sort themselves out. There are no longer any terrible ideas and new initiatives coming down from the men in the Ministry. Mind you, farmers in every country seem averse to that. I noticed the Moldovans hadn't applied to join the European Union. At that time Moldova was supplying vast amounts to Russia. The company we were buying from was doing over 1 million cases to Moscow. And our first shipment from this state-of-the-art Italian/Russian winery (I know, sounds unlikely but it worked extremely well) went down very well with our customers.

Moldova is a northerly wine region, like Burgundy, Alsace, Germany and the Tokay region of Hungary; it has the potential, and indeed the tradition, of making cool-climate wine of the very highest quality and most refined flavour. All it needed was a brand-new, well-designed, well-run winery and some top winemaking talent. All of which it now had. Jean-Marc spent two days combing through hundreds of vats and cherry-picking the best. My role was to distract Moldovan attention from this and attend banquets and press conferences, make speeches, drink toasts and stay upright. Today the Moldovans are still poor, not helped by Putin stopping their wine imports to Russia.

CHILE

Another new discovery was in Chile.

I'd been buying in Chile for over ten years when we suddenly discovered an exciting new region where we thought none could possibly exist. In 2002 we got the first wine made in the Elqui Valley in northern Chile, on the edge of the Atacama Desert. Which still seems illogical to me. Wouldn't we be better off looking to the cool south? But Falernia was

Andean tasting at 5,000 metres with Giorgio Flessati of Viña Falernia, in Chile.

definitely a Wow! To the extent that I remember exactly where I was and what I was doing when I got my first sip. Such intense fruit flavours! How on earth could this be? When Barbara, Tom and I got there we discovered it was due to extraordinary amounts of sunshine, in the super-clean air. They put sunglasses on their horses, it's so dangerously bright. It also never rains – it's all irrigated with channels put there by the Inca. And, crucially, there are freezing night-time temperatures in that thin atmosphere. This is where they put most of those vast telescopes. It's the air clarity. With Giorgio the winemaker we drove right up the valley to cross over into Argentina. The most amazing drive of my life. It's completely barren up there. But there is unsuspected beauty in bare rocks. You get mountains banded with different colours, just like gigantic sweeties. Rock candy mountains. We did a wine tasting of a dozen Syrah samples at over 5,000 metres up. Is this a record? Felt very strange.

PLYMOUTH AND GLOUCESTER

By the time Greg left in 2005 we had outgrown our Theale premises. Both the offices and the Cellars. We had to go elsewhere.

Firstly we opened offices in Plymouth for our burgeoning Wine Advisors. Some would call it a Call Centre. I wouldn't because I saw it as simply us getting more people to do what I once did on my own; wine-chat to customers on the phone. Call centres, it seems to me, are all about 'The Hard Sell'. They pester. I hate them. Everyone hates them. God knows why they exist. We don't pester for one very good reason. Wine is not highly profitable, so you don't make money by making one sale then upsetting people by pestering. You only make money over the long term. Which means you must never upset customers. You must be considerate and learn how only to call them when they want you to, and not waste their time telling them about wines you know they will not want. It's simple really. But what it means is you have to hire just the very nicest people. That's the qualification. Niceness. That's all that matters. Well, also being prepared to learn stuff so as to be able to answer questions intelligently and quickly solve any problems.

I remember the Plymouth office very fondly. I had been worried the nice work atmosphere we cherished in Theale, which we'd nurtured since the Windsor Arch, wouldn't survive the jump to Plymouth. I need not have worried. It didn't just survive, it improved. A team of young people in Plymouth, off their own bat, decided they'd do something about the way in which we talk to customers. They decided our business would talk to our customers in an unusual way. They decided that our customers are actually our friends so we should talk to them just as we talk to friends. So many businesses don't seem able to manage this. They talk a different way; a business-speak way, full of clichés and standard phrases. 'Have a nice day', 'Your business is important to us'... automaton sort of stuff. They decided we'd also do away with recorded voices on the phone. Except maybe after midnight. They created a training programme that gave our staff power... to make quite important decisions quickly, on the spot. The result of this is that since then, whenever I chat to a customer the question I'm most asked is not 'Where do you get your wonderful wines?', but 'Where do you get your wonderful people?'. 'Nothing to do with me', I say. But I am secretly thrilled by the compliment.

Where else but New England? Our office in East Avenue, Norwalk CT.

So it was a very sad day when I had to go to Plymouth and tell them all we were moving the office to Gloucester. I hated it, but I know they hated it more. I miss them. Except that quite a lot moved to Gloucester and if you went to our Sydney office until recently, you'd find the Advisors managed by a Plymouth man and in Connecticut, they're there too.

Why did we move to Gloucester? That's a question we all lay awake asking ourselves in 2006. You maybe remember British Airways opening Terminal 5 at Heathrow? Hit the headlines. A disaster that turned out fine in the end. Well, we had our very own Terminal 5-type opening disaster on Hurricane Way outside Gloucester... which had actually once been an airfield. And we did it just the same. We built a splendid great place, installed all the latest kit... and the thing just didn't work. But today it is a superlative operation. A joy to behold. We should do tours. Actually I think we do. But that first month... I shudder. Nothing worked. The forklift truck put a wheel through the too-flimsy mezzanine floor. The various softwares wouldn't talk to each other. The headsets that told the packers what to pack in eight languages, just didn't... in any language. I found a girl asleep on a pallet of wine. Some young Russians had time to dig a tunnel under the security fence. It just went on and on. But... my lot got in there – even Simon who was supposed to be in Australia – got in and sorted it. I wrote a grovelling letter with a wine voucher to every customer who could have been affected. They were so nice and understanding. Some even sent the vouchers back, saying they hadn't really been troubled, and not to worry. We survived... but never again! Today, as I said, it's the jewel in our crown. They cope there with everything we throw at them – even Black Friday.

GOING TO AMERICA

We had decided at a Strategy Meeting to try entering the US market, that well-known graveyard for British firms.

In my early days I'd had a disproportionate number of American expat customers living in London. My most enthusiastic customers. I delivered to them, talked to them. They were extremely keen. So in the 1980s I'd been over to New York and met a couple of people in direct marketing agencies who looked at what we did and said 'That'd work here, no problem. Come over.'

But it turned out that direct marketing of wine in the US is illegal. The US wine industry has what they call the Three-Tier System. The three tiers are importer, wholesaler and retailer. These strict divisions were introduced after the repeal of Prohibition, I believe, as a way of preventing the less desirable – well, illegal – sort of booze merchants who had flourished under Prohibition from taking over the whole drinks industry. Under the system you can be any one of the three, and in a few states you can be two. But nowhere can you be all three. Try it and you go to jail. Every state also has slightly different rules. Anyway, we continued to get encouragement and we started selling to the US. This grew, so we acquired the US company in Chicago that had been importing our wines. We encouraged them to try doing things more our way and to try more of our European wines. After a while we realised we had to be more 'hands on'. So we sent over our most experienced guy: Ade Bentham. Basically what we now do in America is to import all of our great wines that we have sourced around the world (and now also in America). The rest of the complicated business of getting the wine to customers is completed through a series of licensed partners spread across the US. Odd, but it works. Ade's first move was to start a new office on the East Coast. So, during a brief exploratory trip (in a seriously freezing February), he wandered into a realtor (estate agent) in Greenwich, Connecticut and told them he had three days to find an office. Amazingly, they did. He ended up with a converted attic with enough room for about ten people.

The first few months were chaos. On day one, there were just four in East Norwalk, Connecticut. Bev Smith (operations) and Helen Gunn (marketing) were already working with the *Wall Street Journal* and had a launch date of September. It was already late July. They were also putting in a new computer system, building a new website, and setting up a new warehouse and call centre with partner companies. It was, says Ade, 'Stress on steroids'. Reinforcements began to arrive from the UK: Duncan Hurley on creative and Nick Taylor on wine and merchandising, tempted by a huge new challenge over the pond in what seemed a more exciting place than West Reading. The *Wall Street Journal* launch was all-important. As important as *The Sunday Times* had been for us back in 1973. Working with the *Wall Street Journal* was also 'interesting' as this was their first such commercial venture brand and there were plenty of naysayers. Ade had to maintain their confidence. This entailed, amongst other things, keeping them well away from that office in the attic – shades of our beginnings with *The Sunday Times* when we'd had to keep quiet about being under a railway arch. Hitting the launch date was touch and go, as they desperately worked at putting a credible website together for our partners. Approaching the deadline, they were doing daily calls with the *Journal* which had rooms full of people looking for Web bugs. At one point, Ade remembers uttering the desperate line, '24 hours is a long time in online', as they pointed out all our faults and threatened to pull the plug on the launch – which was two big full-page ads running in the Saturday edition. Ade somehow convinced them to go ahead and the first wave produced a huge response: 3,500 orders, more than what *The Sunday Times* had produced with its first offer 30 years earlier. Early chatter on the US wine blogs was like '*WSJ* has sold out, I give it six months'. Ten years later, it is comfortably the No. 1 wine club in the US despite having spawned countless imitators.

The first office was an initiation test. Built for 10 people, it had 23 full-time employees competing for space by the time we moved elsewhere. Laptops propped up on windowsills, meetings held in the corridor. The elevator opened directly into the crowded office space... which always threw visitors. Worst of all, there was just one unisex 'bathroom' right in the middle of the office. Ade remembers that recounting tales of his first days at Direct Wines in a damp Windsor railway arch with no toilet at all didn't help the new US staff count their blessings. He also recalls the *Wall Street Journal* senior management visiting for the first time – looking very out of place in their suits and nervous smiles – with Ade praying nobody would need the bathroom.

The early team were united in adversity. A few people (who are still there) wondered what on earth they had done in joining, but, as always, Ade tried to keep it fun, and share each small success. Helen, Duncan and Ade still remember sitting, hungover, in his tiny office laughing hysterically at the previous night's events while a mad squirrel scratched surreally at the window as if it was cleaning it. They stopped laughing briefly as the realisation of all the things they still had to do that week dawned on them, before dissolving in giggles again.

It was a crazy, all-consuming first year. However, by the end of the year, they were in a new, cool office space with a core of talented, hard-working people, in a cleverly converted industrial building. A lot of the old equipment including a massive rusty boiler was left in, as decor. A young country like the US doesn't have a lot of historic stuff, and so treasures anything even vaguely old. Most importantly, the office had developed a happy culture based on good old Direct Wines values that would withstand some major challenges over the years, and create a highly successful business. If the US continues to grow at its present rate, one day soon it will overtake the UK in sales.

OPENING IN AUSTRALIA

As if that wasn't enough, we then decided to start selling wine – as well as buying it – in Australia. I can't clearly remember why.

Except there was this bright young Australian who had worked with us for years, who wanted to go home and asked if we could help him set up a business to sell our wines there. I had already helped David Thomas set up Cellarmasters over there, ten years before. They now dominated the wine direct sales market and, under new management, were not talking to us any more. So of course I said 'Sure, go tweak the lion's tail.' We gave him some money and off he went and joined up with a winemaking mate. But... here's a business tip: if ever you finance a start-up and hear that

Wine education in action – Nikki, Tricia, Scott and Adam in the US office.

the first thing they've done is go out and buy two big BMWs, you'll know, as we learned, it ain't going to work out. Ah well.

So then in 2007 we brought in an ex-publisher, Simon McMurtrie, to be our International CEO. Perhaps an optimistic job title but at least he had a very large field of play. His first day, Simon got on a plane to Sydney in pursuit of the person he rated the finest direct marketer ever. She had worked with him in his previous career as a direct mail publisher in several countries. 'None finer,' he said. I said I reckoned she'd have to be the best because Australia was certainly the world's most competitive wine market. As it happened, we'd just lost our finest young writing talent, an Australian who had got homesick. Andrew Stead is actually Barbara's nephew but that's always been irrelevant. People who can write about wine in a way that appeals across the spectrum from enthusiast to newcomer are rarer than Icelandic Chardonnay. Andrew is an excellent writer. (Has a first-class degree in it.) He writes:

> *I'd just moved home to Sydney. I'd enjoyed selling wine in Britain for Direct Wines. I was wondering what to do next. Then I got a call, and Rachel Robinson and I met at a café. She climbed down out of her 4WD, a tiny foot stretching for the pavement. She's 5 foot nothing. Can that really be her? I'd expected someone bigger. An Amazon.*

They went for a walk from Mona Vale to Warriewood along the beach and agreed that as neither of them were naturally corporate people, they would probably enjoy getting something going in the funny old Direct Wines style.

> *The first office was a single room down a dark alley. Shared an outdoor dunny with other little businesses. [... What is it about our Company and no proper toilets?]*

> *First day we drove to IKEA and bought some basic desks. Then we screwed them together. Sense of accomplishment. Initially we used Wi-Fi from a neighbouring house until we could get set up. They never twigged. Conference calls to the UK would be in the balmy evenings – and a local kid would frequently call things off by playing his bagpipes.*

> *I wore flip-flops and shorts to work unless we were meeting business partners. Then out came what I called my 'McMurtries'. Beige chinos. Rachel was Managing Director and I was Wine Director. In reality there was no one else, but potential business partners didn't know that. I had the song 'Mrs Robinson' in my head for weeks. Goo-goo-ga-choo.*

They moved around the corner to a new office in a converted terrace house.

> *We had a kitchen and a bathroom; so clearly we'd made it. Rachel and I sat down on the blue carpet (there was no furniture yet apart from a white board), feeling very nervous, and wrote a flow chart of what were the best and worst things that could happen. Elizabeth was born the same month. I definitely won't start up a business and a family in the same month ever again.*

Laithwaites.com.au had for some reason been registered by Cellarmasters so we had to look elsewhere for a name. It was 2007 so most decent domain names had been bought but WinePeople.com.au was available and seemed to fit what we do.

Australia did prosper. Not immediately. But the thing with a family business is you can be patient, if it's something you really want to do.

And we did, not only because we do very much enjoy working with Australians, all of us, but because the place has been, over the last 20–30 years, the most creative wine country in the world. Not just in wine production but in wine marketing. So it's given us a lot back. France, as I've said, was my first teacher, but Australia was certainly my second.

OVEREXTENSION

Simon in his role as our internationalising CEO also took us into Germany, Switzerland, Poland, India and Hong Kong.

It was all very exciting at the time but maybe too optimistic. Our talent got spread too thin, or perhaps those cultures didn't quite 'get' us. Suffice to say we tried but we clearly weren't good enough. In business, as I now realise, you have no hope unless you can put everything you've got into it. But we just couldn't, there weren't enough of us. So in the end we pulled out of all those places. As Barbara said at the time, 'Being in seven countries but only making a profit in one just does not add up.'

With so many overseas operations to run, Simon needed more help to run the UK business. The first UK Managing Director was Glenn Caton. He did exciting things like getting our name up on the scoreboards by sponsoring England Cricket and on the airwaves by sponsoring a programme on Classic FM. He really put our name out there. Then, alas, left to go run Cadbury's. We stay in touch. The second was an experienced direct marketer of the old school from the US called Mike Brennan. He postponed retirement for a year to give us his experience. The ex-West Point man gave our troops some hard times, but is still remembered fondly for it. He retired to the town next to where we have our US office. We also stay in touch. Our current UK Managing Director is Philippa Strub. That is certainly not because we feel we must do the equality thing in this day and age. Direct Wines has always been equal opportunities, though I know we've never thought about it much, or planned it. Just looked for the best.

Teresa Graham and Liz McMeikan brought so much fun and smart thinking to our Board that even after they left we still meet up regularly for a jolly. The only reason today's Board is a bit male-heavy is that Barbara and I failed to produce any daughters.

With good grace, Simon pulled us out of most of the countries he'd worked so hard to get us into, which cannot have been enjoyable. He then decided to move on in 2015 but not before he had found us a brilliant new UK Managing Director, David Thatcher, who after a year in that job, seemed effortlessly able to move up to replace him as Group CEO. David is extremely clever. But it's his work rate – I've never seen one like that before. In a man. Funnily enough he'd been recruited by Rowan Gormley to run Naked Wines. But just before he joined them, Rowan changed his mind. So David could come to us. I must remember to thank Rowan.

So not everything works. Still, in today's uncertain times we are happy that our eggs are in the baskets of several nationalities around the world because, like most people, we haven't the faintest clue what the future holds.

PASSING THE TORCH

So what is Direct Wines doing now?

Well, we keep on steadily improving our performances in the UK, USA and Australasia. That last name we use because we are now working well in New Zealand and we didn't pull entirely out of Asia: we operate a franchise model there in both Taiwan and China itself. China is very exciting. Inspiring. But a wild ride!

We do still have a company in Chennai, India, called Redgrape. But they don't sell wine, they write our computer programmes. Generally I only go where there is wine but I make an exception for our delightful and clever people at Redgrape.

I think I mentioned that Barbara and I are now Doctor Barbara and Doctor Tony, thanks to Durham University. And thanks to the Windsor Great Park vineyard I've met the Queen, Prince Charles and Prince Philip and not always in a line-up but informally. As I said when CBS interviewed me, 'If only my mother had lived to see this!' Nana Florrie too – she who started it all off. She'd have been speechless. For the first time ever.

We've won Wine Merchant of the Year, which meant a lot to me because I felt we had at last been accepted by our peers in the wine trade, and I have become a Liveryman of the Worshipful Company of Distillers which means I am also a Freeman of the City of London and can drive sheep over London Bridge. You never know...

I continue to travel and am still discovering new wine places like Georgia. When I say 'new', that's just to me – there isn't any wine place older than Georgia.

But, basically it's now 'handover time'. The next generation have all stepped up. It's their turn now. Our sons launched out on their own. Henry, with Kaye, set up Harrow and Hope winery on the slopes above Marlow and make English sparkling wines, including his mother's Wyfold. They are very dedicated and very skilled, so there have been lots of medals won. Will, our second, who went over to the Dark Side (beer) and set up his brewery Loose Cannon in Abingdon, collects plenty of medals too. His beers have been runners-up in five national competitions. This frustrates him. He feels he's doomed always to be No. 2. But I am sure his single-minded determination will soon get him a No. 1 slot. Our youngest, Tom, went his own sweet way as usual and disappeared to Australia for years until he did a prodigal, returning home to take over as the voice and maybe even the soul of Laithwaite's. Cousin Andrew also returned from Australia to resume working on our writing and creative side, and Cousin Iain returned to us from being head buyer at Bibendum to take charge of the Company's own wine production. He and Tom and a group of Aussie winemakers and growers have recently been engaged in building a new permanent home for the previously peripatetic RedHeads studio winery right in the heart of the Barossa Valley. That's very exciting. The sheds are now up and the tanks are done. Latest news though is frost damage to budding vines. I pray we'll have enough grapes in 2019! It should be open by the time you read this.

Back in Sainte-Colombe we continue to improve La Clarière. The original vineyards we planted are now approaching 40 years old and may be considered *vieilles vignes*. They are in very good health, however, due to the input from an excellent agronomist who nurtures them as they have never been nurtured before. They blossom under her hand. A joy to behold. And the wine they produce is better than it's ever been. We have, over the years, expanded the vineyard from 3 to 30 hectares, allowing us both to welcome more Confrères and to offer all an even better deal. Castillon wines can now sell for as much as top Saint-Émilions. Monsieur has been proved right, as some are getting up towards £40 a bottle. That's from a vineyard with which we share a border. Finally the message about the incorrect geography that I've banged on about for 50 years is getting through. Prices could rocket. Certainly the price of Castillon vineyard land is already rocketing. But we, especially for our Confrères, are keeping our price low. That seems only fair; their loyalty makes us strong. And anyway it's what I stubbornly want to do. I don't interfere much in Company affairs these days. Except when it involves my Château La Clarière and its Confrères. Perhaps strangely, very high-priced wine does not interest me very much. Personally. (I'm very happy for my lot to supply high-priced wines. There is considerable demand.) I have tasted plenty of legendary wines and they are usually very nice. But a £1,500 bottle is never 100 times more enjoyable than a really good £15 bottle to me. In fact I would certainly enjoy it less if I was paying. That's the Boltonian in me, I guess. I can ensure we lavish all possible care and attention on our La Clarière and it still need not cost more than £15. As a result, the number of visits to the château from Confrères is expanding rapidly every year. We have to apologise that there are usually works going on as we upgrade the cellars and buildings, but actually the Confrères like seeing the work in progress and always say they'll be back to see the finished result. This is precisely what I want and have wanted for over 50 years: that people should not just drink my wine but actually join the world that produces it. La Clarière, the vineyard where it all began, is the part of our business closest to my heart. If I'm not there in person, I'm there in spirit, daydreaming about it. Makes me smile. It's my paradise. I share it with many. They dream about it too. I devote most of my time now to it, and also its 'annexe' down the road, Le Chai au Quai: my special bits of our wine world now. So the very centre of my world is still little Sainte-Colombe, making wine from the first vineyards in which I ever set foot.

So where do I actually live? It is mostly the UK but I consider I have never really left Sainte-Colombe since 1965. I still go there as often as I am allowed, miss it badly if I'm away too long, and still get excited every time I go back. It's not just loving the region and its people, it's the La Clarière project. There's nothing on earth that could excite me more at my age. I was there, standing by the winery in the morning sun, just recently. To my left a tractor was deep ploughing where we had uprooted a big patch of vines that were no longer performing. We will plant that bit with radish for a couple of years then put in healthy new vines. Ahead of me, on the steep 'Black Run' vineyard, Vincent our Estate Manager was

Henry, Kaye, cousin Iain, Will and Tom, crushing at Harrow and Hope.

showing a new tractorman how to manage the steep turn at the bottom, which is right on the edge of a 30-foot drop. Get that wrong and we'll need another new driver. To the right a bit were sounds of sawing, as trees were being thinned between our three terraces to let more light in on to the vines. To the left the masons were heaving about massive pieces of stone, renovating the second part of the barrel hall. Jean-Philippe our *gardien* and gardener was mowing the grass up the drive, and Dumain et Fils, the local carriers, were delivering boxes of something, like I've known them do for 53 years. Behind me a painter was risking his life on the winery roof, painting the eaves, breaking every possible safety rule. I was just waiting for Jean-Marc to turn up so we could taste the 2016 wine before it was bottled. All around me the vines were showing their first tender shoots. Such a delicate green. With the sun behind, they looked like thousands of little green lamps. I was thinking, 'Life doesn't get much better than this.' That afternoon, Simon, the local lad who looks after visitors, would be bringing round the day's visiting Confrère couple and I'll be able to show off all of this.

With all this, I really had no problem recently relinquishing my Co-Chairman role after 45 years. There was no need of a shove. I was happy, instead, to become President and Founder, a very undefined role which I

can make up as I go along. Barbara, though, has carried on successfully steering things alongside our new, younger, but more experienced Co-Chairman, Angus Porter.

Henry, Will and Tom continue to take on more and more Direct Wines responsibilities. When the boys were young they hated being dragged around wineries and swore that when their chance came they'd sell the Company and buy a Lamborghini each... just winding me up. But a few years later, in response to a serious enquiry, they said they were in fact all keen to pick up the baton and look after Direct Wines. They didn't say it to us but to the avuncular Peter Happé, who, on Simon McMurtrie's wise suggestion, we'd hired to go round the world, find them and interview them without any influence from us. He knew from previous experience that if family firms don't get the succession right they will not survive. All three have now been sitting on the Company Board for some years. Silently at first but now getting quite vocal. Especially when Barbara and I aren't there. The books we have read about how successful family businesses have managed the generational transfer all advise the same

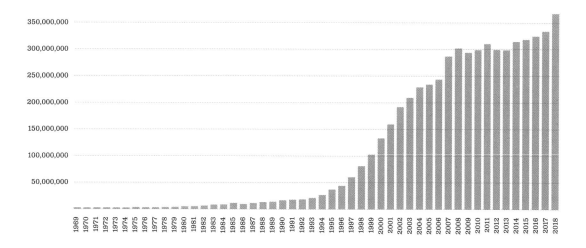

Direct Wines Group –
historical sales in £.

thing: (1) show how, (2) let do, and (3) let go. We've pretty much done all three now, Barbara and I. We are in the process of letting go. But we will never totally leave. This is wine! It is impossible to leave. Who would? We are just doing that generation-passing-the-baton thing the way we've seen it done on many small wine estates in France and elsewhere. By now, I'm well used to turning up at a vineyard we've worked with for years, to find I'm now talking to the son or daughter while old dad is pushing a broom around in the background. I suspect this is what the boys have in mind for me. Barbara and I already get called in to help on bottling days. Well, a bottling line is where I started and it looks like that's where I'll finish.

We've certainly grown. Numbers aren't my thing but I can manage graphs – easier. Here's one that shows how we grew. You'll see we didn't rush things. We are no overnight success. The revenue way back in 1969, by the way, has been estimated at £500 (estimated because I kept no accounts for the first two years. They'd have been too depressing). Anyway, according to the number-crunchers we now sell that amount every 43 seconds, 24 hours a day!

While writing this book, our amazing IT (computer) department put in a new operating system and decommissioned the old software, called WineSeller, which had served us well for the last 20 years. So I was sent some precise numbers. In its 20 years, WineSeller processed 43,877,395 orders from 3,550,230 customers. How many different wines have we sold over that time? We can consider every vintage is a new wine so... Maybe 50,000 or 60,000? Is that how many wines I've drunk? And I'm still alive?

They have even worked out that the cumulative wine sales from day one are now up to £5.6 billion. It would not be unreasonable to assume that the average price of wine sold during that period is a fiver, which suggests that we have now sold over a billion bottles of wine. And of course in doing that, we've done our bit for our country too. Last year alone we handed the UK Government, via taxes and duties in all their myriad forms, something over £100 million. I expect they liked that.

I have tried to explain how our Company got this far, but I have probably failed. Because I really don't know how it happened. I do, however, hope I've shown how a huge amount of luck was involved. It's true, you have to capitalise on your luck, which involves much hard work. Yes, but generally not by me. It's my lot who work hard. Very hard indeed. They really do amaze me and I cannot thank them enough. Personally, I've just never felt that I work hard. I have always thought I was just playing.

I get on very well with my lot, my Company. We all get on rather well. As far as anyone tells me. We have had hardly any serious fallouts. In its entire lifetime our Board has never once been forced to call a vote. Never. That must be unusual, going on what you read in the City pages. There have been disagreements but they have always ended with one side or other giving way. I'm only talking about the senior level in the Company. But that's the only bit I really know about. Elsewhere in the Company I suspect there have been fallouts but I endeavour not to know about those. Basically, we all get on, and people stay with us a long time. Our statistics for customer and staff longevity at Laithwaite's are, they say, only beaten by the better sort of high-security prison. Hundreds of customers have been with us from the 1970s, and are still going strong. (It's the wine that does it.) Monsieur and Madame would be pleased by that. Every month we celebrate anniversaries of 10, 20, 30 or more years in the Company. Well, it's an excuse for a glass of fizz.

I write now as a 72-year-old. I no longer have the perspective of a youngster. Or the energy. I try and keep fit. It hurts but I want to try and be around some years yet. I'm generally optimistic about the world generally but then I don't watch the news any more. I'm relaxed about the future of Direct Wines. Not totally relaxed, mind. Dropping our guard now would not be a good idea.

Family Laithwaite.

We must watch we don't get complacent. We must reinvent, then reinvent again, keep on discovering new wine delights, keep on creating them too, every day. It's what we are here to do. Not that we necessarily know where we are going... but then we never have. That's just not important, in wine. As I realised early on, the journey in the wine business really is more important than the arrival. Our journey has gone past in a blur so far. It's been 50 years in the great tumble drier of life, just going where things led us. 'Where are we?', 'Where next?', 'What's happening tomorrow?' When I was young, baffled and probably a bit drunk, I would say to anyone who'd listen, 'Just keep bumbling on.' (Completely unaware then, that Churchill and Roosevelt always signed off their wartime communications to each other with something roughly similar: 'KBO'.)

So that's our story told. Well, everything I could actually remember. You want some analysis? Reflections? Lessons learned? Advice? Oh please, no. I haven't a clue.

I do believe wine and the wine way of life will go on despite all today's puritans. It's notched up 8,000 years so far – which is to say as long as civilisation itself. So which came first? Wine or civilisation? You may well ask. I do. Can we be truly civilised without a little drink to calm us down, relax things and make us quite friendly?

In so many ways, over our 50 years, we've not gone far at all. I think of that when I'm over at the Windsor vineyard. Windsor is where I started the business and we are back there again with our vineyard in the Great Park. My UK work today also remains much as it was: I regularly do tastings close to Burnham where I did my first ever with my half-bottles in my sample case in 1969. I have lots more wines these days. We still tell our stories. We still pour lots of wines. They don't turn up just for us.

Barbara and I say we are doing less. But as I write these final words we are both in a completely knackered state having just done two days at the 39th Vintage Festival. That is like we just did a 16-hour drinks party. Four sessions of just sipping and talking and talking about wine with well, maybe not every one of the 5,000 attendees but many, very many. It's lovely, it's inspiring, but a little hard on the body. However there is no finer life.

'Thank you, Mr Laithwaite, I want you to know you've changed my bluddy life' said the tall, rather severe-looking customer... from Yorkshire I'd guess. I'd seen him determinedly heading over to me through the throng and braced myself, expecting a bit of a going-over about something we'd got wrong. But no, seems we had seriously brightened his life. I don't think he'll have been the only one. 'A meal without wine is like a day without sunshine' they always remind you in France.

The Company story has not ended here, and won't for a long time yet. Fingers crossed. We've done a lot to ensure it carries on. Direct Wines is now mostly owned by a trust on behalf of our sons. They are most definitely in charge, today, and at least one grandchild has been on the Marlow bottling line already... yes, child labour, but she insisted. The future is here already.

That's our little story. I made my deadline... just. Lots of words. But I've always known that my wines talk better than my words.

I've already mentioned Hugh Johnson's words. So I'll end with words from the very first paragraphs of his very first book. They say it all:

Think, for a moment, of an almost paper-white glass of liquid, just shot with greeny-gold, just tart on your tongue, full of wild-flower scents and spring-water freshness. And think of a burnt-umber fluid, as smooth as syrup in the glass, as fat as butter to smell and sea-deep with strange flavours. Both are wine.

Wine is grape juice. Every drop of liquid filling so many bottles has been drawn out of the ground by the roots of a vine. All these different drinks have at one time been sap in a stick. It is the first of many strange and some – despite modern research – mysterious circumstances which go to make wine not only the most delicious, but the most fascinating, drink in the world.

Now, where's that corkscrew?

GLOSSARY

AOC (Appellation d'Origine Contrôlée) in France a guarantee that a wine comes from a specific region. Now replaced by AOP (Appellation d'Origine Protégée).

ARSOUILLE a yobbo or hoodlum, ne'er-do-well... sounds remarkably like an English word with the same sort of meaning but is not a literal translation.

BLEUS from *bleu de travail*, the French working jacket (and trousers) once worn by every man working in the vineyards and everywhere; it has now become a rather trendy fashion item (I have one).

LES CAVES COOPÉRATIVES many were started in the 1920s and 1930s. The Depression brought winemakers together to pool resources and share the cost of winemaking. They built big ugly wineries but to me they have their charm.

LES CHARTRONS the wine trade district of Bordeaux, along the waterfront. Still going when I started. Now all gone. The waterfront is a big – and excellent – tourist attraction.

CIVB Conseil Interprofessionel du Vin de Bordeaux.

LE CONCASSEUR machine used to break or crush stones into something approximately like soil. Much needed on the stony hills of Provence where the best vineyards are planted.

LES COURTIERS not the beruffled nobility that used to inhabit the palace at Versailles... no, they are much grander than that. They act as the link between the Bordeaux winegrowers and the merchant *négociants*. They charge 2 per cent and are sometimes known rather disparagingly as 'Monsieur 2%' but they are key to the historic wine-selling by the famous houses.

CRÉMANT slightly less fizzy sparkling wine made by the *méthode traditionnelle* of in-bottle secondary fermentation. Nothing outside the designated Champagne area can be called champagne, or they will sue, but it can be called Crémant, so it is in many other areas, e.g. Crémant de Loire.

EN BROSSE a spiky upstanding haircut (*les brosses* are the spiky bristles of a brush)... a bit like the Mohican so popular during the age of Punk.

FAIRE SA CUVÉE to make a blend... usually of champagne from different vineyards and varieties of grape. Vital to maintaining a recognisable house style.

LE FOUDRE a large wooden vat, about 10 feet high, can hold 1,000 litres of wine or more.

LA FRANCE PROFONDE I suppose Sainte-Colombe is as much *La France profonde* as anywhere... the 'heartlands of France' is one translation but it represents all parts of local life, a perhaps rather outdated but jolly nice concept.

GOULEYANT roughly translates as 'succulent aroma'; a 'fat', rounded, unctuous style of wine that slips down very easily... a style I have been keen to get for my customers for the last 50 years.

LA GRANDE BOUFFE a very large meal, a feast or blowout, not for faint-hearted or picky eaters... certainly not for vegans.

LES GRANDS FAÇONS in the past, the more physical jobs in the vineyard, ploughing, pruning, requiring more muscle, splendid if rather self-important. Machinery has changed this.

LES GRILLADES grilled meats, but quite something else in the hands of Madame Cassin... the simple word does not do justice to her grills over vine embers.

LE GROS PAIN DE CAMPAGNE big, crusty country bread, half a kilo or more and never ever those small little baguettes which are for the soft townies.

LA GUEULE DE BOIS a hangover – not to be encouraged but sometimes unavoidable... literally a mouth like wood... or a GB Brit.

GUIMBORA a deep, dark rich soup consisting mainly of pig's blood, beans and spices... delicious and very nutritious.

LIQUEUR DE POIRE a colourless fruit brandy made traditionally from Williams pear. It may be colourless and is so delicious it seems harmless, but is in fact a powerful drink not to be taken lightly. New wine buyers in our Company are initiated by being 'poired'.

LA MACÉRATION CARBONIQUE a technique where whole bunches of grapes are not crushed but first macerated in a carbon dioxide environment. The grapes then ferment whole, sort of, from the inside out, and produce a juicier style of wine.

LE MAÎTRE DE CHAI literally a cellar master but much more than that, the man responsible for the care and ageing of wine. A god to his staff.

LA MANIF, LA MANIFESTATION a demo... popular French pastime on the streets of Paris and even Bordeaux in the 1960s. Still popular today!

LE MEC a guy or a bloke or, if you are from East London, possibly a geezer.

LE MÉTAYER sharecropper or tenant farmer... divides the spoils of the land between himself and the owner of the land.

LE MILDIOU downy mildew – the dread of the grape grower... well, one of them.

MOUSSEUX sparkling wine, but slightly more foamy and frothy than Crémant.

MW Master of Wine.

LES NOUILLES long flat noodles; also an insult roughly the equivalent of fathead.

OXIDATION a curse of the wine-drinking fraternity. Oxygen rapidly changes even the best wine into a dull brown liquid, the same way a forgotten, cut apple goes brown.

PERLANT/PERLÉ down at the bottom of the sparkling descriptions; such a delicate fizz it barely tickles the tongue .

LES PETITS FAÇONS the lighter, smaller jobs in a vineyard, not requiring brute strength, like tying vines to wires, leaf stripping or tucking-in... the opposite to *grands façons*.

PÉTILLANT how many words do the French need for describing fizz in wine? Another word for sparkling, just not very.

PHYLLOXERA BUG hard to think now that in the 1850s and 1860s the aphid known as grape phylloxera nearly destroyed the French wine industry. It started out in America and was carried across the Atlantic. Fortunately clever grafting using vines resistant to the aphid meant the industry recovered slowly but surely... thank heavens.

LA PICOLE booze, slang for a drink... as in *picole* drunk. Is it the source of our word pickled?

LE PIED DE CUVE a method of starting the fermentation process using a small amount of warmed juice or water and juice with yeast in a small container. Get it really fizzing, then put into the tank.

LE PINARD a slang, often derogatory word for wine apparently dating back to the wine ration for soldiers in the First World War... of course they were going to have a wine ration, probably rough old stuff, much as British sailors had their rum. *Courage, mes braves!*

RD *route départementale*.

LE ROUGE QUI TACHE wine which stains, so hardly complimentary; describes cheaper and younger red country wines pretty accurately – the colour leaches out very easily. Black teeth problems.

LE SARMENT bundle of the old vine shoots that are collected and used as a basis for cooking as in Madame Cassin's fireplace. A faggot.

SCHIST metamorphic flaky rock like a *millefeuille* or volcanically compressed clays of many colours on which the vines produce grapes with superb flavour, possibly because their roots can penetrate deeply between the rock slivers.

LA SIESTE the postprandial nap so enjoyed in the past by the French working folk – and me – during the heat of the day. In summer they started – still do – at first light and finished late in the cool of the evening... the midday *sieste* helped them keep going.

LA SOUPE the midday meatl in the vineyards to restore energy and give you the fuel to carry on... but only after *la sieste*.

LE/LA STAGIAIRE the dictionary translation is trainee; can be applied to an intern. In my teenage years in France, whilst not quite slave labour, was certainly hard-worked, cheap labour.

LA TIREUSE a syphoner... a drawer of wine by gravity.

TRANSPORTS INTERNATIONAUX ROUTIERS (TIR) international road transport.

VARIETAL applied to wine that comes from a specific variety of grape.

VDQS Vin Délimité de Qualité Supérieure, now integrated into Appellation Contrôlée but once the Second Division of French wine. Below AOC and above Vin de Pays (country wine) and Vin de France.

VIEILLE FRANCE old-fashioned, traditional, country-style France.

VIEILLES VIGNES phrase used in winemaking and on some wine labels to show that the grapes used have come, simply, from old vines but there is no definition as to how old they actually have to be. And there is now some doubt as to whether older vines do, in fact, give better wine. They certainly produce less wine, which is therefore more concentrated.

LA VENDANGE the harvesting of grapes or the grape harvest.

LE WATER colloquial word for a flush toilet from the English 'water closet' WC. The most useful phrase in French is: *'Pardon, où est le water, s'il vous plaît?'*

INDEX

With thanks to Jon Ryan without whose encouragement and threats this book would never have been finished. TL.

First published in Great Britain in 2019
by Profile Editions, an imprint of
PROFILE BOOKS LTD
3 Holford Yard
Bevin Way
London WC1X 9HD
www.profileeditions.com

A CIP catalogue record for this book is available from the British Library.

ISBN 978 1 78816 125 1

Cover design and styling by David Eldridge,
  Two Associates
Layout by Jon Allan, TwoSheds Design
Project managed by Jamie Ross
Printed and bound in China by 1010

The sources, photographers and/or copyright holders of the images in this book are listed below.

Every effort has been made to contact copyright holders. In the case of an omission, please contact the publisher.

pp7, 8, 10, 18, 20, 27, 28, 40, 44, 48, 53, 55, 69m&b, 71, 72, 78, 85, 86, 88, 91, 99, 102, 105, 112, 116, 117, 123, 135, 144, 159, 163, 169, 172, 184t, 190l, 205, 210, 220, 222, 254, 259 **Laithwaite's archive**; pp13, 15, 16, 23, 32t, 35, 39, 47, 68, 69tl, 77, 114, 127, 130, 132, 141, 143, 156, 164, 193, 253 **Tony Laithwaite**; p11 **Moviestore collection Ltd/Alamy**; p12 **Interfoto/Alamy**; pp22, 76 **Anne Linder**; p32b **Sheppard Day**; p51 **Judith Spalding**; pp56, 67, 96, 167, 189, 198, 200, 216, 228, 235 **Piotr Gradziel**; p61 **Corbis via Getty Images**; pp50, 69tr, 106, 190r, 257 **Steven Morris**; p103 © **Sunday Telegraph**; p109 © **VINEXPO**; p110 © **The Sunday Times**; p121 **Weingut Dr Loosen**; pp129, 184b, 231, 240 **Yves Gellie**; p147 **Bella Spurrier**; pp150, 177 © **RedHeads**; pp154–5, 197 **Jo Denis**; pp160, 213t **Vincent Paris**; p165 **Richard Nourry**; pp180–1 **Emily Shepherd**; p202 **David Thomas**; pp208, 242, 246 **Scott Lander**; p213b **James Bentham**; p227 **Lucy Pope**; p249 **Beth Willard**

Thanks to Hugh Johnson for permission to reproduce the extract on p.259.